About the

Chris Wadsworth began her career as an art teacher and graphic designer, until she moved back north and became an accidental gallerist. During her 25 years at Castlegate House in Cockermouth, Cumbria, she mounted many exhibitions including solo shows by L. S. Lowry, Sheila Fell, Winifred Nicholson, Mary Fedden, Elisabeth Frink, Percy Kelly, Barbara Rae and many more. She contributed articles about art and artists to magazines and, being a keen observer of humanity and its eccentricities, began to write things down. In 2012 with four published books behind her, she sold the gallery and now writes full time. She lives near Keswick in the Lake District with her partner Michael.

If you would like to view any of the pieces of art which feature in *Life Class*, you can do so by visiting the following web page:
<u>www.chriswadsworth.net/lifeclassimages</u>

Also by Chris Wadsworth

LIFE CLASS

The memoir of an accidental gallerist

Chris Wadsworth

PROSPERO

First published in Great Britain in 2016 by Prospero Press.

Copyright © Chris Wadsworth 2016

The right of Chris Wadsworth to be identified as the author of this work has been asserted by her in accordance with the Copyright, Designs and Patents Act, 1988.

A CIP catalogue record for this book is available from the British Library.

ISBN: 978-0-9928972-4-6

Set in Times font

Book design and layout: Katharine Smith, Heddon Publishing

Cover design: Laura Bamber

Front cover
Dream Valley; Setting Sun
Michael Bennett
Oil on canvas

For June and Michael Bennett, for 25 years of friendship and loyal support

LIFE CLASS
CONTENTS

Prologue: Autumn 1986

The estate agent's young assistant was already waiting on the impressive front doorstep, jiggling a big bunch of keys nervously when I arrived.

'It's this way,' she said, leading me to a small gate let into a wall at the side of the house.

We made an ignominious entry across the yard, past the dustbins, and into the utility room to knock off the antiquated alarm. The place looked bigger, bleaker, darker, colder, and much shabbier than I recalled. The air smelt dank and stale. Had I just done something very foolish or very clever? I suspected the former, but I'd soon find out. My husband Michael and I had just completed on the sale. Castlegate House was now ours to love and to cherish from this day forth.

'Oh heck!' the assistant said as she looked around. 'I've never been inside before. You've got your work cut out, haven't you?'

Yes, I had. The dirty green walls in the hall made me feel seasick. In places there were darker rectangles where pictures had been removed. The stair carpet had been left in situ but it was threadbare and dangerous. Our life savings and the proceeds of the sale of our old house in Bristol had been absorbed and swallowed by this gloomy place. It didn't look one bit like the house I'd viewed enthusiastically two months before.

'What are you going to do with it?' the girl chattered on. 'It's very big and there's so much work. Have you got a big family? You could do B&B: a lot of places round here do that. We're nearly in the Lake District, you know.'

'Oh, thank you,' I said firmly, getting a grip of myself, 'but I've already got a plan. I intend to open an art gallery here.'

She gave me a funny look which was either incomprehension or horror. I had to admit it sounded idealistic - and a bit pompous - even to me.

The first time I had seen Castlegate House, I knew it had to be mine. I liked the way it had stood for 300 years opposite Cockermouth's Norman Castle: four-square, solid, dependable.

Clutching the estate agent's brochure, I had made my way up the steps and through the big front door with its brass lion's head knocker, my pulse quickening and my heart fluttering with desire. As I stood in the hall, the floor seemed to shift as I admired the elegant Georgian plasterwork, the staircase flooded with light, the perfect proportions of the rooms. Through an open door at the far end of the hall there was a tantalising glimpse of a walled garden.

It had been a life-changing moment.

The asking price for Castlegate House was exactly the same as that of the house Michael and I had just sold in Bristol. How lucky was that? But how could I justify the purchase of an eight-bedroomed house (and the rest) for just two people to live in? How could we afford to run it? What could I do with this house to make it viable? A small guest house was the obvious solution, but that was my idea of hell. And what did I know about business? What did I know about anything?

Well, I did know a lot about art. I'd taught it for many years on various levels. I'd studied graphic design. I'd hung out in the big public galleries and visited the landmark exhibitions. But I had to admit I'd usually avoided the commercial galleries. I'd found them daunting and unfriendly. I felt I was there under false pretences, given that I wasn't in a position to buy anything: with three children to get through university, Michael and I couldn't afford original works. But now, I argued with myself, things had changed. Our children had recently left home and were independent and so was I. Michael had come up here to organise the privatisation of the company he worked for and we were both ready to make a new start. Was it now time to be totally self-indulgent and open a gallery in this beautiful house – fill it with works of art of my choosing? I could visualise the rooms and walls hung with glorious modern paintings. I could see sculpture in the garden.

It sounded wonderful, but I had no idea how to start. There was no training manual, no business template. I knew next to nothing about what running a gallery involved.

***

I was born and brought up in the north of England but I'd never been to Cockermouth, famous as the birthplace of William and Dorothy Wordsworth, before. I didn't know anyone in the town and no one knew me. To the friends I had left behind in the south, I appeared to be moving to the edge of civilisation as they knew it. I was on the fringe of the Lake District National Park, the fringe of the art world, and the fringe of my resources and experience. I felt exposed and vulnerable. Was this all simply a mid-life crisis; a dreadful mistake?

I'd always been a risk-taker, never opting for the easy way out, but opening a gallery would be by far the biggest risk I'd ever taken. I'd always worked within the security of rules and a framework; had a career path, a higher authority, a headteacher or a line manager to report to. Now, I *was* that higher authority. It was dizzying; terrifying. I felt as though I was on the very edge of the highest diving board, poised on tiptoe as it trembled and flexed. I must not look down.

To those outside it, the Art World appears romantic. It seems to be a glamorous, sexy world of culture, money, fashion, celebrity and excitement; a place where men in suits and young women called Fiona and Annabel swan around in designer clothes, selling beautiful things for lots of money to lovely rich people. As if! I was under no illusions. I knew that starting a gallery would involve hard physical work, risk and rivalry – but in my innocence I had no idea how much.

I was determined to make Castlegate House a warm, friendly place where everyone was welcome. I wanted it to be somewhere for people to meet. I wanted to have music and poetry and I wanted it to feel to others like the home it would be for me.

First, however, I had to make it more user-friendly. Then I had to persuade the council that Cockermouth would benefit from an art gallery and get them to grant permission for a change of use.

***

Within the space of a few weeks, Castlegate House had become a slalom of hazards, a grade one obstacle course. A team of electricians and plumbers were taking up floorboards everywhere, falling over each other's pipes, while rolls of new wires were creating a spaghetti junction of various bright colours.

'Your boiler's buggered,' the plumber said. 'Come and have a look, love.'

He cautiously put a match to the pilot light and a flame shot horizontally out of the side. I jumped back.

When the foreman of the builders appeared, he was as solemn and pale as Banquo's ghost.

'You know the roof...'

I quickly interrupted. 'The roof is sound. It has been recently re-slated. The surveyor said...'

'Yes, well come and look in the loft,' he replied. 'Did this surveyor go up there then? I think not. It's full of roof rubble. It'll bring the ceilings down. They're cracking already. We'll have to clear it out before we can spray for the woodworm.'

And so it went on – exciting new discoveries every day.

The planning officer was doubtful; grey suit, grey face, bored and uninterested. He clearly saw me as another of those daft offcomers who have a romantic view of living in the most beautiful corner of England; one of those idealists who start or buy a business and think it will look after itself while they run up mountains or go fishing. His cynicism had built up layer upon dusty layer, like the cobwebbed attic windows. He had seen it all.

'This house is in the conservation area, Mrs Wordsworth,' he announced. 'And it has always been residential. You'll have a hard job to get change of use to commercial.' I decided to ignore both the negativity and the flattering Freudian slip.

'We're at the end of the main shopping street,' I argued. 'And hey, I'm not proposing to open a nightclub in the cellars or an Indian restaurant, am I? A gallery will bring people to the town - not just tourists, either. People will come long distances. They will eat and sleep in the town. They'll wander round the shops. They will spend money.'

The planning officer looked even more doubtful. Blandly, he suggested perhaps an existing shop in a more tourist-oriented town would be better. Then I wouldn't need any planning permission. (Also, I thought, I would be off his patch so that he could go back to his tidy office and resume pushing papers about). I was offended. I didn't want a shop. I wanted a way of life. Nor did I want to sell 'views' like the framing shop over the bridge and all the other galleries I'd been to in the honey-pot tourist towns.

He went on lugubriously to tell me about a gallery that had opened in Cockermouth a year or so before.

'It was at the bottom of the hill,' he said, 'where's there's now a greengrocer. Gallery went bust, but the greengrocer's doing all right. Folk always need apples and potatoes and such.'

Oh joy! This man really gave me the wobbles. I gently informed him I was proposing a serious gallery run on London lines, not a hobby and not a shop. There would be at least ten exhibitions a year. It would be advertised nationally. He looked even more sceptical.

'Do you paint yourself?' he asked, changing tack.

I bit back my flippant answer. This was not the right time. I'm glad I didn't know how many times I was going to be asked that question in the coming years (and how many times I would resist the urge to indulge in body painting for the sheer hell of it). Instead I walked him round the beautifully proportioned rooms, stepping over the builders and the mess as we went.

'You can't put any illuminated signs outside,' he observed. 'And we'll need you to submit a plan for the lighting system – oh, and you can't touch the ceilings.'

I did realise this. As they were fourteen feet high to my five foot six, I didn't intend to try.

He looked up. 'Those plaster mouldings are precious – original Adam.'

I realised from his solemn tone that he wasn't talking about the Garden of Eden, though I could have been taking ownership of the Sistine Chapel the way he was carrying on.

We both craned our necks.

'That one's an original Adam as well: rare, irreplaceable. That's what earned the star.'

'What star?

'The star on the your Grade II listing,' he enunciated as though I was dense (which I was). 'That ceiling is starred.'

I looked up, expecting a galaxy.

'And you'll not be able to do food or get an alcohol licence without an extra application, and that's not easy to come by. That's the trouble with listed buildings: you can't just do anything.'

It was still all negative but I was hopeful. At least we were now talking about what I couldn't do when the house was a gallery. And anyway, food was the last thing I wanted to be involved with, and I had no plans to sell alcohol – just drink it. But I didn't tell the planning officer that. I was trying hard to look respectable and responsible, although probably failing.

A few days later, he returned with a colleague and they snuffled about the house, grunting. They stood out in the street for ages, pointing and making notes, then they measured the car park.

'You're not intending to use that as a car park, are you?' he asked when he came back inside.

As the space he was indicating was already full of

6

builders' vans and lorries as well as my car and his, I guessed this was a rhetorical question.

'It's access, you see,' he continued. 'Out onto the main road. You can only do domestic parking.

I smiled and nodded, grinding my teeth. Domestic? So be it if the gallery depended on it.

***

The letter granting permission for change of use arrived six weeks later. I couldn't believe it. It was now March and I planned to open in the summer. The builders stepped up the pace and there were days when I could stand the banging and drilling no more. Leaving them to it, I chased round the country in search of artists. I followed every trail and began to build up a mail list. I knew I had to find artists and buyers in equal proportions and although one would generate the other, starting the cycle off was going to be tricky. We had no spare capital after buying the house so the artists I found would have to put their trust in me and allow me to handle their work on a commission basis. What a huge responsibility. They too had to make a living. They couldn't leave their precious work with a gallery just for fun. This was not fun. It was deadly serious.

Two months after completion, Michael and I moved into Castlegate House from the security of the bungalow we'd been renting. It seemed cavernous by comparison, and our furniture looked as though it was meant for a dolls house when it arrived out of storage. I had reached the end of the renovation budget, although there was still a lot more to do. It would have to wait. I had to find my artists and get the gallery up and running. Meanwhile, Michael was more and more preoccupied with his job. The nationalised bus company for which he worked was being split up into small units to be sold off individually, thanks to the government's zeal for privatising national assets. As Chief Executive, Michael was now leading a management buyout of the Cumbrian sector. I knew he was capable of doing

7

it. He had already been parachuted into several failing companies and saved them. I was less sure about my own abilities.

'Are you certain you want to do this?' Michael asked me at breakfast one morning a few weeks before the opening. I'd tossed and turned restlessly all night.

'What do you mean? Do what?'

'Open a gallery. When I have the new company up and running we won't need your income and you don't need the worry.'

He saw my face.

'Well, you could do another course…'

'First of all, I do need to do it,' I replied sharply. 'This isn't a hobby! I have the chance at last to do something I'll really enjoy, something that is mine. I want to be self-employed. I need to measure myself against the commercial world. I also want to see these walls full of original paintings.'

I paused.

'Secondly, this is a fall-back plan in case your buy-out goes horribly wrong.'

He laughed.

'It's not going to go wrong. You'll see.'

I did.

A few weeks later, just days before the grand opening of the gallery, I heard Michael's car scream into the car park in the middle of the afternoon. This was unheard of – he was a workaholic. He was never home before seven. I heard the front door bang and felt the house shudder. I ran downstairs. He had dumped his briefcase on the kitchen table. He was pale and his face was gaunt.

'We were outbid,' he spat. 'We've lost it. To a little company nobody's heard of called Stagecoach. It's a brother and sister operation: they run a small bus company up in Perth. They've offered me my job, the cheek of it. I've resigned.'

'You've what?' My eyebrows shot up. 'Did you really

8

have to? It might be all right if you stayed on for a bit, you never know.' Inside, I was panicking like mad. 'Can't you stick with it and give me five years to get the gallery established and into profit?'

'No. Impossible. They want me to start by selling off half the assets to cover the price they've paid. They want me to recoup their over-spend and I'm not doing it. I'm sorry love, but I'm taking no part in any asset stripping. Let's just hope this gallery venture of yours succeeds.'

No pressure then.

The Reluctant Exhibitionist

'Hello, my name's Chris - Chris Wadsworth. I've recently moved to Cumbria and I'm going to open a gallery in Cockermouth in the summer.'

This sounded implausible, even to me. Would I entrust my precious work - if I had any - to myself? I had no sales record, no client base, and no reputation.

At the other end of the line there was a too-long silence. I held my breath.

'Oh yes?' came the almost inaudible reply at last. Then silence again. Michael Bennett was clearly not a chatty person.

'Isobel Watson has given me your contact details,' I pressed on. 'Hope you don't mind. She speaks highly of you. I saw one of your seascapes in her sitting room yesterday and I really liked it. Would you care to be part of my opening show in July? Perhaps you have two or three paintings you can spare.'

I waited.

I prayed.

There was another long pause.

'I'm sorry,' came the reply eventually, 'but I'm not painting at the moment.'

I was devastated. Was this just an excuse - had I said the wrong thing?

'But... my wife's just started painting again. She was a jeweller, but she could be interested.' I could hear Michael's voice lightening; becoming warmer, more enthusiastic. 'Perhaps you'd like to come over and see her work? She's not here at the moment, but can you come on Wednesday? Come for lunch.'

I put the phone down, disappointed. I felt I was being fobbed off. Could a jeweller metamorphose into a credible painter? I doubted it. I might not like June Bennett's paintings and then I would be trapped in an embarrassing lunch ordeal: once in the artists' domain, I was learning, it was difficult to retreat with honour.

I had begun to gather artists as soon as I had planning permission for the gallery, but those I wanted to show most were the hardest to track down (and to nail down when I'd found them). Most of them already had a gallery to whom they were loyal and a programme of exhibitions booked for a few years ahead. Often, as I'd just discovered with Michael Bennett, my original objective would somehow be transformed into something quite different and there were times when I felt I was in danger of losing sight of my initial intention.

I was looking for artists who would provide the stock, the reputation and the future of the gallery. These were people that needed to be wooed, persuaded and cosseted. I wanted artists whose work gave me a buzz, with whom I could make a connection; artists that I knew I would get along with. The gallery would be a cooperative effort with no place for resentment, inflated egos, or prima donnas – and that included me as well, of course.

In the months before I opened the gallery, I did a lot of searching and researching. Suddenly, I had the entrée to people whom I had admired from afar. I was invited into studios I would never have got anywhere near in my previous life. These were the days before web pages had been invented so there was no chance of previewing work and I ended up driving thousands of miles. But it was a cumulative process: one artist led to another. There was a network, a chain of informers, a passing-on of information. Artists are generous people but they also cast a sharp, critical eye on other artists. They trade and swap and they gossip. They go to exhibitions. They compare and contrast. And they recognise talent when they see it.

During my travels, several people had mentioned a flower painter called Isobel Watson who lived and worked in the Newlands Valley, about twenty miles away from Castlegate House. After making an appointment, I set out on a sunny spring day to see her in her studio. Leaving Cockermouth, I turned south off the busy A66 trunk road and soon found myself rumbling over a cattle grid onto a quiet, single-track road. It twisted and turned, creeping alongside unstable-looking grey slate screes and quarries, revealing new mountain vistas round every bend. I knew the names of most of the peaks - Michael and I had climbed them on holidays up here - but we had approached from valleys the other side of these fells, the valleys with lakes in them: Buttermere, Derwentwater, Crummockwater.

As I looked across to Cat Bells, I mentally retraced my every step along the ridge: Maiden Moor and High Spy and back down to Manesty and Derwentwater. It was hard to keep my eyes on the road and at a passing place I pulled in to savour the moment. I was thrilled to think that I now lived and worked here. I was part of it. I was no longer an outsider, a tourist, a visitor. Michael and I had already started crossing off all the Wainwrights on the big map of the Lakes which hung in his office.

The narrow road clung to the fellside as I resumed the drive further towards the head of the valley.

'You can't see the house from the road,' Isobel had helpfully told me. 'Look for a wooden gate on the left.'

I drove past the gate twice before I noticed it. It bore a small name plate: Emerald Bank. Abandoning the car in the layby, I descended into a wonderful wild garden in a verdant valley. It was full of interesting plants and flowers - some rare, some in bloom. This was the source of Isobel's work: botanical studies in the form of detailed drawings and beautiful, translucent watercolours. The house itself was built into the bank on several levels, and every room was full of wonderful paintings, ceramics, sculpture, wood carvings and fabrics. It was a treasure house. Every bit of wall and every surface was covered. My eyes began darting from one interesting piece to another and I was beginning to feel dizzy when I caught sight of an unusual seascape in the corner. The horizon was high, there was a hazy suggestion of people on the shore, and the deep, glorious colours and grainy texture clearly came from multiple layers of paint and impasto. I couldn't take my eyes off it.

'Who painted that?' I asked Isobel.

'Michael Bennett,' she replied at once. 'Lovely man, lovely painter. He lives in Cumbria – up on the Solway. I'll give you his phone number if you like.'

My pulse quickened. It was a familiar name. I was sure he had exhibited with some prestigious artists.

I wanted it - I wanted that painting. It excited me more than anything else I'd seen on my search so far. Isobel's flower paintings were beautiful and accurate, but this oil painting imprinted itself on my soul. I could have walked out of her sitting room and still described it in fine detail. When I did come away, I was clutching a precious bit of paper with Michael Bennett's telephone number.

The following Wednesday, I found myself driving north for lunch at the Bennetts' house. True, I was going to see his wife June's work, but I had liked Michael's voice and his diffident, modest manner, and had a suspicion that he had far more to give than he was letting on. I didn't realise how marvellously true that was going to turn out to be.

The landscape of the Solway estuary is totally different from the lakes and fells of the central massif of the National Park. There was an inherent sense of danger when I took to the narrow causeway through the salt marshes, cattle wandering haphazardly onto the unfenced road. The estuary tide runs fast, right up to and sometimes over the tarmac. White marker poles indicate the height of the tide at its extremes, with warning notices about Springs and Neaps:

WHEN WATER REACHES THIS POINT MAXIMUM DEPTH IS 1 FOOT/2 FEET

A deviation from the road and the marshes might gobble

the car up without trace. This was Riever country; bandit country – the bad lands of old. I looked across the narrow waters - I was looking at Scotland from this rarely visited, secret land.

My destination was a small, stone Georgian terrace on the defensive line of Hadrian's Wall. The Bennetts' house was at one end of the terrace and there was a Post Office at the other with a pub and bowling green forming an exclamation mark beyond. I parked on the cobbles outside the Bennetts' house. The front door was open. Peering through the stained glass panel of the inner front door, I could see a harlequin figure approaching in response to my ring. It was Michael, tall and handsomely lethargic, with a soft voice that I had to strain to hear. I soon realised it was worth persevering: every word, like every mark he made, was significant.

As Michael welcomed me in, he saw my sideways glance into a room that was lined floor-to-ceiling with books.

'That's my business now: collecting and selling rare art books and catalogues,' he explained. 'But come into the sitting room. It's lovely to meet you. I'd love to hear all about your new project.'

The comfortable room he showed me into was dominated by yet more shelves of books, as well as a grand piano and walls hung with interesting paintings. I could see a Keith Vaughan oil, some intriguing portraits, and several oil paintings that I recognised as coming from the same hand that had painted the seascape in Isobel's sitting room. I was about to comment when a petite woman came through the conservatory from the garden. She was a tiny, colourful bundle of energy with bright pink lipstick and blonde hair swept back in a chignon, her jewellery glinting like quicksilver as she moved.

'This is my wife, June,' Michael said with obvious relief as he handed me over. My first impression had been right: he was clearly not a man for small talk. By now, he had probably used up his quota of chat for the whole day.

Almost immediately, June whisked me off up two flights

of stairs, chattering nervously as she went. The smell of turps, linseed and oil paint insinuated itself like smoke through the whole house: it was part of the atmosphere.

There was barely space for both of us in June's attic studio, and certainly none to turn round: the room was crammed with oil paintings as colourful as she was. As I studied them, she explained that she had been a silversmith for the past ten years or more while she was bringing up children, but now that both her boys had left home and the house was quiet again, she had settled back into painting. She told me that she had originally trained as a painter. I had seen that instantly. My fears of an uncomfortable lunch evaporated: I loved her textured, jewel-like work.

'Is that a real place?' I asked, pointing.

It was a painting called *Cumbrian Cottage,* an impression of a small white cottage, its windows shuttered, half hidden by a high hedgerow of cow parsley and wild flowers. In the background, the estuary glinted. June laughed.

'You drove past it on the way here,' she said. 'It's just before the dog-leg bridge.'

'And that one: *Red Chapel*?'

'The red chapel's just up the road,' she said, smiling. 'You must have seen it. Look out for it on your drive back.'

Over lunch, June readily agreed to be part of my opening show. We found we had a lot in common: our children had recently left home, leaving us free to start new ventures, and June felt the good timing was an omen. Meanwhile, Michael was attentive, quietly supportive, and offered me much good advice about running a gallery. He had a wealth of experience of the art world and knew how it all worked - which was a lot more than I did. He was knowledgeable on every aspect of art: fellow artists, famous artists, galleries, critics. His was the voice of common sense and although I didn't know it then, I would be turning to him a few times in the next twenty years.

Having said my goodbyes, I set off home, eager to spot

Cumbrian Cottage and Red Chapel. I didn't see the first and I barely recognised the second: it was a very ordinary, dull, brick-built place on the bend of the road, which June had transformed into something interesting and exciting. She hadn't recorded what was there – she had painted what she saw. In fact, I saw so many things from which she had drawn inspiration on that drive that I almost ended up in the marsh. In the course of a few hours, she had completely changed my perception of the area. There were June Bennett paintings in disguise everywhere.

***

Castlegate's opening exhibition the following summer was a great success: I sold all of June's paintings. The Bennetts came to all the subsequent gallery openings and generously gave me lists of people who might be interested in buying not just June's work, but other artists' as well. We spent some jolly evenings together at Castlegate and I always enjoyed going to their house for supper, the talk of art and books.

Then, at the end of one particularly good evening, June stopped me at the door as I was leaving. 'Michael hasn't really stopped painting you know,' she whispered. 'He paints every day.'

She clearly wasn't going to say any more, but I thought about her words a lot. I could not forget that seascape at Isobel Watson's.

The Sofa Hunter

As the opening of the gallery had drawn near, I'd become increasingly apprehensive. What was I thinking? I was inviting, nay *encouraging*, complete strangers and random passersby into my home. Nobody actually needs a painting. Would they like what they saw? And how would Michael feel? Would he resent the invasion into our privacy? Would he fit in? Would he want to fit in? Was I throwing my happy, 25-year marriage on to the sacrificial altar of art?

I needn't have fretted. From the moment I opened my front door to the public, and placed my shiny new 'GALLERY OPEN' sign on it, I enjoyed my new life as a gallerist. I loved the variety, the unpredictability. Each day was different. Each day brought challenges to be faced. Having moved to Cockermouth knowing no one, I quickly began collecting like-minded people – people who welcomed and supported me. Within a few weeks of opening Castlegate House as a gallery, I had made more new friends than I could easily cope with and had a full diary of social invitations. I had been accepted and integrated into the local community, albeit sometimes in the guise of 'that funny woman in the big house up the hill with all them paintings'.

The locals were overjoyed at having somewhere new to visit, somewhere to meet friends, and something different to gossip about. The art world welcomes eccentricity and is disappointed if there is no drama, no oddity, no outrageous behaviour. It's easy to get away with odd socks, inside-out clothes, mismatched earrings – and I have done many times, although mostly by accident. It takes a lot more than that to faze northerners. Cockermouth was proving to be a lively, friendly town and not as old-fashioned and traditional as I'd feared. I already had a sense of belonging, and as for Michael, once he had adjusted to his new-found freedom – which took some time, after being a full-on workaholic for 30 years - he also settled down. Although he was offered other jobs in the

17

south, he opted for quality of life, finding the time to walk and join organisations and charities. He decided that he was going to enjoy himself and I am so glad he did. We neither of us realised how little time he had left.

I quickly discovered how much I had to learn as soon as the visitors to Castlegate began to arrive. They were an eclectic assortment of locals, artists, tourists and rivals, and I had no idea into which of these categories they fell when they walked through the door for the first time. I kept getting my approach wrong. Some people liked to chat - some would tell me their life history if encouraged - and others preferred to be left alone, anonymous. I had to be intuitive in my 'meet and greet' routine, making everybody feel welcome and comfortable.

The sofa helped. It was a very nice sofa: a Chesterfield in mulberry linen strewn with sprigged flowers in cream. Tasteful, though a bit chintzy in a classic Georgian house, perhaps - but no matter. I had bought it five years before in a posh furniture shop on Whiteladies Road in Bristol, and it had come with us from our now almost forgotten previous house.

Galleries can be cold and daunting, exuding an austere, reverential atmosphere which makes people tiptoe about, whispering. I didn't want Castlegate to be like that. The sofa gave a homely, informal touch – it was somewhere to relax; to look and think, and it was well-used as people began to pour in.

One afternoon that first summer, just a few days after the opening of the gallery, two people came in separately. The man hurtled in first and roared about the gallery, chattering noisily to me all the time as I followed, striving to keep up with him. He was self-assured, dark and handsome, with a small, neat moustache and twinkling eyes. He carried a sports bag and had just been for a swim. I knew that because he immediately told me. The woman followed at a more sedate pace. She had not been for a swim and she definitely didn't want to talk. Her body language made that quite clear.

She was tall, slender and contemplative and wandered around quietly, giving a lot of thought and attention to each painting. Meanwhile, the man rushed round the gallery twice, opened the glass door marked 'PRIVATE' and shot off into the garden. He disappeared out of sight beyond the raspberries, quickly ricocheted back inside, and began to fire questions at me about countless irrelevant things, hardly waiting for the answers.

'Love your garden,' he said. 'Have you been here long?'

'I moved in last year. It's taken over nine months to get it all sorted out...'

'What did you pay for it?' he continued. 'The house..?'

Hey! He was very direct – some would say cheeky – but I couldn't take offence.

'We just bought a place down near the lake,' he went on. 'We live in London but we come from these parts. Carlisle. Good to come back and see our folks. We come up for the summers – get away from the city. We had a small place over Caldbeck but decided to sell and get something bigger.'

The woman called softly from the adjoining room before I had the chance to comment. 'Come here and just look at this, Hunt,' she said quietly. 'I like this one.'

I hadn't realised they were together until she spoke. Ah, now I'd got it. I knew who they were. 'Hunt' was the clue – he must be Hunter Davies. I'd read an article by him in *Punch* a few months earlier, recounting his success in buying a house near Loweswater at an auction. Then I remembered that as a young housewife and mother - many years ago in another life - I had read a light-hearted novel by him entitled *Here We Go Round the Mulberry Bush*. It was about a randy delivery van driver and had made me laugh a lot - never had I thought I would meet the author.

So if the man was Hunter Davis then this quiet, elegant woman must be his wife, the novelist Margaret Forster. I recalled how Hunter sometimes referred to her as the Old Trout in his columns in *Punch*. She wasn't a bit like that. I felt indignant on her behalf as a frisson of delight quivered through me. I'd read all her books and loved her writing, especially her first novel, *Georgy Girl,* written soon after she had graduated from Somerville College, Oxford. That book had hit the bestseller list and been made into a film, and she was now in my house! And she was possibly going to buy a painting from me.

The work she had called her husband to look at was *Morning Coffee at Binns*; a small, well painted oil of two women taking coffee and cake in a café. It was by Ceri Allen, a talented young Cumbrian artist fresh out of college.

'It reminds me of when Mother and I used to go to Binns in Carlisle on a Saturday morning,' Margaret said wistfully. 'It's all changed now, taken over by a chain.'

'Well if you like it, pet,' her husband replied, 'why not have it?'

I withdrew a little, giving them space to discuss it. After a few minutes, Hunter swiftly approached me with a faux-confidential air.

He's going to buy the painting for her, I thought. *Isn't that lovely?*

More fool me.

Hunter sidled up to me, hand shielding his mouth so his wife couldn't hear.

'What do you want for the sofa?' he whispered, spiv-like. He nodded his head at the Chesterfield in the other room.

I was taken aback. This was not what I was expecting to hear. What had sofas got to do with anything?

'We just bought this house down by the lake,' he told me again. 'That sofa would go really well in there. It's just what we need.'

He gave me a dazzling and persuasive smile: he was charming, handsome - and confident he'd get his own way.

'Excuse me being nosy, but are you Hunter Davies?' I countered, trying to gain some thinking time.

He nodded proudly, glad to be recognised.

'Well,' I continued cheekily, 'this is an art gallery. Didn't you notice? We sell art. We don't sell sofas. It's there for you to sit on while you're thinking of buying something we do sell – like a painting or a pot or a piece of sculpture.' I grinned. 'This isn't a secondhand furniture shop, you know.'

He laughed loudly. He didn't mind the put-down. I'd judged it correctly for once. He appeared to like being challenged and he was delighted with a bit of banter.

'Yes, but…' he began, anticipating some friendly bargaining.

'Come along, Hunt.' Margaret appeared beside him. 'You heard what she said. We'll go on looking. We'll find one somewhere.'

She turned to me and smiled apologetically. 'I really like the gallery. It's a real asset to the town. I'd also like to reserve that lovely little oil in the other room. I was born and brought up in Carlisle and Binns isn't the same now it's House of Fraser.'

Having arranged to collect the painting a few days later, she said goodbye and made her way to the door, which Hunter rushed to open and gallantly saw her through.

Then he turned back to me. 'It doesn't go in here, that sofa. Better in our place. Think about it.'

With that parting shot, his embarrassed wife dragged him off.

A few days later, I got a postcard of a leafy city garden. I turned it over.

Whataboutadasofa?
Hunter

There was a London address and phone number too, although the postmark was local.

I ignored it.

Another arrived, and then another. I ignored them as well.

Then I thought about it and… maybe Hunter was right. After the fifth postcard, the sofa was beginning to annoy me. It was the wrong colour, the wrong shape. It didn't fit in. He had worn me down - as he knew he would.

After an amusing avalanche of postcards I gave in and began negotiations. I mentioned an amount and weighted it with a request for a mention in *Punch* or the *Sunday Times* as Hunter wrote for both. I needed national publicity and I knew Hunter couldn't resist a bargain - ever. He was an excellent journalist and a skilled haggler: he would do well in the souks of Marrakesh.

As soon as we'd struck our deal, Hunter arrived in a flamboyant red estate car with roof rack. He shifted the sofa and tied it onto the car, enlisting the help of anyone in the vicinity - impressive, but such was his determination to have it that I reckon he would have taken it away in a wheelbarrow if necessary. And, a month or so later, I got my – rather tenuous - mention in *Punch*. It was in a piece that Hunter had written about the new Cumbrian house: a crow had fallen down the chimney, scattering soot around the place and especially onto a painting he and Margaret had just bought at - *da dum* - Castlegate House Gallery. It was a bit obvious, but it was exposure nevertheless, and not to be underestimated at this crucial developing stage of the gallery's life. As for the *Sunday Times*, I had to wait fifteen years for my mention there. It's a day I will never forget. It cost me close to £20,000.

The Knob Man Cometh

Within a few months of opening, I could tell the gallery was going to survive. I knew I must be doing something right and I was enjoying myself. Castlegate was becoming an arts centre, a meeting place. It was buzzing with life. I was making friends at an alarming rate but there were also times when I felt vulnerable manning - or womaning – such a big place on my own, especially as autumn arrived and the afternoons became darker. In the early days, I could only afford a part-time assistant to come in when I needed to go out. I was always wary, despite the red panic button by the desk in the hall which would silently summon police at the press of a finger. Happily, I never needed to use it. There was usually a fairly constant stream of people passing through and we didn't take cash: art isn't instantly translatable into ready money. I doubt you could sell a Picasso in a pub, though I must confess I've never tried it. I also tried hard to make everyone who came into the gallery feel welcome, no matter who they were or what they looked like. But it wasn't always easy.

The second Saturday of the gallery's existence brought a strong, stocky man through the front door. In one hand he was carrying a very big axe with a glinting blade and in the other a loaf of bread. Oh dear. The bread was reassuringly domestic but I didn't like the look of that axe. He didn't look like a murderer, but then I don't suppose any of them do. I looked around. There was no one else in the gallery. This was a tricky situation. I approached him cautiously, but in doing so realised I was leaving the security of the panic button.

'May I look after your shopping for you?' I asked, attempting to take the axe from him.

What a daft thing to say, I thought. The axe looked shiny-sharp and threatening. He was curiously reluctant to let it go and a minor tussle broke out but I won – I had to win, didn't I? I took my confiscated trophy through to the kitchen, all limbs and digits intact, and laid it carefully on the table.

23

After he'd wandered round for a bit he appeared at the desk and said: 'May I have my axe back now, please?'

We both burst out laughing.

It turned out he was a local teacher who lived up the road and had just taken his axe to the ironmonger's at the bottom of the hill to get it sharpened. He went on to become a regular visitor and we still laugh about our little bout of Cumberland wrestling.

'The axeman cometh,' we say now when he walks in, *sans* axe.

Darth Vader made his noisy entrance by motorbike wearing a black helmet which he soon removed to reveal a closely shaved head. He strode across the car park as I dodged behind the shutters. This tall, sinewy, middle-aged skinhead came dressed in full leathers: gauntlets, studs, buckles, everything. I greeted him, feeling very insecure. He ignored me and walked straight into the West Room, then strode round the other gallery rooms, examining everything in great detail like a valuations expert (or a burglar casing the joint). It was impossible to engage him in conversation. He didn't want to talk at all - he just nodded in a dismissive manner and moved on. His body language shouted 'Go away!' So I did. I left him alone but observed him closely through a crack in the door, although he still managed to slip out when I wasn't looking.

I wonder who he is, I thought uneasily.

A week later, I heard the deep, throaty roar of a powerful motorbike again. As before, its shiny-headed owner didn't communicate. He didn't smile. It was unsettling.

On his third silent visit, I was ready and determined to memorise everything about him, even down to the small scar on his shiny head, shaped like a CND symbol. I was just surreptitiously writing down the number plate of his black Ducati so that I would be able to give a full description as and when necessary when he approached my desk. I flinched and

24

blushed as I hastily put an exhibition card over my scribble.

'I'd like to buy the sculpture over there,' he said in a soft, Scottish-accented voice. He was indicating a very expensive bronze sculpture. 'Leave it where it is at the moment. I'll collect it next Saturday. Oh, and will you gift wrap it please?'

He handed over a gold credit card and the four-figure amount was immediately authorised. He left without another word.

The following week he returned but in place of the Ducati and leathers there were smart jeans and a woman. I handed over the large, gift-wrapped box to him while she looked around. He caught up with her in the Adam Room and quietly presented it to her: it was a wedding anniversary gift. I disappeared to open the bottle of bubbly we kept in the fridge for such occasions. His wife was sociable, delighted with the sculpture, and ready to chat. She told me that she and her husband had a weekend cottage in the Lakes but lived in Manchester, where he was a heart surgeon.

I chastised myself for being so judgemental. I was learning fast.

'Watch out for the knob man,' said the note on the kitchen table. I recognised my assistant's clear, rounded hand.

What's that all that about? I wondered, and discreetly scrutinised everybody who came into the gallery that morning, searching for enlightenment.

By the end of the afternoon, when I'd forgotten all about it, a tall, smartly dressed man came in. He was wearing a dark suit and carried a briefcase. Jehovah's witness? Advertising salesman? Instantly forgetting my new resolution about not judging by appearances, I braced myself for either sales patter or Bible-bashing, but was surprised when I turned round again to find he'd disappeared.

Where's he gone? I asked myself and leaned over my desk to find him hidden in its shadow, kneeling on the floor. *Maybe he's a carpet salesman.*

'Have you dropped something?' I asked.

He looked up. 'No, I'm looking at your knobs.'

I laughed out loud. Then I remembered. 'Ah - you must be the knob man! I was warned about you.'

We both began to laugh at that. It was impossible to hold an innuendo-free conversation. The smut was implicit. A knob is a knob – there is no polite alternative. I began to have some sympathy with the 'Knobs and Knockers' hardware retailers who had recently had an advertisement banned on the grounds it was lewd.

'You do know your knobs don't match?' he reprimanded me, resuming his serious face.

I tried to resist the temptation to look down at my chest.

'Look at this one, for example: it's loose and wobbly,' he said as he jiggled it, 'the knob, I mean.' It came off in his hand.

By now I was hysterical. I couldn't suppress my laughter any longer. My cheeks were damp with tears. My stomach was aching.

'Is this your job then? Selling kno... er, door furniture?'

'No, not exactly. My day job is a psychologist.'

Now why did this not surprise me?

'But my over-riding interest is Georgian houses,' he quickly added.

A perfectionist, he had noticed the parlous state of my interior fittings on his first visit. Inconsistent would be a good way of describing them – or random. I confessed to him that I too had noticed the deficiencies of the knob on the Adam Room door: especially since the inside bit kept coming off in my hand, leaving me trapped inside. I agreed with him that this was disconcerting, and found myself embarking on a tour of the whole house to see what else was awry. I had never noticed before the astonishing variety of fittings throughout. But did mismatching knobs matter? I had spent so much time and money trying to ensure that the building held together, I had ignored anything which worked. He strongly disagreed, of course (being a Georgian expert). Halfway round the bedrooms

- and they are numerous - I wondered if I'd been a little foolhardy to invite a strange man into my private quarters alone, especially after the rather salacious conversation we'd just had. Was he really a shrink? What was in the briefcase he was holding onto so carefully? Knives? A silk scarf? Oops - too late.

Back in the safety of the hall, he placed the briefcase on my desk, opened it, and produced - not implements of murder, but a genuine pair of Georgian knobs. He then proceeded to fit them on the large gallery door.

Did he simply wander the streets with a bag of knobs, looking for opportunities to use them?

'There. You won't get locked in now,' he said with some satisfaction. 'Don't you feel better?'

No, you do, I thought as I smiled and thanked him, then handed over £35 in cash.

A few weeks later, we were showing a film in that same gallery room about the recent terrible floods in the town. People were getting very emotional as they relived their own experiences, but just at the really poignant bit where the newsagent's small daughter is seen tearfully waving goodbye to her mother as she is being handed into a dinghy, a mobile phone with an irritating comedy ringtone went off. The culprit leaped up and rushed for the door, wrenched it open, and both the new knobs, interior and exterior, fell off. Ignoring the catastrophe, she stumbled clumsily out of the front door, slamming it hard enough for the brass lion's head knocker to cringe. Meanwhile, the tiny grub screw which had held the knobs in place had flown off down a crack in the floorboards.

Henry, one of our regular clients, came to the rescue, grubbing out the grub screw - now we know where the name comes from – and, having been supplied with tools, quickly fixed it. All was soon peace again, but I decided that I didn't want a matching set of knobs throughout the house. Variety was acceptable.

The following day, there was another message awaiting me: 'Watch out for the Barefooters.'

I just couldn't wait!

Early Works

It was people like June and Michael Bennett who kept me sane that first year. I was making new friends all the time, gathering many loyal artists and clients, and my social life was hard to keep up with, but an evening with the Bennetts was always relaxing. I found out a lot more about them, mainly from the more loquacious June. She came from Grange-over-Sands, and Michael from Windermere. They had met at art college in Lancaster decades before, and moved on together to Leicester College of Art. By the time they left college in the early 1960s, married, and took up teaching posts in London, Michael was gaining an enviable reputation as a painter and was soon exhibiting with people who were to become Royal Academicians.

'He'll never tell you himself,' June said, giving her husband a challenging look. 'But he exhibited alongside David Hockney, Sandra Blow, Sheila Fell, and Lucien Freud, among others.'

She told me what an exciting time the Sixties were to be in the capital: Ivan Hitchens, Keith Vaughan, John Piper, Graham Sutherland and Henry Moore were all evident in the galleries of Bond Street and Cork Street, as well as in the public galleries. The couple made the most of their time there, but after they had children they decided to move back north: first to the Midlands and then to Wakefield, where Michael taught painting at Bretton Hall (now the Yorkshire Sculpture Park). However, he became frustrated: he took his job seriously and genuinely cared for the students, but it was to the detriment of his own work. The couple's big break came in 1970 when Michael was left a small legacy and resolved to take a year's sabbatical to paint full-time. They decided to come back to Cumbria when they found a house to rent on a clifftop in Seascale on the Cumbrian coast. It looked out over the sea but was very close to the Sellafield nuclear power station, which meant it was a reasonable rent. Michael never went back to teaching and that one year turned into a lifetime of painting. The seascape I had seen in Isobel's sitting room and others like it were done during that time.

June's jewellery sold very well and Michael sold enough work to keep them solvent. As their boys got older, they decided to settle permanently in Cumbria. The sea had become important to them, and eventually they bought the terrace house overlooking the Solway, where I was now a regular guest.

As June told me all this, I thought time and again what a pity it was that Michael no longer admitted to painting. What a waste. Then a marvellous thing happened. At the end of a simple supper one evening, Michael asked me in an almost inaudible whisper if I'd like to see his studio. Studio? It was an invitation just for me and I felt as if I was being let in on a secret as I followed him up the stairs to the first floor room on the right. It was a room I had never entered – I had always bypassed the first floor on my way to June's attic studio. The door to this room had always been firmly closed and it still was, but Michael now opened it shyly and stood aside to let me in. As I entered the private world of Michael Bennett for the first time, I was awkward and embarrassed: I felt as if I had barged into the bathroom by mistake, catching him naked. It had taken time and patience to get there, but I had earned his trust and his thoughts were now laid bare before me.

I stood still in the doorway and looked around in astonishment. The small room was littered with work in progress. There were so many ideas and images – more than I could cope with. I held my breath in case I broke the spell. Every surface was covered. Paintings were stacked three- or four-deep against the wall and I hardly dared move for fear of treading on the precious things underfoot. Michael silently melted away as I picked my way carefully over the floor. A large unfinished oil, the paint still wet, stood on the easel by the window. It was quite dark, rich browns and ochres, lit by a silver moon. As I stepped towards it I could see it was a garden. It drew me still closer, promising more. Against the almost black hedge, the vague figures of two running children emerged. They were chasing a white bird which stood out against the dark hedge. The boy was within a fingertip of touching the bird, the girl close behind him straining to reach it too. It engaged me. I was waiting for him to grasp it. There was movement in that painting, ambition, failure, perseverance, and all so subtle. Nothing was defined but I wanted them to touch the bird but not catch it.

I could faintly hear muffled conversation from the real world downstairs. It wasn't important. This was important. This was another world - a wonderful, alternative world into which I had been invited.

It was some time before I left the studio to rejoin the supper party. I didn't make any comment. It would only have been superfluous and crass. To offer Michael an exhibition would have broken the spell; I mustn't appear too eager. I was excited and impatient, but I would have to bide my time: I would have to learn to adopt the reticence that he displayed and play the long game. That was going to be hard for me.

Two years later, in the spring of 1990, I was sitting on the stairs winding down at the end of the opening of the gallery's Spring Exhibition. Once again, June had given me work for it, and once again I had sold it all. She now had two very successful solo shows behind her and we had built up a loyal following.

People were drifting off when Michael Bennett, wearing his habitual blue jeans and sandals, joined me on my perch.

'This is a good show,' he said quietly and, after a pause, 'Do you think you could find room for me some time?'

I tried hard not to show any eagerness or excitement. I had to control myself or I would blow it.

'A solo show?'

He nodded.

'I don't know, Michael. I'll go and have a look at the calendar, shall I?'

I went through into the packing room, turned round slowly

three times in delight, did a few star jumps, counted steadily up to twenty, then strolled back to find him still sitting on the stairs looking nervous.

'I've looked at the diary, Michael. I think I could fit you in next October - if you could be ready by then?'

There were at least three exhibitions strewn about his studio if he would just call them finished and let them go, but Michael was retentive by nature. His dogged pursuit of the perfection that would always elude him had held him back from fame and fortune – but he didn't want those ephemeral, self-corrupting things anyway.

There is a serenity about Michael's work which is almost tangible. It is very different from June's. She is the extrovert of the pair with her quick, bright oils; Michael the quiet introvert who will work on a painting for months, even years, painting out and adding on. He is still never satisfied with what he has created.

Many of Michael's paintings show indistinct figures or an ethereal woman reaching out to grasp an elusive bird. The bird is never caught, it is always a whisper out of reach. The bird is Michael's muse. He confessed one day that he'd had a picture in his head since the beginning of his college days in 1954: his perfect picture. He had tried to paint it many times and had been close to capturing it – but, like the bird, it always escaped.

'Will you ever manage it?' I asked

'No,' he said sadly. But we both knew that if he did, the painting would stop. He would have nothing left to strive for.

I have often been surprised by the weight of Michael's paintings, the result of multiple layers of paint and impasto built up over long periods. I once joked that I would be better selling them by the pound like potatoes, and June sometimes complained that if they had all the paintings he had painted out, painted over and obliterated, they would be millionaires. I knew how she felt. There have been many times when I have visited his studio and asked where a certain painting I wanted for the gallery had gone.

'It's there,' Michael would answer, indicating something quite different.

'No, I mean the one with a group of trees and a gritty pink sun. It was just here.'

'It still is - I painted over it. It wasn't very good. This one is better, isn't it?'

'No, it's just different, Michael. It would have been good to have both - on separate canvases!'

I could hear my headmistress voice emerging and I hated it. However, what I have come to realise is that the painting underneath informs the next layer. It gives depth and substance. If Michael's paintings are ever subjected to ultra-violet analysis in the future, the results are bound to be interesting.

On a Sunday morning that following October, I was preparing to open my first Michael Bennett exhibition. I was trembling with excitement. Michael hadn't had an exhibition anywhere for at least ten years and the illustrated invitation and glossy catalogue had created a stir. When I opened the door at midday to the art critic Peter Inch, who had come at the bidding of *Art Review*, I was astonished to see a queue forming. This was my very first queue. It was to be the first of many.

When Peter had finished wandering round, taking notes, I opened the exhibition to the public. It was half past two. The crowd rushed in eagerly, dispersed in all directions clutching price lists, and then fell completely silent. It was uncanny – this was different from any previous opening. No pleasantries were exchanged; no glasses of wine were touched. The atmosphere was charged. Everyone was concentrating on this collection of 30 exceptional paintings.

What's the problem? I thought as I waited anxiously for some sort of action. *Don't they all share my passion for his work?* I knew people had travelled long distances to be here – were they disappointed?

They weren't. After a tense ten minutes, the spell broke. The first red spot went up and was followed by an avalanche. Requests came so fast that I struggled to keep up. I dashed from room to room, from wall to wall, followed by a retinue of anxious buyers fearful someone else would get in first.

90 minutes and 28 red spots later, it was all over. People had retired to the garden with a glass of wine and were now calming down, discussing their purchases volubly. There was gossip and laughter. The party had begun.

The Chief Executive of a global business based in London approached me. He had bought three of Michael's paintings.

'These are real quality, Chris,' he said. 'Get a contract on this guy.' Then, seeing my diffident look, 'I mean it. You'd be crazy not to. Tie him down. You must have an exclusive.'

Most of the London galleries with whom this man was familiar had a common practice of binding artists to them with a contract. The artist agreed to produce a certain number of works each year and not sell anywhere else, and in exchange received a small stipend and were looked after by the gallery. I felt this was wrong, like caging a bird; it stifled creativity and curtailed initiative.

I laughed lightly, shrugged my shoulders in an enigmatic manner and moved away, smiling. If I tried that with Michael Bennett, I would surely lose him. I would have to win his loyalty, not buy it.

Throughout the afternoon of his first show at Castlegate, Michael drifted about shyly in his faded denims and sandals. The strain of the last few months was showing on his face. June and I had coaxed him along, trying to persuade him that certain paintings really were finished, but he was never convinced.

'Can't you get that one from him before it's too late?' I would sometimes whisper to June outside the door of his studio. She rarely managed it. It was like tussling a bone from a strong, stubborn dog.

The last painting to arrive for hanging had been one I

hadn't seen before, not even as work in progress. It was different from all the others: pink and orange flowers wrapped first in dark tissue paper then in cellophane, set against a pink sky with a perfect circle of hot, orange sun. There was a hint of pink stripes - maybe curtains - down each side of the painting, and a slight horizontal band below the bouquet – maybe a window-sill. The colours were subtle, the shapes indefinite and vague. It was a very small painting, but its heavy mount and frame bestowed a sense of importance. All the other paintings in this exhibition were in Michael's habitual plain, light frames. This one was in a heavy antique frame with an elaborate gold lace-like slip. 'Bouquet for the sun 1990; oil' it said on the back of the canvas, and it was just that: a gift-wrapped offering to the sun. When it arrived at the gallery, the paint still wet, I looked at Michael with a raised eyebrow.

'It's my thank you to the Muse,' he explained. 'For being able to finish the work for the exhibition: a sort of votive offering.'

It had only been painted when the rest of the exhibition had been complete.

I couldn't resist the urge to buy the bouquet, and it now hangs on the wall of my office. It was my thank you for a remarkable exhibition - and all those that were to follow.

Michael Bennett is now in his late 70s and frailer than ever, but he is still painting, still chasing the Muse.

While arranging his next exhibition - and after the outstanding success of that first one, there had to be a second - I again spent some time at the Bennetts' house on the Solway, photographing work and offering encouraging words. I always felt cruel wresting work from Michael: each was part of him. He always looked so sad and wistful as I extracted his treasures, loaded them into the car boot and drove off.

Over lunch one day when I was on a mission to relieve him of yet more paintings, he made an oblique reference to some early works. I was instantly onto that.

'What early works are those, Michael? How early?'

'Oh, when we lived in the Midlands. That was where my painting really began to develop.'

'He showed with the Midland group,' June intervened. 'He was showing alongside Ben Nicholson, William Scott, Mary Fedden, Julian Trevelyan, Prunella Clough and - within a few years - Sheila Fell.'

Michael's work had appeared in open shows of Modern British Artists at the Graves in Sheffield and Bradford City Art Gallery, among other places, she said.

'He got good reviews. I think we have the catalogues somewhere.'

I already knew all of this. I'd been waiting for an opportunity to discuss those days. Meanwhile, Michael gave a modest but uneasy smile and made no comment.

'Do you have any images of your early work?' I asked. 'Do you know where any of them are?'

'He's still got some of them,' June blurted out.

Michael frowned at her.

I really sat up now, hearing this.

'So where are these early works?' I was trying hard not to sound too interested.

'Oh, they're not worth looking at,' came the reply. 'They're in storage.'

He gave June a warning look. He wasn't going to show me or tell me where he kept them. They were definitely not in his studio. Maybe they were in the loft? But they hadn't got a loft: June's studio was up there in the rafters under the sloping roof. Maybe there was a storage facility somewhere. But where?

'They're very big and abstract,' he added. 'Nobody will want those now. Would you like some more crumble?'

From time to time after that, we indulged in a little friendly badinage about Michael's early works. It became a joke between us. But however much I enquired, however subtly I delved, Michael wouldn't tell me where they were stored and

36

June wasn't allowed to either. Nevertheless, although many years would now pass, my quest was far from over...

Legless

Having made a good start with the gallery, I was well aware that I had to keep the momentum going. I had to provide a series of changing exhibitions and they had to be good. I could not sit back complacently. Many people believe that if you open a gallery, artists will appear like magic with no effort involved – and they sure do: in double figures. There were times when it was easy to believe that every other person in Britain was an artist and what's more, like salmon to the Sargasso Sea, they were all making their way unerringly to the gallery.

Some would arrive hauling paintings proudly with them and scatter them liberally around the hall and the gallery rooms. A 'pop-up' exhibition would be in situ before I realised what was happening. Others arrived with three-dimensional pieces which they placed strategically for people to admire - or fall over. And it would be hard to stop the flow once it had begun. They would be back out to their car before I could protest, getting ready to bring in the next batch. It was really hard to refuse politely without causing embarrassment or offence or, even worse, being forced to give reasons or prompt an argument about the merits of the work.

I was pleased about the attention the gallery was attracting: I wanted artists to come and was happy for them to use it as a meeting place. It was good to have them buzzing about, discussing the works on show, but most of them wanted me to give them an appraisal of their work and, above all, they wanted to be hung.

In the middle of my second opening, I failed to see a sculptor arrive with a large cardboard box. It was the size of a washing machine. She dumped it in the hall and promptly started to unpack it, sending white polystyrene bows floating everywhere. By the time I came on the scene, the hall was like a paperweight snowstorm. Visitors were arriving, struggling through it, treading it everywhere, trying to brush it from their clothing. I lost my decorum and shouted.

'Get that mess cleaned up and get it out of here!'

'But I've been invited,' the sculptor said, waving her crumpled invitation card at me.

'Not to bring that in you, haven't.'

'But you haven't seen it,' she pleaded. 'It's one of my best!'

'I've seen enough,' I whispered. 'Send a photograph if you wish, but remove it now - whatever it is.'

I was fast becoming a hard woman. I had to be, or the gallery would be full of amateur paintings, lopsided pots, corn dollies, tea cosies, and horrendous papier-mâché articles which defied description. I avoided looking at anyone's work unless they sent images and a CV in advance, and if I thought they were a possible, I would invite them to bring no more than three items to show me. It sounds autocratic, but it was self-preservation.

Nevertheless, I was submerged. A fairly new commercial gallery in a very beautiful house with an impressive sales record and a reputation for paying artists promptly is good news, and word soon spread quickly via the ultra-efficient artists' communication system.

Photographs, slides, floppy disks and CVs arrived in every post, but although I looked at everything, only a small percentage engaged my interest. Galleries each have their own character, so a rejection from one gallery doesn't mean that the work in question isn't any good. However, I had a finite amount of space, limited exhibition slots, and not enough time to deal with everything I was being sent. It would have taken a full-time member of staff who knew the gallery and knew what they were looking at to keep up with it all. Yet artists would sometimes only wait three days after posting their stuff before ringing to ask what I thought, or complain that I hadn't let them know their slides or floppy disk had arrived. Some would wait a little longer and then ask why I hadn't returned their things to them if I didn't want their work. Others asked for an appraisal and wanted to know why I hadn't rushed to offer an exhibition.

Something had to be done. Realising that I had to toughen up, I composed a gentle acknowledgement/rejection letter that could be personalised, signed and sent. It was polite and I avoided the words 'don't like' or 'don't want', which I thought were too negative and damaging. Art is subjective; who was I to condemn? But I knew what I wanted as soon as I saw it and the opposite was true. This cover-all letter, together with a request for an SAE if anything was to be returned, would surely solve the problem.

Apparently not. I was still too soft! My refusal letter was too ambivalent for some, who wilfully misinterpreted it, and one day things inevitably caught up with me.

I had received some photographs of ceramic sculptures which I, even at my most charitable, thought were truly awful. They were of animals: ungainly, stiff, heavy and lifeless. There was no movement, no soul in them. The artist lived way south of London and had never been to the gallery, but thought he would like an exhibition. The 'Dear Sir/Madam' at the beginning of his letter told me he had possibly approached dozens of galleries from a list: at the very least, a prospective artist should do some research and find out the name of the proprietor. They should visit anonymously, if they are close enough, get a sense of the place, and look at the work of current exhibitors. Then they should ask themselves honestly if their own work fits in. They should be as discerning in choosing a gallery as a gallery will be in choosing them. If you do marine paintings, for instance, find a gallery that specialises in them. Likewise wildlife, photography, abstract work, figurative work, portraits, textiles... But since when have artists been logical? Creativity makes for divergent thinking. Let's celebrate that.

My standard, politely discouraging letter of refusal went off to the ceramicist immediately. It ended with this sentence:

'I am sorry we can't take your work, but if you are ever in the Lake District do come and see the gallery. Yours etc.'

A few months and dozens of applications for exhibition space later, I returned from a meeting to find a campervan in the car park, back doors wide open and the gate into the garden open too. I hurried through to investigate. There stood a ceramic hare, rearing upright on its hind legs above a crouching beaver. They were fused together, having been fired all in one piece, and the beaver was looking up at the hare from roughly crotch level. The sexual connotation was not nice - or was that just me? A man I didn't recognise had just finished placing the piece on an empty stone plinth and as I approached he turned and gave me a dazzling, disarming smile.

'What are you doing?' I asked.

'I've brought the sculpture you asked for,' he said, full of confidence.

I searched my mind. Yes, we were awaiting the arrival of some sculpture, but this definitely wasn't it. I had never met this person before. He introduced himself. Hell, it was the ceramicist from the south!

'I'm sorry, but I didn't ask for this. I wrote you a letter. I returned your photographs.'

His face fell, his shoulders drooped. I felt sorry for him. He did seem nice and very sincere.

'But it looks good, doesn't it? I like this garden. It's the perfect place to show sculpture. I like the gallery too. You did invite me.'

'I think you'll find I invited you to visit if you were in the area, but I definitely didn't offer you a show,' I said, gently. 'I'm afraid I don't have the space.'

'Oh, but yes you do. And there's another spare plinth over there. I'll just fetch my wolf. You'll really like my wolf.'

He strode off to the van before I could stop him. My assistant Wendy and I exchanged despairing glances.

'I didn't know what to do. He told me you'd asked for it,'

41

she said. 'I must say I was surprised.'

The wolf was even bigger and uglier than the hare or beaver. I wouldn't have known it was a wolf if I hadn't been told. I was horrified. Wendy and I stood transfixed as he struggled through the gate with it and made for the most prominent stone plinth: the plinth we used for the most outstanding piece in any garden sculpture exhibition. It was empty because it was awaiting the arrival of a large abstract bronze by David Howarth. The sculptor plonked the wolf down on it enthusiastically – whereupon one of its legs fell off.

Thank you, God, I said silently.

'Oh dear,' I said aloud. 'Look, I'm sorry but I'm afraid you'll have to take these elsewhere. They're not suitable here.'

The time for gentle had passed.

'But you asked for them,' the artist began again. 'I'm on my way to Scotland and I haven't room in the van. I'm sleeping in it tonight. I've got a van full of my best work that I've brought specially for you. You will have to keep it. And look - one of them's now got broken.'

A wise London gallery owner once said to me: 'You know, artists are quite neglectful of their work. When it's in their studio it's worth nothing. They rarely insure it. But as soon as it's in a gallery, it's suddenly worth a massive amount of money and even a small scratch on a frame is a major repair job.'

I thought of this as the man looked at me as though the wolf's mishap was my fault. His smile had disappeared. This handsome, pleasant young man had now put his injured and upset face on, and there was a slight hint of menace.

I was annoyed. It was time for hard talking.

'No, I don't have to keep them at all. I didn't ask for them and I don't want them here. That one is damaged and the other is obscene. Take them away. Do not get any more out of your van!'

At that moment, dead on cue, the telephone rang. Wendy answered and called me in. It was urgent. As I took the

42

telephone from her hand I said, 'Can you please get rid of that sculptor? Don't let him bring any more in and don't take no for an answer. Be firm. Tell him I'm an ogress and you'll lose your job if I come back out and find it still there. You won't of course,' I quickly added, 'but say anything to get rid of him.'

When I came back out, the sculptures had gone, the van had gone, and the gate was locked. Wendy had made a pot of tea.

A few weeks later, a visitor came in from the garden, laughing.

'Why have you hidden your best sculpture in the bushes?' he asked.

'What sculpture is that?'

He'd found the hare and beaver in the rhododendrons! He had pulled them out, but after one look had hastily put them back again. Luckily he wasn't prudish and had a wicked sense of humour – and, mercifully, there had been no sign of the three-legged wolf...

The Life Class

'What a lovely gallery,' the man said, looking around. 'May I say a poem?'

I hesitated for a moment. He looked like an escapee from a tramp farm but he sounded posh. The two things are not mutually exclusive, of course. He was wearing a very old tattered and stained overcoat and looked dishevelled. His thin grey hair was straying in all directions.

Without waiting for an answer, he took a small, well-used notebook from his pocket, strode confidently into the West Room, and began to read from it in a loud, clear voice. His poem was about Scotland and the clearances. It was about an old shepherd who died in exile miles away from his croft in his beloved Highlands. It was strong and compelling and deeply moving. People came in from the other rooms to listen. When he had finished they applauded discreetly.

Who is this man? I asked myself. Maybe he was an eccentric farmer. Maybe he had fallen in love with an Englishwoman and come over the Border for her – a sort of Gretna Green wedding in reverse.

My thoughts were interrupted as he reappeared beside me.

'Thank you so much for that,' I said. 'It was lovely…'

'Do you have a husband?' he abruptly asked.

I bit my lip. People often assumed there had to be a man in the background running the place and it annoyed me.

'Yes, I do,' I said shortly. 'Why?'

'Where is he?'

'He's working in the garden.'

'What's his name?'

For goodness' sake! I thought.

'Michael,' I said.

'May I go and talk to him?' he asked, looking out of the window.

What a cheek, I thought.

'Yes, of course,' I replied doubtfully. 'But please will you sign the visitors' book first?'

I wanted to know who this untidy, inquisitive person was before I let him loose in the garden and inflicted him on a husband who was still withdrawn, depressed and fragile with the shock of experiencing unemployment for the first time in his adult life.

The man's signature didn't tell me much. 'Patrick of the Hills', he simply wrote.

'Do you have an address?' I asked quickly. 'Then I can put you on the mail list.'

'Muncaster' he wrote in the address column. I wouldn't have been surprised if he was of 'no fixed abode'.

'I can do mirror writing, you know,' he then said proudly. And he wrote his name again, this time in reverse.

'That's clever, you must have been educated at Eton!' I said, with some measure of irony.

'How did you know that?' he shot back, before setting off outside.

Ah! Now I'd got it. My visitor must be Patrick Gordon Duff Pennington of Muncaster Castle near Ravenglass. It had been the Pennington family home since 1208 and was famous for its owls, rhododendrons and ghosts. I hadn't found time to visit it yet although I'd read quite a bit about it. It was Patrick's wife Phyllida who had inherited the estate and when she married, her husband had been legally obliged to adopt her surname. As the couple then had three daughters, whose husbands also had to adopt the Pennington name, their story was a good slap in the face for the feudal system of primogeniture.

As soon as Patrick was out of the garden door I could hear him calling, 'Michael, Michael, where are you? I'm coming! I'm coming!'

I smiled. Clouds of white smoke were billowing across the garden: my husband obviously had a good bonfire going and was either hiding behind it or simulating deafness in the shed. But when I made some tea and went out to find them half an

45

hour later, they were sitting on a log in the smoke, chattering away like old friends.

***

Opening and running the gallery was an education for me – it was a crash course in human behaviour: a Life Class. The person walking through the door might be the chairman of the Arts Council or a local pottery teacher, a motor mechanic or a famous actor – my customers fitted no standard profile. Titles or wealth didn't interest me – a passion for art was the significant quality, the quality I admired. In fact, the social status or wealth of visitors to the gallery turned out to be no guide to whether they would leave with a painting: titled people have often got stately piles stacked with more than enough dark portraits of ancestors, while the extremely rich are looking for investments or 'look at me' show-off paintings of the kind I had no desire to display at Castlegate House.

With a gallery, as in life, the socialist maxim of 'treat everyone the same, whether a prince or a pauper' just didn't work: every one of my customers turned out to be extraordinary in some way. On the other hand, art could sometimes be a great leveller...

Early in my career, I travelled miles to see a Mary Fedden show, only to find that everything had sold from the catalogue long before the opening date. This was a steep learning curve for the new kid on the block.

'Never turn down a sale,' many gallery owners who were older and more experienced than me urged. 'Keep the cash flow going.'

Maybe that was good advice, but I wanted to be fair. I didn't want others to have the experience I'd had of travelling so far only to be disappointed. What's more, I also wanted to feel the drama, the sense of occasion, that surrounded each opening – there was none of that if the works on show were already covered in red spots.

I never envisaged or expected people to queue for art outside the gallery, but they did. After that first queue for the Michael Bennett exhibition, they continued with Marie Scott and peaked with Percy Kelly.

The first Kelly queue in May 1994 started early at the front door of the gallery, snaked round the car park, out onto the pavement and down the hill. By midday it was 50-strong, everyone chattering and laughing. When I opened the door at half past two, there was a stampede of eager people who snapped up every single painting. I'd felt a bit guilty making people wait outside for so long and asked myself whether it was fair. But the feedback from the participants gave me to understand that they'd enjoyed what had become part of the story of their particular purchase. There had been debates, exchanges of addresses, friendships formed and life histories retold in that queue.

On the morning of the second Kelly solo exhibition two years later, I woke early to hear chattering outside, below my bedroom window. I was ready for this by now, but I was surprised and amused when I took out coffee and chairs to see Antonia occupying the coveted first place in the queue. She was an elegant, well-dressed woman who lived in the Home Counties and always visited the gallery with her sister, who lived locally. She desperately wanted a Kelly – well several, actually – but had previously missed the ones she wanted because she lived so far away. She was petite and fragile with glossy, well-cut dark hair. I doubted she'd ever queued for anything in her life before this. Regularly during the morning, a long, sleek black limousine pulled into the castle gateway opposite. Antonia's husband got out and came over with a flask of hot coffee, solicitously checking on her welfare. Over the next few hours this was followed by smoked salmon sandwiches, a slice of gateau, strawberries and cream, and chocolate biscuits.

All the while I could hear Antonia entertaining the queue with her stories: she was enjoying herself immensely and so was everyone else. Previously, I had considered engaging a busker to entertain people while they were waiting - this time he would have been redundant. Of course, the growing number of people behind Antonia were anxious to know what she was going to buy so they could adjust their wish list accordingly. There had been two viewing days prior to the opening, so they had marked up their catalogues with what they wanted in order of preference. When I took out the first batch of hot coffee, Antonia told me which ones she was after in a confidential but loud whisper; she needed reassurance and asked my advice. The queue leaned forward attentively and messages were passed backwards - but a little while later a roar went up. It was like a football crowd when their team misses a goal. I went out to see what disaster had happened only to find Antonia had had a change of heart. Sitting on her stool, erect like a queen, she suddenly said, 'Oh no, I've changed my mind. I think I'll take number 32 and number 47, rather than 15 and 26!'

Immediately it was all heads down to see which paintings those numbers were. There was a mass mental rearrangement of choices which was relayed up the queue, rippling like a Mexican Wave, but such were Antonia's dramatic waverings, wobblings and changes of mind over the next few hours that after a while nobody knew what they were doing any more. There were frequent phone calls to her husband, son, sister and various friends and family with the queue behind her straining to hear what she was saying. It was a game of Chinese Whispers. Finally, the doors opened and she got what she thought she wanted - or at least, what she wanted at that moment.

***

After his first visit, Patrick of the Hills often called in at the gallery. Sometimes he was killing time, having dropped his car off for service at the nearby Volvo garage; sometimes he was on his way from the Butcher (his name for Meredyth Bell, the local dentist) and had to speak through a frozen mouth. His memory for names was excellent. He remembered all the staff at the gallery and treated us all with equal respect. Once I got to know him much better I took the opportunity to tell him how off-putting the old coat he always wore was.

'Prince Charles gave me that,' he replied indignantly, as though it explained everything. Maybe it did. He was a man totally without pretension. He was a good example for me to follow.

Ours developed into a firm friendship and on every visit Patrick would entertain us with talk of his native Scotland, sheep-farming, parliamentary committees, poetry, and birds – the owls and raptors he kept at Muncaster as well as the migrating swallows which nested in our tumbledown shed and in which he took a keen interest. He talked of bears - one of his ancestors was eaten by a bear in Siberia - ghosts, and the discomfort of living in a cold, mediaeval castle; discomforts that Michael and I were soon invited to experience firsthand.

Sitting round a fire in the castle library after the paying visitors had gone, we resorted to swaddling ourselves in blankets to keep warm, while Patrick himself was buried in a quilted sleeping bag. We discussed the castle ghosts and he told us that he was arranging a themed evening with a talk by two ghost specialists who had dared to stay several nights in the haunted Tapestry bedroom. He was thinking of hiring some local thespians to provide some surprise special effects. On his desk, I smiled to see a Christmas card from Prince Charles, his mate.

'Do you know,' Patrick said suddenly, looking around the double-height room, 'what I'd like to do is build a little centrally-heated bungalow in the middle of this place. Leaving the retaining walls, of course - then the planners and English Heritage wouldn't know, would they? Unless they have a helicopter! What d'you think?'

We laughed at the thought – however, a few years later, his roof work was in fact checked out by helicopter and found wanting, much to his disgust.

The next May, I took my two granddaughters to the castle to frighten them with tales of ghosts. Isn't it the duty of a grandparent to do things the parents wouldn't do for fear of the consequences?

The gardens were full of rampant rhododendrons in full flower and inside the castle was just as impressive. From the hall we made our way up the oak staircase to the bedroom corridor, where most of the rooms were still used by the Pennington family. There was a pair of trousers casually left over the back of a chair which gave the place a human touch. We peered through the open door of the roped-off Tapestry Room at its heavily curtained four-poster bed: this was the room where the sounds of children crying could supposedly be heard at night. I was just telling Natasha and Sylvie the blood-curdling story when Patrick suddenly materialised through a connecting door.

'Hello Chris,' he said. 'How lovely to see you. Who have we got here, then?'

The girls squealed and hid behind me, convinced he was an evil ghost that somehow knew my name. My credit rating in the grandmotherly stakes went right up to the top: it was as though I'd hammered the 'Test your strength' game in a fairground and rung the bell. I could imagine the girls at school saying, 'My grandma knows a ghost – he's called Patrick!'

Bit by bit they became bolder and more curious and finally emerged from inside my coat to tentatively shake his hand.

'Now,' he said, 'would you like to see Tom Fool?'

Of course they would. They were quivering with excitement - or was it fear?

Patrick led us back down the corridor towards a life-size oil painting that hung in an alcove at the top of the stairs. It was impossible to pass: Tom Fool's evil eyes were piercing, compelling passersby to stop and pay him some attention. He had been the castle's steward and jester in the seventeenth century and was painted wearing a bright yellow and blue chequered gown. But although the terms 'Tom Foolery' and 'Fool's errand' derived from his name – which in fact was Tom Skelton - he wasn't a fool but a mendacious and sadistic man. He was a jester without a jest in him. His face in the painting was pure evil: thick, fleshy lips; cold, penetrating eyes, and legend has it that, if he took a dislike to travellers who stopped at the castle to ask directions to London, he would direct them across the nearby quivering bog and they would never be seen again.

As we looked on, Patrick recounted the story of a castle carpenter who had fallen in love with one of the Pennington daughters. Tom Fool lured the unlucky man to the Tapestry Room under false pretences, hacked off the man's head, and buried it under the chestnut tree outside the castle's front entrance. After Patrick had finished telling us the tale, we all went out and stood under the tree, the girls shivering delightedly.

It was a day to remember.

The Big Apple

My first big outdoor sculpture exhibition arrived unexpectedly in the early hours of a Monday morning. Midwinter isn't an ideal time for an al fresco exhibition, but I hadn't planned it that way: I hadn't planned it at all. It just turned up on the doorstep in the night, a 'ready made' – my one and only.

It was my first winter as a gallerist. I was going at a cracking pace and loving every hectic minute. I fell asleep the moment I got into bed and knew nothing until I woke to face a new day and a new adventure. It was November but I was already working on the coming year's programme of exhibitions. Sales of paintings were massively beyond my expectations, my mail list was growing all the time, and I knew I had to keep the momentum up and provide new things, keep the interest going. I had all the inside exhibitions planned, artists and dates were agreed, and I had now turned my attention to the three-dimensional. I had worked out that I had a limited market for paintings here in the far north west, and that in a few years the walls of all my new clients would be full at the rate we were going (I was mistaken – but then I did once say I didn't think the World Wide Web would catch on...). So I decided I must have some spectacular sculpture – particularly outdoor pieces – for the summer.

The gallery's walled garden was the perfect setting for large pieces, but sculpture is awkward: difficult to transport, difficult to handle, and difficult to source. Painters, potters and printmakers were approaching me all the time but never outdoor sculptors. I'd have to seek them out. Where should I start?

The answer arrived one cold, bright, morning. In that dozy warm time between sleep and awakening, I was subconsciously aware that there was something different. It was an absence rather than a presence. It was like an itch I couldn't reach and it gave me an uneasy feeling. There was something not right.

There wasn't any traffic noise. That was it. There was no chatter of schoolchildren outside walking up the road, no school buses charging past.

What day is it? Is it Saturday? I thought. No, I knew it wasn't. Maybe it was a school holiday? But no, Christmas was some weeks ahead. I was drowsily working this through my brain when a loud whooshing noise intruded - and then another. Instantly alert, I rushed to the front of the house and looked down from the upstairs window to see gravel pouring from a lorry to form an unstable pyramid in the road. A large pipe then came into view, hovering gracefully outside the first floor window. I could have leaned out and touched it. Slowly, it rotated in an anti-clockwise direction before the crane from which it was suspended deposited it with a clank across my front doorstep.

Quickly pulling on some clothes, I stumbled down the stairs and out of the door, just as the crane deposited another swinging pipe next to the first. Another heap of gravel was sliding from the back of a tipper lorry with a deafening clatter. With difficulty, I scrambled through all the rubble and surveyed the scene of devastation from the other side of the road. My beautiful house, my shiny new business, was being obscured by pipes and pyramids. The front door entrance was inaccessible without steel-toed boots, hard hat and protective clothing. A large red board announced 'ROAD CLOSED' in big white capitals. There was another 'ROAD CLOSED' barrier at the bottom of the hill, and a row of wide gauge concrete pipes lay head-to-tail all the way up. It was impossible to reach the gallery from the town centre. We were cut off, afloat in a sea of pipes.

I heard a pneumatic drill start up and rushed towards the glass-shattering racket to find two men in ear defenders making a hole in the pavement at the narrow entrance to the gallery car park. Their high visibility jackets bore the legend: 'KEN CONSTRUCTION MANCHESTER'.

In full flight, I went in search of Ken to demand an explanation.

The foreman was defensive. Pleading ignorance, he said he was unaware that he was dumping materials in front of a working business; he hadn't noticed that I couldn't get any cars in or out of the car park, or that nobody could reach the entrance to the gallery on foot either.

'You had a letter,' he stated tersely. He pointed to a lamp post. 'It's there. I thought you were just a private house or something.'

Yes, I had received the standard letter a few weeks ago. I did know they were replacing the old Victorian sewage system throughout Cockermouth, but I had also been informed that disruption to businesses would be kept to a minimum. Work had begun some months previously, but there had not been any road closures as yet and I'd had no idea about the extent of the work and the timescale. It had come as a shock that Monday morning.

'Don't worry, love,' he continued, more cheerfully. 'We'll be done up here by Christmas. Then we'll re-open the road.'

'What?' I exclaimed. 'That's seven weeks away. This is a disaster.'

My first Christmas exhibition was due to open on Sunday. What could I do? I would have to work round it somehow. Perhaps I could even work with it. But how?

We had a quiet week in the gallery: no visitors and no sales. After some persuasion and mugs of strong sweet tea, Ken repositioned the hole a few feet further down the hill and I was able to get my car out, although where I could go from there was contentious. I had also negotiated the placing of the pipe across the entrance gate: it was nudged by a few feet to allow pedestrian access to the front door. But there were no pedestrians and there was still a slalom of obstacles to negotiate in order to do anything at all.

I'd just felt confident enough to take on my first part-time assistant. This would be her third week. By the time Wendy arrived on foot that Monday morning, picking her way through the debris, I had formed a plan. Our Christmas exhibition had suddenly taken on a new dimension. There is no such thing as bad publicity, they tell me. I was about to test that theory.

I chose my time carefully. On Friday afternoon, as soon as Ken's men left early for the weekend back home in Manchester, Wendy and I flew into action. We hauled out a pre-prepared large piece of mount board which announced:

'PIPES FOR CHRISTMAS
An exhibition of modern sculpture
by
KEN CONSTRUCTION
of
Manchester'

With a little imagination, the massive, debris-filled hole now adjacent to the car park entrance had all the makings of an entry for the Turner Prize. We had just rearranged it more artistically, with a bit of tinsel.

The label read: 'ON LOAN FROM THE TATE GALLERY LIVERPOOL'.

All this activity after a week of nothing happening made me begin to feel a bit better. A large board which stood at the bottom of the hill read:

'NEW EXHIBITION
PIPES FOR CHRISTMAS'

An arrow pointed up the pipe trail to Castlegate's Christmas Exhibition. The first pipe, labelled 'THE PIED PIPER', had a flute stuck on it and a toy mouse led the way up the hill.

We spray-painted a wobbly but colourful Scottish tartan on

the next pipe, stuck a large bin bag on the end and labelled it 'BAG PIPE, £142,000', adding a very big red 'sold' spot (just in case anybody turned up with a chequebook). Likewise, we adorned the next pipe with J-cloths and a mop and bucket and it became 'PIPE CLEANER' (price £123,500). We made a 'PIPE FISH', 'PIPELINE', 'PIPE DREAM' (with pillow) and 'PIPED MUSIC', which featured a blaring radio concealed within. We put big red spots and price tags on everything. That'd be sure to get 'em out.

I had warned Wendy at her job interview that the unexpected lies in wait ready to pounce on a daily basis in a gallery. We had a laugh as we discussed clause thirteen in her job description, which stated that she must be prepared to do anything (within reason) asked of her by the management. She was now facing the reality of having agreed and was really enjoying herself – she told me she'd never had a job like this before. Banksy, just beginning his graffiti career in Bristol (and having his future, potentially priceless, efforts obliterated by the council), would have been proud of us.

A phone call to the local press brought photographers and a headline article, and when our exhibition hit the national press, we had streams of visitors - far more than we would have had with conventional advertising - to the opening of our unique exhibition and our planned Christmas show. They picked their way cheerfully through the chaos, enjoying the joke, and disaster became triumph.

However, there was consternation from the workers of Ken Construction when their convoy rolled in from Manchester the following Monday morning. They stood and scratched their yellow helmets until they realised what we'd done and, happily for us, saw the joke. More press and television cameras arrived and asked them what they thought of it: were they proud of their exhibition? Did they like being part of the art world? They replied with enthusiasm that they too had never done a job like it before - ever.

Not all exhibitions arrived ready made like that one.

My trip to see the exhibition by the American sculptor David Smith at Tate Modern was inspiring. Hailed as the greatest American sculptor of his generation, he transformed machine parts, tractors, shovels and broken tools into things of interest and beauty. His first job was as a welder and riveter for a car manufacturer, so his first sculptures were made from waste iron and steel parts picked up from the factory floor. In 1962, he had an exhibition in Italy and was given the contents of a huge, abandoned welding factory in Spoleto. He set up a workshop inside the derelict building and worked happily for months, like a child with a giant Meccano set.

As a Yorkshire woman, I felt empathy: I deplore waste. It's in my DNA. I recycle everything I can and find it hard to throw anything away. With walls of cupboards on every floor of Castlegate House, a huge labyrinth of cellars and several sheds and outhouses, it was easy to accumulate.

Living in a market town among the farming community, I soon realised that many farmers were the same - they held on to every bit of junk they ever had, although usually for different reasons: maybe inertia; maybe because they had fields and barns so it was easier to abandon items rather than recycle or destroy them; maybe because there could be cost involved in having it taken away. A few farms in the area were surrounded by dead machinery, and the worst looked like scrapyards. I could have taken you to a stream in an idyllic spot in the National Park, a few miles from the gallery, and shown you the old car that had been dumped in it and nearby a field full of slowly rusting machinery. Some useful money could have been made if they could have bothered to load it all on a trailer and take it down to the scrap merchant. In fact, the scrap man would probably have come and collected it. Or, of course, they could have made sculpture out of it themselves – in an ideal world!

Given that I was still on the lookout for sculptors, I was

particularly thrilled when I found one who scooped these rusting pieces up. Norfolk-based Anna Williams cannibalised discarded agricultural implements and bits of old farm machinery and welded fantastical sculptures from them. Anna's 'horse', made from an old metal plough and various tractor bits, was an impressive exercise in recycling. A 'cow' made from the bucket, pistons and doors of an old tractor was brilliant (especially the udders made from the leather seat). This was not swords into ploughshares, but ploughshares into pieces of art and imaginative beauty.

I was even more excited when Anna agreed to a summer show in the garden. By now I had drafted a contract for artists with dates, commission rates, deliveries and general conditions - essential to the smooth running of the gallery. I'd learned the importance of it the hard way: artists need a definite framework of dates to guide them. Anna signed and returned her contract straightaway. She provided photographs at the right time, the invitations were printed and ready for posting, and I was sure everything was sorted: I could now concentrate on other things.

It was ten past one in the morning when the telephone by my bed woke me up. I answered on about the twentieth ring, sleepily trying to pull myself into the real world. I braced myself for bad news. Had someone died? Had there been an accident?

No, it was Anna the sculptor.

'Hello,' she said in a dull, flat voice. 'I'm a bit worried about how I'm going to get my work to Cumbria.'

'What?'

I'm not good at that time of the morning. I was tetchy. My badly needed beauty sleep had been brutally disturbed. We had thoroughly discussed this months ago. She'd already told me she had her own transport and she preferred to bring her pieces and place them herself. She had seemed keen – then.

'Do you know what time it is?' I asked sharply.

'No, I don't bother with time.'

'Well I do, and it's quarter past one and I was asleep. Can we talk about this in the morning? I'll ring you back then.'

She ignored this and carried on in the same dreary tone.

'I've just looked at a map and Cumbria is a long way from Norfolk now.'

The 'now' annoyed me further.

'It's just as far as it was when you agreed to do the show,' I snapped. 'It hasn't moved!'

I could see where this was leading and I didn't want to know - not this side of eight a.m., anyway.

'Well, I can't do it. It's too far. I can't drive that far.'

The opening of Anna's exhibition was two weeks away. The invitations had gone out and there had been many enquiries about the scrapyard lion with a motorcycle chain spine, as well as the horse welded from bits of tractor. I told her this. I was fully awake now.

'I'll send a carrier,' I offered more gently. 'Or I can send someone to pick them up. There's a lot of interest in your show, you know.'

'No, I like to bring them myself. Things get broken with carriers. Even when I deliver them myself, I often have to do a bit of assembly or welding on the spot. I place them as well. I'm really particular about presentation and position.'

I offered every solution I could think of - I tried hard to accommodate her - but alas, there was no solution. I tried to reason, help and persuade, but she wouldn't shift. She was determined to reject any solution I put forward. We reached deadlock. She had made her mind up. She wasn't going to do it, was she? Maybe she had double booked. Maybe she'd had a better offer. Maybe she did place her sculptures well, but that was assuming she ever got them to places where they were supposed to be. The gallery contract wasn't practically or legally enforceable. My bluff had been called. What was I to do?

People were now travelling long distances to our openings. It would not be good for public relations to have an empty sculpture garden. These were the days before email, Twitter and Google, and I couldn't just conjure up an exhibition. Nor did I want Ken Construction, nice as they were, scattering pipes about in the road again.

What do you do when all else fails? You panic and then phone a friend. The most helpful solution came from a friend who taught at Glasgow School of Art who suggested I come to the Glasgow Sculpture School to see what they had. I was not hopeful. I'd never heard of this sculpture school. This was too important to just get something that might be randomly kicking about. I didn't want 'pot pourris of broken dreams', as Grayson Perry has described in his Reith Lecture the skips outside the Sculpture and Applied Arts departments of art colleges. But I was desperate. *My* dreams had been broken ever since that telephone call. I'd once scrabbled through a dustbin for some work by a recalcitrant painter, so if it had to be a skip scavenge, I would do it. I drove up to Glasgow.

Maryhill Road was not pleasant that day. In an energy-sapping May heatwave, with scenes from Taggart passing before my eyes, I found the old tram shed workshop I was looking for, tucked away on a dusty backstreet. It was in a rundown area: a succession of massive, ramshackle buildings situated next door to BBC Television Scotland. Inside, it resembled an amalgam of a huge dismantled funfair and Dante's inferno. There was machinery, noise, sparks, fibreglass models, welding equipment, hoists and people in masks making golden showers.

Joe and Russell emerged from dark corners at my call: I had their names on a scrap of paper which, like me, was crumpled and damp with perspiration. We chatted and they showed me round with enthusiasm. They loved the tram shed because the council let them have it rent-free and the television centre next door brought them business. When BBC Scotland needed a twenty-foot pink crocodile or an ugly, one-eyed slimy alien in a hurry - which must happen all the time - they tended to rush and ask the guys next door to put something together for them. For recent graduates such as they were, this was a valuable source of income.

I explained my ridiculous situation and tried to look desperate and pathetic – easily achieved because I was - and they showed me what they had available. Russell only had one piece: a massive, red-skinned fibreglass apple in two halves, each half measuring five feet in diameter, with letters of the alphabet cast into the pale green plastic flesh. Maybe it had been on a television set. It would look good in the gallery orchard under the apple tree. I found myself calling him Russet!

Joe was a metal man with huge welded abstract chunky pieces. I liked him and his work. He said he could bring four sculptures. 'Bring' was a good, welcome word - it sounded hopeful because these were big, heavy, awkwardly shaped works and we had only three days before the opening.

I tentatively mentioned delivery. They were relaxed about it and went off to check whether the communal transit would be available. It was - on Saturday, the day before the opening. This was cutting it fine but they told me they would set off really early and put their work out in the garden for me. This was pure joy! I photographed the accessible pieces that would be coming, shook their hands, gave them a map, offered to cover the cost of diesel, invited them for lunch, tea, drinks, caviar and chips – anything they desired - and returned to Castlegate House in a better state of mind to a night of deep sleep – the first since the one a.m. phone call.

Saturday was soon upon us and Wendy and I were really on top of it all. The paintings were hung, the gallery looked wonderful, the garden was in full early June bloom - swathes of bluebells, poppies and roses - and the sculpture was on its way from Glasgow. But was it? We spent the morning in a busy mist of anticipation and nagging doubts. The lads had been very quiet since my visit. This was 1995 when mobile phones were still an expensive, cumbersome rarity. I rang the Glasgow tram shed but there was no reply.

It was a lovely day and we had lunch in the heavily perfumed garden. Bees and butterflies were madly busy but we were in a restless state of limbo. I was edgy and worried. People were expecting a recycled lion and a horse, among other things, and I was hoping to present an alternative apple substitute and some abstract metal pieces and get away with it. I couldn't face a double let-down.

By three o'clock, Wendy and I were rifling through the garden sheds and pulling out bits of dismembered bike parts and old garden implements to see if we could improvise some sculpture. We both had art degrees so surely we could knock something up.

'How about these for a lion's mane?' I shouted, waving some bicycle chains. 'Do you think we could make a lion out of it like the one on the card? The pedals might make good feet.'

Wendy was busy dragging a well-rusted garden roller, a steel double sink and a draining board she'd unearthed into the yard, and I was assembling the rest of the two old bikes and a broken wheelbarrow into something truly awful. The place looked like a set from *Steptoe and Son*. We badly needed a welder. No, we needed more than a welder – we needed a miracle. We were just about to start on our new careers with a debut exhibition when the phone rang. I dropped everything with a clatter and ran indoors. Thank goodness! It was Joe.

'Hello Chris. How are you?' he said calmly.

'A bit worried about you to be honest, Joe. Where are you? Are you nearly here?'

'Erm, we've broken down actually. The transit's clutch has gone. We've tried to mend it but we can't. We're waiting for a breakdown truck.'

'Where are you calling from?' I croaked in panic.

'A phone box.'

'Where?'

'I walked to a village.'

'What village? Where's the van?'

'On a roundabout.'

'What? You've broken down on a roundabout?'

My voice was rising in hysteria. Wendy had come in and was standing close, trying to hear what was going on.

'Afraid so.'

'But where? Are you in Cumbria yet?'

'Oh yes, we're south of Carlisle. Oh, there's a sign. I'm ringing from a place called Thursby. The roundabout's about half a mile away from this telephone box. Will you wait for us? Oh and by the way – we couldn't get the *Big Apple* on the van. We'll go back and fetch that tomorrow.'

This sounded foolishly optimistic. I had used the photograph of that apple in the new publicity to replace the farm machinery lion that was still in Norwich. It had been used in press releases. Local television was coming to film it on Monday. And it was still in Glasgow. My mouth went dry.

'Well yes, of course I'll wait. Good luck.'

He rang off. I had a moment of despair. I went into the back yard and screamed a silent Munch scream. Other artists who had contributed to this Summer Exhibition were coming that evening and we were all going out for a meal. I'd booked a table for eight at the Quince and Medlar, a very nice restaurant conveniently opposite the gallery. They'd surely be here before then...

A lot of nail-biting followed. At six p.m., when our nerves were vibrating like hornets' wings, there was an almighty flurry of noise and fuss outside. We dashed out. A low loader was trying to negotiate our narrow drive. I was so relieved to see it. The lorry tentatively and carefully nosed its way forward. The big white transit van was sitting on the low loader and the metal sculptures were sitting in the white van.

Joe and Russell were sitting in the cabin of the low loader, next to the driver. It was like a massive Russian doll, waiting to be unpeeled and revealed layer upon layer.

The low loader backed up to the fairly narrow entrance to the car park, bringing my grumpy neighbour out shouting, swearing and complaining. I ignored her. I feigned deafness.

When it couldn't get any further, and after a lot of chain jangling and positioning of ramps, the broken transit, containing about ten tons of welded steel, was liberated. Or rather, it broke loose and catapulted off the back of the lorry. It hit the ground running. We all scattered as it hurtled across the car park, fortunately grinding to a halt in the gravel rather than demolishing the wall and dropping the ten feet onto pedestrians and the main road below.

We were still unloading as the other artists began to arrive, dressed for dinner. When all the work was out on the plinths, Joe collapsed in a heap of exhaustion and emotion and made a little speech, saying his work had never been in such a beautiful place. There was no possibility of he and Russell getting back to Glasgow that night so I offered them beds and dinner. After they had gratefully accepted both, I looked at my watch and I looked at them. They were in dirty, tattered clothes. They were covered in oil. Their hands and faces were black. I rang the restaurant and asked for a bigger table - in the darkest corner if they had one. How I wished we were going to the pub. Luckily, The Quince and Medlar's owners were good friends and, having seen and heard the palaver in the car park from their window, understood the problem perfectly.

I dug out a couple of large, clean t-shirts for Joe and Russell, and they scrubbed up quite well, but there was nothing we could do about the rest of their filthy clothes and the heady perfume of oil and diesel that clung to them. We must have looked a motley group to be out dining together when we made our entrance, but we had a hilariously memorable evening - one of the best. When we got back to the gallery, I showed the boys to the top floor of the house where there was a two-bedroomed studio, sometimes used for artists in residence. At the time, we were in the process of cataloguing and photographing the Percy Kelly collection of paintings which had recently come up from Norfolk after Percy's death. There were piles of unframed paintings everywhere in the studio and Joe, seeing them, stopped dead and stared.

'Is that by Percy Kelly?' he asked in astonishment, pointing at a painting.

'Yes, it is. Do you know about him?' I asked.

I was surprised because Percy, a recluse, was still virtually unknown - his work had rarely been seen. My friend Joan David and I had not yet unleashed him on the world.

'Yes, I do. He used to write to my parents. He sent them a handmade Christmas card every year until a few years ago. They've kept every one. They worried when they stopped. The cards were important to him, you know – and to them. We wondered if he was all right. He must be getting on a bit. They still send him a card, though.'

'I'm afraid it's because he died last year,' I said. 'The dead don't really do the Christmas card thing, you know.'

I don't think Joe slept very well that night – he was too excited to be among the Kelly collection.

Very early the next morning I drove Joe and Russell to Carlisle where we hired an Enterprise van (theirs remained in the gallery car park). They then set off to Glasgow to get the *Big Apple* and I returned to the gallery. The opening began at 2.30 and the Apple arrived at 2.40. We made a ceremonial procession of its journey to the orchard as though I had always intended it to be like that, a windfall apple.

Mean with Money

It was Autumn 2003. Cumbria was recovering from a disastrous foot and mouth outbreak, and everybody needed cheering up. We were all desperate for good news rather than the habitual bad of the last two years - desperate to erase the acrid smell of the animal funeral pyres and forget the stench of rotting carcasses which stuck in the nose, the throat and the memory. The fields were being re-stocked and the footpaths were open again when a client I knew well approached me with a small collection of paintings by L.S. Lowry that he wanted to sell. I had a really good look at them – especially the labels on the back – and checked the paperwork and the provenance as a matter of course. All was in order, so I quickly accepted.

When I first became a gallerist, I had never imagined I would ever be able to put on a Lowry show. It was way beyond my reach; a show like that needs a lot of planning and a lot of capital. Unless the owner of the gallery is super-rich – and I can assure you I wasn't in that category - it is difficult to amass enough works to put a solo exhibition together. And if the artist is as popular, celebrated, in demand and as dead as Lowry, the works usually have to be bought in.

I had watched as the prices achieved for Lowry at auction had risen in the past ten years beyond anything I'd ever anticipated. If only I'd been in a position to buy ten years earlier when the collection of Lowry's friend, the Reverend Geoffrey Bennett, had been auctioned at Christie's (see *The Fish and Chip Shop at Cleator Moor* in *Hercules and the Farmer's Wife*), I'd have been a millionaire by now. But that's what we all say after the event - hindsight is a wonderful thing.

Nevertheless, I had acquired a few small, modest Lowrys over the years and so was now in a position to stage the first Lowry exhibition in a commercial gallery in Cumbria.

It turned out to be the most popular show I had ever put on. That wasn't a surprise, but what was surprising was just *how* popular – we had more than 20,000 people through the door in six weeks. No matter how early I got to the gallery, there was always a jostling crowd outside, impatient to get in. Footfall was so heavy, it wore out the hall carpet and it wore me out as well; I had to take on extra helpers.

Lowry had close links with Cumbria. He was a regular visitor from the early 1950s when he came to visit Geoffrey Bennett, who had been promoted from his job at the National Westminster Bank in Manchester to the position of manager of the Cleator Moor branch. Cleator Moor itself is a small, somewhat rundown satellite town on the eastern fringe of Whitehaven. It appealed to Lowry: he loved the decrepit, disfigured working class industrial scene. He painted the Co-op, the church and the fish and chip shop in the main street, all populated with lively matchstick figures and cats and dogs.

A few years later, Lowry had another reason to visit Cumberland when he came to stay with the parents of the artist Sheila Fell, who lived in nearby Aspatria. Sheila would come up from London where she lived and worked, and she and Lowry would go off drawing and painting together. He made several drawings and paintings of Workington, Allonby and Maryport on the industrial west coast, so local interest in the exhibition was strong. As many of the visitors weren't people who normally visited galleries, it was even more important that they had a good experience.

I partnered the show with a newly acquired collection of works by Cumbrian-born artist Percy Kelly. It was an ironic pairing. In life these two eccentrics had never hit it off. Lowry, as a regular visitor to Cumberland, had visited Kelly at his home in Allonby several times, but Kelly always regarded him as a rival, a foreign interloper who had no right to paint and draw on his patch. When Lowry met him in Allonby one day, he boasted about some steps in Maryport he had found interesting, and which he was painting.

'I've painted those steps many times,' Kelly later wrote to his friend, Rosanna. He was enraged. 'I've known those steps since I was five years old. The locals call them the Zig Zag steps. He doesn't even know that!'

Kelly went on to tell Rosanna that he would hide his paintings if he had advance warning that Lowry was visiting his cottage, in case the other painter stole his ideas.

They were too similar in background and character to ever get on, but they sat together very nicely in the gallery, providing I kept them in separate rooms. It amused me to imagine what might have happened at the opening if they had both been alive. The atmosphere would have been explosive.

With the exhibition hung and opening day approaching, I became extra nervous. It had made a splash in all the local press and also gained television coverage. The *Cumberland News* even ran a front-page story with the headline 'OUR LADY OF THE LOWRYS' and a photograph of me. This was embarrassing, but there's no such thing as bad publicity – or so I thought…

***

'I've always wanted a Lowry,' the man said. 'Which do you think I should buy?'

This is always a difficult question and one I deflect or avoid.

'Which do *you* like the most? Choosing one from those within your budget, I mean.'

I handed my prospective buyer the rather frightening price list. He was tall, broad-shouldered, and looked smart in a nice tweed suit and soft, grey-checked wool shirt. His face was brown – evidence of his healthy outdoor life – but the deep wrinkles suggested stress over the last few years. I suspected he'd never been in a gallery before.

He glanced at the list. 'Hey, I don't know. I just got me foot and mouth money. Compensation, like. I want an investment but summat I can look at as well, eh. I don't trust banks these days. I like that one there. What do you think?'

He gestured toward a detailed pencil drawing of a young woman.

'Do you really like it?'

He laughed nervously. 'Yes, I do. And sheep are a poor investment anyway these days. They're fetching next to nowt in t'auctions.'

'Yes, well a piece of art should only be bought if you like it and don't need an immediate return on your money,' I said. 'I'm not a financial adviser, you understand, but Lowry has a good auction record. In fact, Lowry has recently broken the million pound mark for a big oil called *The Football Match*. Possibly, it has been bought by a Man U player.'

That really grabbed his interest. I decided to clarify lest he'd misunderstood.

'Personally, I've never seen a Lowry take a drop in value,' I continued. 'But to be honest, I don't think there's a hope in hell that this drawing will ever get to a million - although you never can tell. But you must buy it primarily because you like it – see it as something you can do with your money that's reasonably safe and that you can enjoy on your wall as well. It's nicer to look at than a bank statement or share certificate. But if you buy it and then decide to sell it straightaway, you'll almost certainly lose out. There are fixed costs involved in buying a painting – VAT and commission. Art is a long-term investment you know, and there's always a risk factor.'

The man took all this in, but he had made his decision: the beautiful, early pencil drawing of the woman had clearly captivated him. I understood the attraction: she was Lowry's 'Ann' figure and as I told my new client about her he hung on my every word.

'Lowry often painted and drew a woman whom he called Ann,' I explained. 'There has been much debate among Lowry scholars and biographers as to whether she ever existed in the flesh. She's his mystery woman.'

Lowry had once told a reporter for the *Manchester Guardian* that Ann was 25 years old, lived in Leeds and was the daughter of some people who had been very good to him. One of Lowry's friends said that he had told him Ann was a pupil of his mother's and she had died when she was 25. Lowry's artist friends Harold Riley and Pat Cooke both claimed that Lowry told them Ann was a friend from Lytham St Annes who died in her early twenties. None of it added up. Maybe she was a fantasy girlfriend: Lowry never married, and lived alone. He was lonely. He wanted company and he was attracted to a certain type of young woman: slender with large eyes and long dark hair, just like the woman in the drawing. As far as anybody knew, there was no sexual relationship.

He had spent much of his life trying to gain the approval of his mother, who had been convinced during her pregnancy that she was carrying a girl. Her son was a disappointment to her from the moment he appeared, but he had been devoted to her, caring for her up to her death. It was his way of compensating her for being a boy.

'These young women,' I continued, 'were Lowry's companions. He took them out for meals, bought them gifts, and travelled with them to art exhibitions. One of them was Sheila Fell, who fitted the Ann description perfectly. He was her friend and patron.'

'Oh yes,' the farmer interrupted. 'I know about her - she came from Spatri didn't she?'

He was proud to show off some knowledge of art.

'Yes,' I agreed. Aspatria, Sheila's home town, was just a few miles away from the gallery.

'Another girlfriend was Carol Ann Lowry - no relation - who inherited his estate.'

The farmer liked the story and, no doubt, the attention. He was disillusioned with sheep.

'Hey, I like Art,' he said as I put a red spot on the drawing for him. 'It's got a bit of class about it.'

Thanking me profusely, he left the gallery a happy man.

70

I didn't see the article in the *Sunday Times*, but Hunter Davies sent me the clip the day after publication with a little hand-written message at the top: 'To Chris – in case you missed the mensh – Hunter. Sun Times Sept 22, 03'.

I wondered why he'd posted it to me. Hunter's and Margaret's house in the Lakes was on my bike training circuit, and I'd occasionally stop off for liquid refreshment during their summer sojourn. The sofa still looked well in their kitchen-diner, and they had since succumbed to other purchases from the gallery – works of art rather than furniture, though.

I eagerly read the item he had sent. Hunter had had a weekly slot in the financial section of the paper for years called *MEAN WITH MONEY*, because he was - and he was proud of it. It was usually a light-hearted, tongue-in-cheek piece about his latest crazy money-saving idea: cutting your own hair, for instance, or using the toilets in McDonald's without buying a burger. One of my favourites involved the time he lost his prescription sunglasses while swimming in the Caribbean. Being too mean to buy goggles, he claimed to have painted an old pair of specs with brown varnish as a replacement. Sometimes he wrote about Margaret and her extravagant ways - which of course were only extravagant in his opinion. I reflected that he must be a nightmare to shop with. He had once written about how upset he became when Margaret rejected the free element of a BOGOF, and there had been spectacular rows at the checkout when she refused to use a loyalty card. He was well known in the Sainsbury's in Cockermouth.

I settled down to read, knowing it would be a laugh.

The headline for this week's column was 'STAND BY YOUR BEDS – HERE ARE MY TOP TIPS FOR INVESTORS'. This was followed by five, mostly ironic, suggestions. The first was to invest in a pension, although Hunter ruefully went on to point out his was with Equitable Life, who had just gone bust.

The next was to buy stamps – he had invested £4000 in 1979 on the advice of Gibbons' stamp dealers... and just sold them at Sotheby's for £1500. The third was all about football memorabilia – Hunter is a devoted Spurs fan and a keen collector himself. He was beginning to lose me at this point when I noticed his fourth tip was to invest in Art. I perked up – but was he going to rubbish it as an investment too? No, he endorsed it, bless him. He wrote that he'd spent £100 at auction twenty years ago for a Lowry drawing of a couple of matchstick men.

He went on: 'Last week I went into Castlegate Gallery in Cockermouth as I heard they had a Lowry drawing for sale. It's a very nice one of Maryport, much bigger than mine. I enquired about the price, which also turned out much bigger than mine - £29,500. Cripes, I had to lie down. You thought I might be going to say I'd made a mistake. Obviously I didn't. Except I should have bought loads of them at the time.'

Hey, this is good, I thought – a much better 'mensh' than last time. But then came the rub: 'If I sell my little one now, how will I invest the money I will have made? Buy more Lowrys? You must be mad. Not at those prices.'

Well, I thought, I obviously wasn't going to sell him another Lowry – though I resolved to try next time he came in. Perhaps I could do a deal with his little £100 drawing... In any case, though, it was clearly his best investment so far and really good publicity for the exhibition at Castlegate House. But wait - what was Hunter's final recommendation? Had he kept the best until last? I read on: 'Perhaps the best thing to do as you are standing by your bed is to keep your spare money under it.'

I laughed out loud.

An hour later, I wasn't laughing. There was a kerfuffle in the car park followed by the entry of my farmer client, who came storming through the door clutching the *Sunday Times*. His face was an unhealthy mottled red and he was spluttering incoherently. There was no smart suit today. Quickly, I ushered

72

him through into the kitchen. He was breathing heavily and I wondered if I should ring for a nurse or a defibrillator. I sat him down and Angie, my assistant, hastily put the kettle on.

'Whatever is the matter?' I asked. 'Are you all right?'

He obviously wasn't. He held out the paper and pointed mutely at Hunter's column on the crumpled back page of the financial section of the paper. He was speechless with anger, and it was immediately clear he didn't understand Hunter's penchant for irony. He had believed every word of it.

'Look,' he said eventually, pointing with trembling fingers at the first paragraph. 'He's a financial expert.'

I shook my head. 'He's not really, you know. He's a journalist.'

The farmer wasn't having this. 'He's in the financial section of the *Times* so he must be an expert. They wouldn't have him write things if he wasn't.'

'But it's a joke,' I tried to explain. 'Hunter was joking.'

He just looked at me blankly. What could I say? I attempted to talk him through it. We looked at the article in detail and I pointed out that the Lowry was the only investment of the five mentioned that had increased in value well above inflation. In twenty years or so, Hunter had turned a £100 investment into thousands: you didn't have to be Einstein to work out that was a massive percentage gain.

'Yes, but he says your prices are too high. He says he wouldn't buy another from you.'

I sighed. 'Hunter and his wife come here regularly...'

He cut me off. 'Well, he's not doing you much good wi' this then, is he?'

Disheartened, I walked the man round the exhibition and pointed out the number of red spots. People wouldn't be buying the Lowrys if they were overpriced, I said. I wouldn't be in business. But I gave up when I could see he didn't believe a word of it. I couldn't win. I had lost his trust.

'Look,' I said. 'It's your decision. I'll take the red spot off and give you your deposit back. You don't have to have the picture. It's entirely up to you.'

His mind was made up. The spot came off. His deposit was refunded.

After he'd accelerated away in a spray of gravel, leaving behind a strong smell of burning rubber, I rang Hunter.

'Hello Hunter, thanks for sending me the article.'

'Hi,' he said chirpily. 'I thought you'd like it. How's it going?'

'Well, I found it very funny, but do you realise that your 'mensh' just cost me nearly twenty thousand quid?'

'What?'

I explained. I could do irony as well.

Hunter was mortified and at once full of apologies as he protested that he had been misunderstood.

'It was just a bit of fun,' he said. 'I'm not a serious financial advisor like those other boring old columnists.'

'I know that, Hunter. I love your column. I read it every week – it makes me grin. But this guy's taken it seriously. Daft, I know, but you live among the rural community half the year so you can understand the, er, confusion.'

'But the Lowry was the best investment of the lot,' he kept on insisting. 'Couldn't he see that? Have you got his phone number? I'll ring him straightaway and explain.'

I demurred. I couldn't hand out clients' numbers without their permission. That would make me doubly suspicious in the farmer's mind - he might start thinking I'd got someone to impersonate Hunter.

'Tell you what, then,' he said. 'Give the man my phone number. Ask him to ring me. I'll tell him. I'll explain.'

I did - but the farmer never rang, nor have I seen him since that day. Meanwhile 'Ann' quickly sold to someone else – although not to Hunter Davis – so no harm done.

I sometimes wonder where that farmer is now, and if he ever ventured into the art world again. I think it's more likely he's at home, guarding the loose floorboard under his bed.

The Chest

Audrey Kelly lived a twilight life. She rarely left her Cockermouth bungalow in which the curtains were always drawn. She was in her late 70s when I first met her but I could see that she had once been very pretty. The dark glasses which she wore to protect a painful eye condition added an air of mystery, as did the dark brown bouffant wig which perched on her head.

I first met Audrey in 1993, shortly after the death of Percy Kelly, her first husband, whom she had divorced more than twenty years earlier. Her only son, Brian, had died in 2001 while the fifth exhibition of Percy's work at Castlegate House was underway, leaving Audrey with nobody to talk to. She was miserable and very lonely.

We had little in common. Ours was an unlikely friendship, but Audrey was my link with Percy and unwittingly helped me understand him better. She was full of complaints: present, past, imagined and real. She had strong opinions, she hated art, and she hated Percy with venom. But she had a phenomenal memory of their life together, which meant we always had plenty to talk about.

One afternoon in her sitting room, she suddenly said, 'I want to tell you something I've never been able to tell anyone before. Only one other person ever knew and she's now died.'

Audrey wanted closure.

I waited in the semi-darkness and listened to what she told me. When she had finished there was nothing to say; nothing to add. I quietly took my leave and drove the few miles to Allonby, the scene of her story: the coastal village where she and Percy had lived for the final twelve years of their 30-year marriage.

The sun was dropping spectacularly into the Solway as I parked by the sea. Like the other little white houses randomly clustered together in this West Cumbrian village, Glen Cottage – the Kellys' former home - was now an intense shade of salmon pink. The windows looked as though the house was on fire as they reflected the bright red orb that now balanced on the Irish Sea like a penny coin.

As I got out and crossed the bridge over the beck to the cottage, I thought about the story Audrey had just recounted.

One dark winter's evening in 1970, Audrey had returned home from her secretarial job at the nearby hospital and was happy to find the fire in the cottage lit. Through the uncurtained window she could see the flames dancing, but when she let herself in it was to see a strange woman sitting with her back to the door. When challenged, this person turned and asked Audrey for help applying her make-up, her voice sweet and artificially high. And this was the sickening moment that Audrey realised it was her husband wearing *her* clothes and holding out a wand of *her* mascara, his smile a grotesque, lipsticked slash.

No way!

Until that night, Audrey had had no idea what had been happening. She was horrified and nauseated. She blamed the art college – Percy should never have gone. He'd been 42 when he went, and it had put silly ideas in his head being with all those younger Bohemian students.

She allowed no room for discussion that evening. Percy tried to explain to her how much he loved bright colours and soft fabrics: how he liked to feel the air around his legs, the swing of a skirt, the sliding of silk against his skin as he walked, the sensual pleasure of pulling a pair of fine stockings onto his smooth, shaved legs. But she wasn't interested - Percy talked too much anyway.

She didn't want to know how much he envied women and wanted to be like one. Perish the thought. He was a pervert, and was out in the cold December night air before he realised what was happening. His feet, shod in Audrey's best high-heeled shoes - the backs cut out to accommodate him - hardly touched the ground. Nor did she care where he went that night - all dolled up in her lovely, soft grey Jaeger wool dress - as long as the neighbours didn't see and recognise him.

At this point Audrey paused. 'It was a lovely, elegant dress – expensive. I wore it one evening when we went for dinner at Sir Nicholas Sekers' house at Rosehill. There were a lot of important people there – titles and such - and I knew I looked good in it, but my dear husband said I was only invited because of him. How do you think that made *me* feel? You should write this story. Make sure you say it was Jaeger. These people who go crazy for his paintings – heaven knows why - should know how he treated me. Why should *he* have all the attention?'

For Percy Kelly, drawing and painting were a compulsion. Every and any available flat surface was used, and when he worked for the Post Office in the 1930s, a complaint was even made against him for defacing the Royal Mail: he had drawn on the back of an envelope and then delivered it. He just couldn't help himself.

Audrey didn't understand it, and she didn't blame the recipient of the letter for reporting Percy: she would have done the same.

The couple were courting in 1939 when Percy joined the army and it wasn't long before he was disciplined once more for his constant scribbling. But although Percy was ordered to send his paints and art materials home from France, he hid them in his first aid box instead and carried on: he would have gone mad without them. And luck was on his side. When his CO realised what Percy had done, he was deployed behind the lines drawing maps, making technical diagrams for training, and sketching accidents. It was a posting that probably saved Percy's life, I reflected.

Percy wrote to Audrey almost every day until his demob in 1946, she proudly told me. But, unlike her retentive husband, she was not a keeper of things. She read and then destroyed every one of his letters, throwing them on the fire. She could see no point in hanging on to them. *What a shame,* I thought as she told me this: those letters would be invaluable now. We only have Percy's account of this time from the letters he sent to others – and quite a time it was, too. Percy had worked in the Cabinet War Rooms in Whitehall for a short time and had even met Winston Churchill, who had sent him to the National Gallery to see a war artists' exhibition. In fact, the Prime Minister had persuaded Percy to submit some of his work to a serviceman's exhibition at the National Gallery where, with many others, Percy was presented to King George VI. He took part in the Normandy landings, serving with the Royal Signals Regiment, and all the while he was writing and sending drawings to Audrey, even though they would be heavily censored if they ever got through at all.

Now, after all this time, Audrey could remember few details of these events. She was only interested insofar as they related to her. But their married life she remembered all too well.

Percy and Audrey married in 1942 when Percy was home on leave, after which Audrey went to live with Percy's parents in their crowded home at Salterbeck, Workington. After the war, Percy returned to his job as a postal worker and in 1951 an opportunity presented itself for him to take over the village Post Office in Great Broughton, a few miles from Cockermouth. Audrey encouraged her husband, who she thought had no ambition, to apply for the job. But, in reality, who had actually ended up manning the counter, filling in the endless forms and doing the accounts?

She had.

And where was Percy all day?

Off gallivanting in his car, supposedly painting and drawing.

If Audrey left him in charge, it wasn't any better: Percy would drag an easel behind the counter and try to ignore anyone who came in. They often came back later and Audrey had to deal with them herself. And then there were the periods of depression and ill health which she suspected Percy invented

78

to get out of work. Those black moods didn't stop him driving off in the car and disappearing for hours.

Art was a hobby, not a career, Audrey constantly emphasised. What was art for, anyway? She hated it. Percy had accused her of being insensitive to his work but she had told him that she just wanted things nice and his paintings were too dark and depressing. He called it art, but to her it was rubbish. She wanted her husband to have a white-collar job with status, not to wander about in jeans all day, sitting outside with paint and paper for everyone to see.

Audrey was very sensitive to what other people thought: as their son Brian, in a rare outburst, once said: 'My mother wanted my father to be Postmaster General, but all he wanted to do was paint.'

To Audrey, Percy was wasting his intelligence - but he took no notice of what she said; he just walked away. That was downright rude, she thought.

In 1958 Percy resigned as sub-postmaster and the couple moved to Glen Cottage. This was Percy's decision: he wanted to have more space, more freedom. What about what she wanted? Audrey complained. She had to get a secretarial job to support both her husband and son, although Percy didn't appreciate her efforts. Moreover, their house was soon littered with bits of paper, boards, drawings and paintings, as well as all the stuff Percy would pick up on the beach. He drew on shopping lists, cereal packets, and even on the back of a mounted photograph of Audrey's mother. Not only that, he then used the photograph as a backboard to protect a drawing he was posting to America. For Audrey, this was the ultimate insult. Ah, her dear mother! She had never liked Percy – she'd refused to come to their wedding - and had warned her daughter against him. Audrey wished she'd paid heed.

One day, Percy came home having seen some exhibition in Maryport and announced that he was going to apply for a place at Carlisle College of Art. This was ten years before their break-up and Audrey was horrified. Percy would look silly among teenagers. Whatever was he thinking of? And who would pay for it? Not her - never! The authorities said he was too old for a grant and they were right, she thought. So that was the end of that then, wasn't it?

But Percy had gone to college despite everything Audrey said, and changed just as she'd feared. His obsession with art had grown worse – not that she was surprised: she knew that would happen. Percy was mixing with students half his age and was influenced by them. They accepted him and admired his talent and experience. He loved that. He took to wearing tight denim jeans – drainpipes, for God's sake! - and brightly-coloured casual tops and scarves. He was popular and in demand – probably because he had a car – and if it was hot and sunny, he and a crowd of students would often go to swim in the River Eden at Warwick Bridge at lunchtime. Sometimes they swam with no clothes, Audrey suspected: Percy would come home and boast about his all-over tan. To her, that was immoral and shameful, especially when she'd been stuck in an office all day.

Percy was an attractive, charismatic man – many people told Audrey this. He was tall and handsome, athletic and fit when she first met him. He played football for a local team. She was so proud of him when he came home on leave from his war service in his khaki uniform: he was fighting for his country and for her. So how had it come to this? Percy wanted to be seen as the greatest artist of his time. She wanted a husband who paid his wife some attention. Now that he was at college she hardly saw him. He'd arrive home late and often stay up half the night in the wash house studio, 'messing about'.

Audrey had put up with so much because of Percy's 'useless obsession' with art, but the final revelation came as a dreadful surprise. Until that shocking, surreal moment when she found him dressed as a woman, she had no idea what had been developing.

Where Percy went that December night after Audrey had thrown him out will remain a mystery forever. He came back to the cottage the next morning, crept in covertly after she had gone to work, and loaded his van up with as much of his precious work as he could cram into it. There was a note of triumph in Audrey's voice as she told me that when he returned for a second load a few hours later, Oscar, Percy's carpenter father, had changed the locks - ironically he never knew the reason for Audrey's request and he didn't ask.

Much of Percy's work was haphazardly thrown outside into the street like scraps to a dog. Percy was frantic as he quickly gathered it up before it got wet or blew away in the sea breeze. His wife could have everything: car, furniture, what little there was in the bank account, but he must have his work. He could live without Audrey but he couldn't live without his work. It was the most important thing in his life. It was as vital to his wellbeing as food and water.

'He said that in court. How do you think that made me feel after all those years?' she asked me from the semi-darkness.

After almost 30 years of marriage, Percy had to fight through the divorce court to get the rest of his work, but he never got it all. Audrey knew what it meant to him and enjoyed punishing him for hurting her and shaming her.

Eventually, the judge in the case ordered Audrey to give Percy his work in exchange for one-penny. This was in response to an impassioned oration from Percy in which he offered Audrey everything else he owned and more - even a grand piano and Dalmatian belonging to Christine, his new lady friend. As the court dissolved into discreet titters, Audrey made it very clear she wanted neither a piano nor a dog.

She never saw him again.

I had heard much of this before, many times, but she carried on talking, telling me things she had not told anyone before. I listened carefully.

After their confrontation in the divorce court, Audrey spent weeks getting every trace of Percy out of the house. To Audrey, he and his work were synonymous. His stuff was everywhere, it permeated every corner of their small house, and in her efforts to exorcise him she indiscriminately burnt him, binned him, and tore him into small pieces. It gave her great satisfaction. Percy's precious printing press was dumped in the alley at the side of the house until he could come with a van to collect it: he was never going to be invited into the house again. No way! If the thing went rusty or was stolen for scrap, she didn't care. Serve him right.

However, Percy's so-called studio - a small scullery tagged on at the back of the cottage – was more than Audrey could face on her own. She didn't go in there very often and had never attempted to tidy it up in all the years they had lived there. Now it was the only place left to clear and it was the worst - overflowing with a jumble of Percy's art junk, not to mention a sink full of the highly corrosive acid he used for etching out new plates. What was she supposed to do with that, then? It was a toxic mess.

Audrey confessed that she was actually a bit lonely when Percy had gone (although she would never admit it to anyone else), and so when Peggy, her sister-in-law – Percy's younger brother Douglas' wife - offered to help with clearing the studio, she was glad. Choosing a Saturday for the job, they worked hard the whole day, stopping only for bread and cheese and weak, milky tea. They thought they'd just about cracked it when they unearthed the chest which had been hidden in a corner. It had been buried under piles of paper, old rags and paint pots, and was battered and shabby - but then, so was everything else Percy had ever owned.

'Ooh, what's in there?' Peggy wondered aloud.

Audrey regarded it with distaste. She was weary with it all.

'Oh, I bet it's only old rubbish like the rest of it,' she said impatiently, pushing another armful of drawings into a refuse bag. 'Just something else to be disposed of, I bet! Come on

Peg, let's have a cuppa. I'm ever so dry. Aren't you?'

But Peggy had already tentatively opened the lid of the chest a crack - she couldn't help herself. Who knew what might leap out and bite her? Emboldened when nothing did, she opened it a bit wider. It was full – and right on top lay a scrunched up yellow cotton dress with a blue floral pattern.

'Hey, isn't that your summer dress?' Peggy asked Audrey. 'What's it doing in there?'

Audrey stopped in her tracks and turned round, aghast. She had never told anyone, not even family, about her reason for throwing Percy out – the village they lived in was a close-knit community where there could be no secrets and titillating gossip would travel fast and far.

'I've been looking for that,' she said with a curled lip, hoping to brazen it out. 'I'll just put the kettle on, shall I?'

She made to shut the lid but Peggy propped it up and began to explore further: she was curious. As Audrey looked on, Peggy carried on rummaging through the chest, pulling items of clothing out, holding them up, gently shaking out the creases, marvelling and exclaiming at the treasures she found.

Audrey was reunited with a lot of old friends that evening – clothes she had sent to the charity shops, shoes she had put in the dustbin, underwear she had forgotten she ever had, and many other things that had mysteriously gone missing. She had searched for ages for that yellow dress during the hot sunny spell last summer. Meanwhile, Peggy was so absorbed that she failed to notice her sister-in-law's discomfort. Eventually, Audrey stomped off and made tea. She was having nothing to do with it. When she returned with the tray, she shuddered at the heap of garments Peggy had piled on the table.

'Hey, it's a sort of dressing-up box,' Peggy said, taking a mug of hot tea from her sister-in-law. 'Did Percy do portraits, then? I never saw any of those. Did he ever paint you?'

Audrey could hold out no longer. She sat down heavily on a paint-splattered stool, put her head in hands, and began to sob.

'A dressing-up box – that's exactly what it is, Peg.' She wiped her streaming eyes and dripping nose on an excavated blouse. 'It's Percy's dressing-up box. Oh, my Lord! Why didn't I realise what was happening sooner?'

Audrey swore Peggy to secrecy that evening and her loyal friend kept her word for the rest of her life. Audrey had only told me, I realised, because we had built up a friendship. We had a bond. She realised that I was probably the only person who understood what she'd had to contend with, the only person who listened to her. She wanted me to sympathise with her and I did. I sympathised with them both. They were a mismatch. She wanted to justify her actions, to put her point of view, to show Percy up to the world who now admired him. She didn't realise that the world had itself changed; that Percy's legacy as far as everyone else was concerned was his work, not his personal life.

I looked out to sea pensively. The break-up of a marriage is always distressing for all those involved, but for Audrey the trauma of discovering Percy's secret had made it even more so. I wondered how I, a liberal-minded woman, would react to finding my husband wearing my clothes, and felt some sympathy with her. However, the thought of all the work Audrey had destroyed and the anguish that must have caused Percy also upset me. How deeply disturbing it must have been for him to live with someone so blind to his extraordinary talent. Artists are rarely conventional: they lead colourful lives, are creative and unpredictable. Their focus is always their work. Percy and Audrey had each been totally caught up in their own egotism; their aims and objectives had always been incompatible.

I sighed at the waste of talent, and the loss of all the paintings, drawings and artefacts that Audrey had destroyed. Judging by the prices achieved for Percy Kelly works at recent auctions and exhibitions, she had got rid of millions of pounds of what she considered to be rubbish.

Revenge is sweet but it can also be expensive.

New Dawn

My friendship with Diana van de Lugt did not begin well. She strode into the gallery dressed in denims and green wellies and glared around her with an air of disapproval. Built on a large scale – she was six foot three or so, with broad shoulders, large hands and feet - her presence was overwhelming. There was something restless, something challenging, about her. Ignoring my greeting, she glanced around quickly before turning on her heel and marching into the West Room. Assistants Angie and Sylvia disappeared, suddenly finding jobs to do elsewhere, and I too took the hint to leave our visitor alone.

A few minutes later, she stuck her head round the door of the West Room.

'Can I have a chair?' she demanded.

I followed her into the gallery and pointed one out.

'No, I want to sit in front of *this* painting.' She was acting like a petulant child.

Silently and carefully, I picked up the nearest chair and placed it rather pointedly where she was indicating, in front of a Winifred Nicholson oil painting called *Moonshine*. I had to concede that this woman had taste: in just a few minutes she had picked out the best piece in the gallery (and one with a five-figure price tag!). I was impressed.

The woman sat motionless before that one painting for a very long time. People came in and out and skirted cautiously round her.

'Who's that?' some of them whispered when they were back in the safety of the hall. 'Is she an installation – a work of art?'

I shrugged: I had no idea. I kept thinking she had slipped out but no, when I squinted through the crack in the door she was still firmly settled in front of *Moonshine*. She obviously wasn't a prospective buyer, I thought, but it's always good when someone really looks at and enjoys what we are showing.

Most people don't look long enough.

After almost two hours of silent stillness, the woman emerged. She rudely walked straight past me, made for the front door, opened it, stopped, turned, and looked at me in a confrontational manner.

'Did you see the Winifred Nicholson exhibition a few years ago in Edinburgh?' she asked abruptly.

'At the Gallery of Modern Art – the Dean Gallery? Yes, I did.'

'I sponsored that,' she said. And with that bombshell she swiftly left.

It was a theatrical exit: perfect timing.

'Exit pursued by a bear,' I muttered as she banged the door behind her and stumped off down the road.

As soon as she was gone, my diminutive assistants came out of hiding, looking somewhat sheepish. I didn't blame them: that stroppy woman could easily have picked them up, tucked them under each arm, and made off with them kicking and squealing helplessly like Lilliputians.

We all confessed how uncomfortable we had felt in her presence, how she had seemed like a dormant volcano that could erupt at any moment. But never mind: she'd probably never come in again.

A few days later, two strangers visited the gallery. They introduced themselves as Izzi Sutherland, an artist, and John, her picture framer. I immediately liked them. They were genuine, open and sincere. They told me they were tango partners, which didn't surprise me: John was tall, strong and taciturn, while Izzi was effusive, blonde, spiky-haired and full of laughter. I imagined they danced a mean tango, full of innuendo, haughty indifference and sexual tension.

'I believe you have a painting here by Winifred Nicholson,' Izzi began. 'I think it's called *Moonshine*? We've been told to come and see it. Which room is it in?'

I indicated the room to the right. They stood in front of it and discussed it for some time in low voices. When they re-appeared, it was with serious faces.

'Diana is interested in buying *Moonshine*,' Izzi said. 'She wants a second opinion. That's why she's sent us.'

'Er, who's Diana?' I asked. But I knew immediately she was the Amazonian woman who had previously been studying the painting. I was flabbergasted.

'Do you know how much it is? Does she?'

The woman had never asked the price: she probably hadn't realised it would take a serious amount of money to acquire. But Izzi insisted that's what Diana wanted to do. She respected Izzi's opinion and keen eye, and was seeking reassurance that she was doing the right thing.

'And I'm here to look at the frame,' John continued. 'I've to offer her some suggestions about re-framing it.'

This made me even more sceptical.

'But the frame is original,' I protested. 'It tells the story of the painting. It gives you its history: it's like the terroir of a vineyard. It's really important, especially as the painting isn't signed.'

I took *Moonshine* down from the wall and placed it face-down on the kitchen table. We gathered round. It was a classic Nicholson. Winifred was a master at creating near and far, and spoke often and enthusiastically about the importance of 'the spaces in between'. This painting focused on a golden sickle moon with its light falling silver on an indistinct building, the frost glinting on its roof and a distant mountain range in the background. Winifred had used silver paint liberally to create sparkle, to give the sense of emerging from a dark tunnel into the light. It was an optimistic painting, promising a new dawn.

By contrast, I had to admit that the frame was pretty awful – she'd splashed some silver paint liberally on that as well. Winifred never bothered about her frames, they were not important to her. Nor did she tend to sign her paintings, saying she wanted to leave something for the art historians to puzzle over and debate after she was gone. This made the frame and the labels on the reverse even more important. It was the labels which testified to the fact that Moonshine had been shown in some prestigious galleries - the Tate Gallery on Millbank and a gallery in Paris among them – which meant it could be traced back through archived catalogues and its all-important provenance could be established.

The three of us spent a happy afternoon together, examining the painting and talking about art. Izzi showed me some postcards of her own work - still lifes and figure drawings, studies of tango dancers that were full of life and movement. I arranged to visit her studio - on the estate of the Buddhist monastery Samye Ling, in the Scottish borders near Eskdalemuir - with a view to maybe offering her an exhibition. But I was still not convinced that their friend Diana was going to buy *Moonshine*. She might have liked to, but I doubted she had the means. I had only met her once but I thought she was maybe a fantasist; an attention seeker. She was probably like those people who go round expensive houses with estate agents, pretending they might buy them but finding small faults afterwards as the reason for not making an offer. Not that I minded going along with it if this Diana wanted to live the dream.

A gallery *is* a place of dreams, a place of the imagination, a place of withdrawal from the real world. 'It costs nowt to look', reads the sign in the music shop in the town, and I felt like sticking one in our window as well. Some galleries are too forbidding and intimidating, but we welcomed everybody. We knew the majority of visitors would just look – we didn't expect everyone who came in to buy. An eighty-odd-year-old woman came in regularly to our exhibitions and always bought a postcard on leaving, apologising she hadn't bought anything this time. That always cut me to pieces. Nevertheless, as she was leaving, Izzi assured me that Diana was a serious collector.

'She's an heiress to a fortune,' she told me. 'She can afford it. If she wants it she will have it: she doesn't need to ask the price.'

Mmm! I know I'm far too judgemental, and I liked Izzi, but I really found this hard to take in.

A few days later, Diana returned. This time she was calmer, but still as silent as before, and again she sat in front of the painting for several hours. She was giving nothing away. We fetched her a chair before she asked, Angie made her some coffee, and we left her alone.

Eventually she sought me out and quietly said, 'Ever since that Nicholson exhibition in Scotland I've wanted to own one, but none of them were for sale. I've looked since then but they don't come on the market very often and I think this is the right one. May I buy it?'

Well, what could I say?

Michael and I delivered the painting to Diana's modest first floor flat in the Cumbrian market town where she lived. As we climbed the stairs with it, we speculated about what the flat would be like. It should be very special to house a painting as lovely as *Moonshine* – but we were surprised when we got inside. This was not at all like the flat of a wealthy woman. It was small and bleak, and a lot of Diana's things were still in packing cases. She had hung a few of Izzi's bright paintings but there was nothing there as spectacular as *Moonshine*.

We hung the Nicholson in a prominent place over the mantelpiece in the sitting room. It looked dull and lifeless until Michael adjusted the lighting, and then it came alive. It danced for us. It sparkled. Its glinting silvers and shining moon transformed what was a very ordinary space, and Diana lit up with it. She became animated and excited, and opened herself up to us.

Over coffee we discovered that it was the Samye Ling monastery which linked her with Izzi and John. Diana also had a small property there, close to Izzi's studio, and John lived nearby. She was fond of them both and trusted them. She also now gave me permission to call her Di, which amused me: she suited the name Diana much better – more imperious, recalling the mythical huntress. Diana was likewise searching for something, but she didn't know what. It was an elusive, intangible, nagging thing: an itch in the small of the back, a tiny bit of gravel in a shoe or a shard of celery stuck in a tooth, refusing to be dislodged. She was casting about for an answer, struggling with Art and Buddhism, which she believed would be able to show her the way. Those two things were her passion. They gave structure to a chaotic life. They calmed her.

Di told me how much the Nicholson added to her life when she came to the gallery again a few days later and accepted the offer of tea and cake in the kitchen. This was a different woman. She settled herself down, enjoying her new status as a friend. She was more relaxed: she was talkative and confident, but there was still a deeply ingrained unhappiness within her. She never wanted to talk about herself and I didn't ask, but I did understand how her inherited wealth had worked against her. It empowered her to go anywhere, do anything, wear anything, own anything, drive anything - but in reality she didn't have the imagination or confidence to do any of it. It didn't give her happiness, it just haunted her and filled her with mistrust. She couldn't work out whether people wanted her for herself or her money. She knew she was ungainly and difficult, so assumed it was the latter and played up to it. She couldn't 'read' people. She had a strong conscience, a deep desire to do the right thing, if only she knew what the right thing was.

A large woman with attitude who is awkward physically and socially is not endearing to the world around her, but endearment was not her aim. She donned her aggressive armour to put off all but the most intrepid. She tried alienation as a test of loyalty and friendship, and disliked men intensely and vociferously. I could sense that she had been hurt badly – possibly more than once – in life.

In spite of that, I must have passed the test, and so did Michael - perhaps because he was sympathetic and not challenging. One day, when he was in town collecting some catalogues from the printer, he arranged to meet her and take her out for lunch.

Apart from Izzi and John, Diana normally paid people to do things for her, so she was surprised and pleased to accept. He was amused when he saw her coming down the main street on a folding bicycle. She looked bizarre: a top-heavy woman on a miniature machine with tiny wheels which she virtually obscured. She dismounted clumsily, folded it up small like a pushchair, and walked into the café, carrying the bike easily in one hand like a shopping bag. Immediately she was thrown out.

'Hey, you can't bring that in here,' the café owner shouted. 'Get it out.'

Diana swung round - almost taking Michael off his feet - and strode out, red-faced.

They were both shocked and indignant but soon found a more hospitable café. They bonded against opposition.

Diana came to all our exhibitions after that and bought many more paintings, most of which she gave away to hospices to enhance the lives of the patients and carers. She bought well and thoughtfully but always tried to barter with the artist, which was annoying. She came to me after a Marie Scott opening to inform me Marie had agreed to a lower price. I pointed out to her that she had far more money than Marie or the other artists and it was unfair. She immediately retracted. But she then went round to the home of the Bennetts on the pretext of being interested in buying books. She soon got into their studios and began bartering for paintings there, as well as asking for the price of re-framing to be deducted from one painting whose frame she didn't like.

June and Michael are - like many artists - quiet, private people who hate contention, so they quickly conceded. I was cross with Diana. It had taken me over a year to be invited into Michael's studio, and I had gently tiptoed in. She had steam-rollered her way in. The Bennetts hated the invasion of their privacy, but were too polite and nice to say so. They were also usually skint. Diana didn't understand how a few pounds could make a huge difference to an artist and how a gallery depended on sales to survive. It had never occurred to her - although she was extremely generous with Izzi and realised how hard it was for her to support herself as an artist. Once she understood the situation, she apologised.

She loved to come into the gallery kitchen after an opening and have tea with the artists. She never dominated, just sat quietly, listened and enjoyed it. She desperately wanted to belong, to be part of the art scene. I had paintings in there that were part of my own personal collection – my large Sheila Fell *Cumberland* (the largest painting she ever did), a vibrant Marie Scott, several Percy Kellys, and a David Martin gouache of sunflowers. There was a lovely oil painting by Mary Fedden hanging by the kitchen window: lustrous red poppies on a pink cloth. The colours clashed violently. They clashed so much that they worked perfectly.

I noticed that Diana always sat where she could see it and that she was studying it just as she had studied *Moonshine*. She was analysing and devouring every square inch of it with her eyes. It wasn't officially for sale but it was definitely a Diana painting - it epitomised her life: an attention-grabbing mismatch of shapes and colours. It had her name on it - albeit in invisible ink - but I didn't point that out to her. I never, ever actively tried to sell her anything. That would not have worked. I would have lost her forever. I just waited. She sat with the Fedden over countless cups of tea and cake on many different occasions. She fell in love with it, eventually asked if I'd sell it, but then spun out the buying process, enjoying the protracted negotiations and the attention such a purchase brought her.

Her flat was still bleak and uninviting – apart from the dazzling Nicholson *Moonshine* - when Michael and I went to help her hang the Fedden. What a time we had finding the right place. Winifred and Mary, both strong women, were obviously not going to get on with each other. Winifred's muted blues and silvers clashed with Mary's blatant bright pinks and reds, so after much serious discussion we decided unanimously that Mary should go in Diana's bedroom. We crammed up on to her bed to appraise it, all three of us, and laughed uproariously when we realised how ludicrous we must have looked: this enormous woman flanked by Michael (wielding a hammer and hooks) and I (laughing loudly and nervously, tape measure in my hand). It's a pity the selfie hadn't yet been invented – or maybe not. We three wise monkeys spent ages over the positioning, but only a few months later we discovered Diana had taken it round to Izzi and offered it to her on loan because she knew she liked it. She loved giving. She loved bringing pleasure to people's lives. Her generosity was staggering.

'You're not going to write about me, are you?' she asked one day in a little girl voice, giving me one of her long, piercing stares.

'Why? Do you want me to?' I asked.

'No I don't!' she said forcefully - but then added a codicil, 'Not now, but you will know when.'

She asked me the same question at some point nearly every time we met after that and I shrugged it off each time. I assured her that I wasn't even considering it. Why would I think about writing about her? She always looked disappointed, giving an exaggerated pout, her bottom lip protruding like a child's. It became an invitation to defy her.

***

Monday morning and the email silently and innocently dropped into my inbox like a stealth bomb. It announced it was from Diana van de Lugt but the subject line was blank. Di's messages, like her conversation, were terse and to the point. She didn't waste time with unnecessary words - but this email was minimal to the point of nothing. There was no message there. There were just two attachments which I casually downloaded - and then wished I hadn't. As the picture slowly appeared, pixels beginning to form and focus from the top down, I was filled with disbelief. It was alarming. This couldn't have come from Diana - could it? Her email account must have been hacked.

A slender female form lay awkwardly on a concrete floor, her arms outstretched in a crucifix pose. Tightly swaddled in several layers of bubble wrap, secured by blue nylon cord and gaffer tape, her head was pulled back and her feet, which were attached to a boulder, seemed to have been impaled. The boulder itself was encased in concrete, and there was an axe leaning casually against the wall. Stunned, I looked again for the sender. The email was definitely from Diana van de Lugt. I ought to tell her what was being sent out in her name. Was this a macabre stage set? Was it the venue of some S&M sex game gone wrong? Or had Di flipped into insanity and sent me the images as a grotesque joke? Anything was possible. We all felt that she lived on the edge of a precipice and could fall off at any moment, and Izzi had warned us about Di's violent temper, which could flare up in seconds.

'If she gets angry, get her out of the gallery quickly,' she told us. 'In a temper, she will break and throw. I've seen it several times.'

I had never seen this side of Di and was thankful.

While I was sitting stunned at my desk, wondering what to do about the poor woman on the concrete floor, there was a ping as another email dropped into my inbox. It was from Diana van de Lugt again. I opened it with a degree of caution.

Dear Chris

As I no longer have a garden I need to find a home for New Dawn. *She is bronze, life-size and very lovely. She would look good in the gallery garden. I'd like you to have her if you can collect her. She's in a garage at Samye Ling Monastery in Eskdalemuir. I will post the legal paperwork if you are agreeable.*

Di

In all my years at the gallery I had never before had such a precious gift from a client. But like so many people in the last twenty years or so, Di was a client who had become a friend. Could I accept it? I would upset her if I didn't and I really didn't want to do that. She deeply feared rejection and she had probably experienced a lot of it in her life.

I showed Michael the attachment – the images of *New Dawn* all trussed up - and quickly explained it was a bronze sculpture, a gift from Diana, before he too became alarmed. He thought we should definitely accept it graciously, in the spirit of Di's giving, but, practical as ever, he immediately realised there was a potential weight problem. I had no idea of the scale of the piece apart from an estimate based on the size of the axe in the picture. Life-size could be anything from five- to six-foot tall. Diana didn't tell us how much *New Dawn* weighed as it probably didn't seem important to her. Other people would have moved the sculpture for her.

Could we solve this conundrum? I, being the optimist, argued that if it had been moved before at least twice it could be done again. Michael, being practical, studied the photographs closely and thought it was not that easy but was convinced that if he could remove her from her boulder as well as from the concrete she would be more manageable.

It turned out that *New Dawn* really was life-size. It took several strong monks in purple and gold robes - and one sinewy, tango-dancing picture framer - to load her into the hired van at the monastery. I had likewise organised a line-up of strong men (minus purple and gold robes) to receive her at the gallery. Still swaddled in bubble wrap and impaled on the granite which was still encased in concrete, she was difficult to unload. I now know four men with hernias who are never going to volunteer to lift anything for me again. They laid her inelegantly face-down on the lawn and hobbled off to nurse their backs and knees, moaning and muttering imprecations. *New Dawn* lay on the grass for some time.

Visitors to the garden were curious and suspicious, just as I had been. She was a very convincing corpse.

'What's that thing lying on the lawn?' some of them asked, screwing up their faces with distaste and keeping their distance. 'Is it dead?'

Michael spent hours sitting on the lawn carefully chipping away at the concrete with hammer and chisel to minimise her weight. He parted her from the concrete, but found it impossible to release her from the granite boulder on which she stood. The spindle screw that went from her delicate tiptoes into the big rock was immoveable. When Diana came to see how we were getting on, she told us that when Dawn had arrived on a lorry at her Scottish house decades ago, she had no plinth. She had selected the big piece of granite for the bronze to stand on, and her gardener had screwed the figure firmly onto it. Then he had prepared a big hole, filled it with concrete and planted *New Dawn*, rock and all, into it while it was still wet. The wet concrete had travelled up into the screwhole and set hard, making it impossible to free her again without damaging her delicate feet. Dear Dawn was now stuck with that massive boulder forever. Of course Diana hadn't envisaged moving her bronze again: she had imagined permanence and once again had been disappointed.

When Michael had finished his careful chipping away of the softer concrete, Dawn was finally unwrapped and erected facing east on tiptoe, arms outstretched to greet the dawn. At last we saw her upturned face for the first time. She was serene and lovely. She was perfect in the walled garden.

Diana was delighted with Dawn's new home and spent even more silent hours meditating in the tranquil garden at Castlegate House. It gave her a sense of ownership, of belonging and sharing in the gallery, especially as she now had no garden of her own. She felt she had justified her place and could come to see us any time - and so she could. She and Michael spent hours quietly talking about Buddhism. It was therapy for a troubled mind and turbulent life.

As for me, I was delighted to have acquired this beautiful bronze – such a significant piece of sculpture. I didn't mind that we had also acquired Diana. We were growing fond of her. She had our cautious respect. It was mutual.

Then we discovered she had another love. He was called Trevor. She had just bought him and showed us the photographs. He was literally a dark horse, a large handsome stallion, and she loved him - though, like us, she found his inherited name hilarious. She couldn't change it because he answered to it, and she went over to his stable nearly every day to groom and ride him.

'How's Trevor?' I would enquire cheekily whenever she came in with muddy boots, smelling a bit 'horsey', then we'd break into laughter while Diana tried to look outraged at my impertinence. Even then she treated me with a small degree of reserve: she was still not sure if our friendship was genuine.

The following October we mounted an exhibition of paintings by Royal Academician Kenneth Draper. Diana loved them and, as she had before, spent time in the garden room, just looking. Dressed as she was in her habitual denims and green wellies, sitting beside the tall window and framed by bright red Virginia creeper and late white roses, with *New Dawn* on the lawn in the background, it made a lovely picture. I wish now I'd taken a photograph because it was the last time I had the opportunity.

Diana van de Lugt left that day promising to come back the following Monday to meet with Izzi so they could see the two Drapers she had selected and reserved. They were destined for a hospice. For the first time Diana was happy with the frames, which was a relief. But that visit never happened. Izzi arrived and we had a coffee while waiting for Diana. She didn't turn up, and coffee turned into lunch. We thought she must have absentmindedly gone off somewhere – she was unpredictable and erratic - perhaps to see her mother in the south of England. Then we began to worry that she might have had an accident –

perhaps fallen off Trevor. Izzi rang her mobile several times, then the stables, then her mother in Bournemouth, but there was no sign of her. She hadn't been to the stables. Trevor was alone.

Diana often went off impulsively so for several days we weren't too worried, but after more than a week of silence and missed appointments, Izzi drove the 80 miles from her home in Scotland to Diana's flat. She didn't tell us she was going or we would have gone too and met her there. She should not have had to do what she did alone.

Diana's small car was parked outside her flat in the usual place, the curtains were drawn and the lights were on. It was midday. Realising something was very wrong, Izzy called the police. When they broke the door down, they found Diana's body on the kitchen floor. She had died suddenly while cooking her supper more than a week previously. The pan was burnt out and the gas was still on and lit. No one will ever know what happened - the inquest was inconclusive but it was definitely not suicide. Diana was 56.

***

In contrast to the shimmering gold and red decoration of the monastery, the stupa is a simple domed building on the Samye Ling estate. It is an integral part of the monastery reserved for Buddhist pre-funeral ceremonies, preparing the soul of the person for the next journey. Diana van de Lugt's body lay there for three days, and it was where we and a few others paid our respects in silence and remembered her sadly and fondly.

According to her Buddhist beliefs she is now far away in a state of total happiness. Maybe she is between incarnations, waiting to be reborn in order to continue her karmic journey, or perhaps she is already reborn and experiencing another opportunity to attain peace and happiness. She deserves it after her turbulent life.

Diana had made a will which was sensible, legal and

specific. Trevor was to be given back to the stables where he had been born, had lived, and was looked after all his life. The Nicholson *Moonshine* was gifted to the Gallery of Modern Art in Edinburgh where it can now be enjoyed by everybody. Izzi has the exuberant Fedden poppies. And Michael and I have *New Dawn*, a permanent reminder of Di's generosity.

The rest of her not inconsiderable fortune was left to the ROKPA Trust* and this story gives Diana the attention and immortality she craved in her life.

* *The ROKPA Trust is the charitable arm of Samye Ling, the Buddhist Monastery at Eskdalemuir, which was set up by Diana's teacher, supporter and friend, the monk Akong Ttulku Rinpoche, to help poor people in Tibet – primarily women and children. This has now broadened to help people in many countries, fulfilling its motto: 'Helping where help is needed'. Rinpoche was brutally murdered in Tibet in 2013, after Diana's death.*

Russian Roulette

'Международный аэропорт Домодедово'

I stare at the sign, trying to break the code. At a guess it says 'International Airport Domodedovo', but I am unable to recognise anything in Cyrillic script, not even my own name in my visa. This is the raw moment of truth, a frightening reality: I am arriving in Moscow alone, unable even to write my name in Russian in a form that officials will understand.

Along the long, grey airport corridors, stony-faced officials are posted every few metres, but when I try a tentative smile, I receive only an intimidating blank stare in return. I'm not going to get any help from them. I work out which is the Diplomatic Lane at Passport Control – small queue, diplomatic bags, superior looks on faces, but I'm uneasy. Having changed to Lufthanza at the Frankfurt hub, there are few British among my fellow passengers, and I hope I'm in the right place. Never mind: once through Customs, my new American friend will be waiting for me.

I push out cautiously into the dimly-lit arrivals hall. There's a surging crowd of people, some of them holding placards above their heads in Russian script. I scan the crowd hopefully, but I can't see Heidi. I'm not sure I'll recognise her. We've only met twice before. Taxi drivers, sensing my unease, begin to home in on me as the crowd thins out and I try hard to look casual and in control. When a swarthy, thick-set man grabs my arm and tries to steer me to his car, I shake him off: guide books warn about these people. I don't want to join The Disappeared, last seen getting into an unofficial car at a Russian airport.

I glance round, looking for a tourist desk, but I wouldn't recognise one if I fell over it. It's late on a Saturday afternoon, almost dark, and I only have Heidi's work telephone number and email address. I begin to panic. The few officials hanging around are apathetic and the taxi drivers are like a pack of hungry wolves closing in, waiting for the kill. I look anxiously at the big clock on the wall – it is now more than an hour since I landed. The cabbies surge forward, sensing my indecisiveness. At last, over their heads, I see a tall young woman with a long, dark pigtail pushing her way through, speaking in rapid Russian. She grabs my arm and bag and pulls me out of the mayhem.

'I'm so sorry,' she says, giving me a hug and a big, apologetic smile. 'I got held up.'

***

It had all begun a year earlier when I met Heidi for the first time. She and her friend Steve came to the gallery, stayed all day, and bought a stack of paintings which we shipped to Manhattan, where Steve was living, because Heidi was working in Siberia, selling futures. Was there any future in Siberia? I wondered. Apparently not for Heidi, because some time after that visit I received an email from her: 'HEY YOU, I'VE JUST LANDED A NEW JOB IN MOSCOW. IT COMES WITH A FLAT – VERY CENTRAL. THIS IS A WONDERFUL CITY, FULL OF ARTISTS. I'M ADDING TO MY COLLECTION. COME AND STAY WITH ME AND MEET SOME OF THEM. H'.

I was really pleased for her, but at that moment I hadn't time to stay with anyone: it was 1997 and I was working hard towards the gallery's tenth birthday exhibition and party. It was going to be a very special celebration: marquee, band, entertainers, the works. The gallery had survived for ten years and so had I.

Politely declining Heidi's offer, I attached a party invitation to my reply out of courtesy, knowing she'd be too busy in her new job to come. Her response was immediate and surprising: 'COUNT ME IN CHRIS. MAY I BRING A MOSCOW GALLERY OWNER AS WELL? BOOK US IN SOMEWHERE NICE. H'.

The pair arrived on the afternoon of Friday 6th July, the day before the party. Heidi, accustomed to an American left-hand-drive automatic limousine, was driving cautiously. Her passenger, gallery owner Natalia, was elegant, beautiful, and spoke perfect English. She was eager to help with the party. I was organising the decorations for the large marquee which had been erected in the garden and suggested that Natalia come with me to the toy shop in town to fill dozens of balloons with helium.

Each silver balloon was printed with a large red eye with a bright blue iris - the logo of Visual Arts Year – and as we walked back up Main Street, we were surrounded by dozens of staring, shining eyes, bobbing around above us in the breeze, valiantly trying to escape our hold. They were a child magnet and we were soon being followed by a growing retinue of children. I felt like the Pied Piper of Cockermouth, accompanied by my exotic foreign assistant.

'Gi' us one, missus!' they called to Natalia, who was frantically trying to keep control of her balloons and not take off in a Mary Poppins moment.

Meanwhile, back in the upstairs studio at Castlegate, a group of artists were busy painting 'forgeries' on large pieces of mount board. These included 'Vang Off's' *Sunflowers*, an 'L. S. Lousy' factory scene, an animal skin bedcover mounted on board by 'Damian Hurts', 'Money's' *Waterlilies* (with pound signs), some cut-outs signed 'Henry Mattress' and a 'Jackson Bollocks' abstract which looked as though Michael Bennett had ridden a bike across it several times. Which he had!

We hung these and many more around the tent, all with ostentatious big red dots on them, and the party began. However, as the evening progressed, the balloons which we'd released into the roof space made a gradual descent until they were within jumping, reaching, sniffing distance. In combination with the flowing red wine, it perhaps wasn't surprising that quite a few of us became a bit slurry of speech and blurry of eye as time went on.

Some of my friends and clients were wandering around the garden laughing and talking in Mickey Mouse voices. 'Speech,' they squeaked at an appropriate interval for the band to get a drink.

My friendly insurance broker was also getting into the spirit of things and decided to do a 'live' interview.

'My name's Philip Jackson of CNN,' he improvised, holding a wine bottle 'microphone' under my nose. 'Congratulations on achieving ten years of the gallery. How does it feel?'

'Well, I'm ashtonished to have shurvived this long,' I replied. 'Of coursh, I have to thank all theesh wonderful artists, some of whom are here tonight. I couldn't have done it without them.'

I looked around benevolently at the smiling crowd.

'Nor could I have shurvived without the shupport of all you art-crazy people. Thank you for coming.'

A cheer went up.

'I believe,' Philip continued, 'That there are people who have travelled a long way to be here - even from as far as Russia?'

Heidi, who had at last figured out how to use the video camera she had bought the day before in Duty Free at Schiphol airport, nodded.

'And will you be paying a return visit?' Philip asked.

And that was when my affirmative answer was captured on camera, although it wasn't until the following day that I was reminded of it. I think I must have been tired and emotional as I'd apparently agreed to go to Moscow that September and I don't go anywhere in September - especially not to stay with someone I hardly know. Autumn is a really hectic time: with back-to-back exhibitions running from March to December, I'm always hanging one show while printing and posting out invitations to the next, and then there's the following year's programme and publicity to plan. The pace of the year gets faster until I collapse in a heap at New Year, close the gallery for six weeks, and take off on my travels. But the evening had all been recorded, in full frontal silliness, and so that's how I came to be at Moscow airport following a near stranger as she led me to her American Chevrolet... and who knew what else.

***

I began to relax and take in my surroundings as Heidi sped away from the airport and down the six-lane highway. She was no longer selling futures, she was just temporarily in charge of mine - and it was suddenly looking brighter until we drew up outside a dismal block of flats directly opposite one of Stalin's Wedding Cake buildings. I stood nervously looking about me on the pavement as Heidi unlocked the heavy entrance door with two big keys and led me into a dark vestibule. It was shabby and neglected. The stone stairs which zig-zagged upwards out of sight had been worn down by a century of dragging feet, the small window at the back was darkly cobwebbed, and the empty baked bean tins attached to the banister rail with string at intervals were apparently improvised ashtrays. The antiquated lift climbed, clanked and hiccoughed its way slowly upwards like an asthmatic chain-smoker.

'It's a bit unreliable,' Heidi said cheerfully as the lights went out for the second time. 'Don't panic if it appears to break down. Just wait. It'll start again. It's never let me down for long.'

I was not so confident. I was having a Le Carré moment. We eventually got out on the fifth floor and walked across to a massive, padded door. The diamond-quilted, cheap black vinyl was metal-studded and pitted – possibly with bullet holes. Was I being recruited to the CIA or MI6?

'This one's steel, it needs to be,' Heidi said as she swung it open, only to reveal another, wooden, inner door.

'I'll be at work during the week, so don't ever let anyone in unless you know who they are,' she added.

Nobody installs these for fun, I thought as she went on to show me how to work the sophisticated alarm and entry-phone system.

Once inside, however, I was in a different world: a bright and spacious flat full of artwork. Contemporary pieces sat alongside ancient icons and interesting antiques; there were paintings and sculpture, fabrics and modern furniture. It was magnificent.

With a glass of neat vodka in my hand, I sank into the sofa, able now to switch off for the first time since I had left Heathrow that morning.

I asked about a massive oil painting facing me that was dominating the wall of the high-ceilinged room: a large, colourfully-dressed woman lying on a sofa, surrounded by food.

'Irena paints and her husband Igor makes furniture,' said Heidi. She indicated a glass-topped wrought iron table and matching chairs in the adjoining dining room which would comfortably seat twelve.

'Igor made those for me,' she said. 'They've invited us round tonight. Are you up for it?'

Drinks with Irena and Igor? Of course I was up for it. I loved 'em already, with names like that.

Irena and Igor lived in a flat that was as fortified as Heidi's, although theirs was much smaller and there was no lift. We had vodka and chocolates as we admired Irena's paintings and Igor's furniture. Then it was straight on to visit a sculptor, Andrei Kovaltchouk, whose studio was in the dripping, damp basement of a similar block. Heidi and I really needed wellies to reach Andrei's workspace: he had to bring a plank so that we could teeter across in our Saturday night shoes. Apparently, Moscow artists don't starve in garrets – they drown in basements.

Ygorshina was different. She was an internationally known and well-respected painter, and her studio, on the left bank of the broad Moscow River, was high in a block overlooking the floodlit Kremlin and St Basil's Cathedral.

She was in her 80s and like a little bird: frail of body but definitely not of mind. Her husband, also a painter, was dead, but she was still painting Matisse-type canvases every day. One wall held a huge painting of a woman in black who scowled back at us.

'She was a black beetle,' the artist exclaimed, following our gaze. 'She was after my husband. I didn't like her at all.'

It showed.

Ygorshina told us that, back in the Iron Curtain days, she and her husband had been invited to exhibit their work in Paris. They had got all the necessary paperwork and permissions, a process which took time and effort as it involved dealing with the Communist bureaucracy. They carefully crated their paintings – this was art that represented more than two years' work - but the day before they were due to be collected, the KGB arrived at their studio and impounded all of it. They never saw it again.

Artists are distrusted by repressive regimes, and with good cause. Revolutions often begin with creatives - artists, writers, musicians, poets - because they can stir strong emotions with their work. In Russia, many of them had been executed, imprisoned or sent to work in camps in the Gulags. Free art such as Ygorshina's and her husband's was frowned upon. What was encouraged was state art, depicting happy – if starving - citizens going about their crippling labour with big, artificial smiles. Sculptors did well, producing massive statues of the Communist leaders and heroes, while Constructivists like Rodchenko and his friends made and printed posters applauding the state. Propaganda was the art of the day.

Ygorshina and her husband had shunned the path of government art which could have made their life much more comfortable, giving them state recognition and the privileges that went with it. They worked undercover, painting because it was their way of expressing themselves. Just occasionally they bowed to the state and produced a patriotic piece of fantasy.

That day, Ygorshina spoke wistfully of the lost paintings. She wondered what had happened to them: they had never been found. To lose all that work was a bereavement like losing a child. Meanwhile, my hopes of putting a Russian exhibition together at Castlegate were fading. It may have been 1997 but it was still very difficult even then to get anything out of the country. The regime had changed, but the old ways, ideas and bureaucracy were still in place to some extent.

***

I thought about Ygorshina again as I looked around Natalia's gallery some days later. It specialised in 'Social Realism', which was not realism at all but idealism: government-approved paintings from the post-revolution days; scenes of contented agriculture labourers and happy factory workers, all enjoying their so-called Communist equality. Ironically, these were now collectors' pieces and much in demand. They commanded high prices and Natalia told me she was finding them ever harder to come by.

What were not hard to come by in Moscow were icons. In the Pushkin and Tretyakov galleries – both treasure houses of Russian and European art – I saw icons by the hundred, as well as work by the likes of Picasso, Braque, Klee and Kandinsky. However, the House of Artists, despite its name, was a disappointment.

The featureless concrete building stood in Gorky Park and as Heidi and I walked there one morning we could hear the screams of Muscovites coming from the funfair that stretched along the river. The rides weren't our idea of fun, but the House of Artists wasn't either. The typical grey Soviet building contained room after room of dreary paintings. There were more lifeless oils of ornate flowers in gold-handled vases, framed in cheap gold rococo frames, than I had ever seen in one place. Many of the artists seemed to have been given 'painting by numbers' kits for Christmas.

I was beginning to suffer from gallery fatigue when I noticed Heidi was falling behind. I quickened my pace; I just wanted to get through and out into the open air, away from this suffocation by art. Then, in the penultimate room, I struck gold (the right kind). Here were real paintings: lovely textured oils, well painted semi-abstract landscapes, a few good portraits, some modern still lifes.

'Hey Heidi, come along here,' I yelled down the corridor. 'I've found something good at last. Come and see.'

We staked out the room. Every room had a minder, and this one was sitting at a table, reading. He looked up for two seconds in a desultory way and returned to his a book.

'I'm going to buy some of these,' I informed Heidi.

She looked at me.

'Which do you want?'

I pointed to an avenue of trees in the snow.

'*I* like that as well,' Heidi immediately said. 'What else?'

I indicated a golden landscape - corn fields with a hint of a red tractor - and another of two children and a goat.

Heidi liked those too.

'I saw them first,' I said truculently.

'Yes, but how are you going to find out how much they cost? Or get them back to the UK?'

True: without Heidi to interpret, I was at a loss.

'Arm wrestling!' I shouted. 'Come on, that'll decide it!'

The man at the table looked up, bemused: he had no idea what was going on. The invasion of his space by two loud, excited, foreign women behaving like five-year-olds must have been disconcerting. Not least because they seemed to be arguing over his paintings – he was the artist, he informed Heidi in response to her enquiries. 'His name is Vladimir Pavlotsky,' she translated, 'and he lives in Turkmenistan. He comes to Moscow each year for this exhibition.'

Heidi and I selected eight paintings between us and made

Vladimir's day, maybe year. Heidi offered to look after my four for a few months until her next visit to the UK; meanwhile, Vladimir invited me to go to Turkmenistan. I had no idea where Turkmenistan was - nor any of the other 'stans' that were emerging from the shadows of the old Soviet Union. So far, I've not followed that one.

***

Heidi's chauffeuse, a bright, attractive and vivacious Russian woman named Lena, spoke good American English, but she also had a contemptuous attitude to law enforcement, as I discovered when we were flagged down by police after an evening out. Snorting and tossing her head, Lena drummed her beautifully manicured fingers on the steering wheel as she waited for the policeman to come alongside us. When he appeared at the driver's door she immediately went into the attack in rapid Russian – obviously protesting at being stopped. He ordered her to get down from her superior position at the wheel. Heidi and I shrank down on the back seat.

'Will she be sent to the Gulags?' I whispered.

Heidi laughed nervously. 'Not these days,' she said, 'but I think she's pushing it.'

In the end, Lena got away with a mild telling off, but she was unable or unwilling to tell us why she'd been pulled over.

Galleries weren't the only places in Moscow to see art. The city centre Metro stations are art galleries - people's palaces.

Heidi had presented me with *Russian in Ten Minutes a Day* on my first morning, but after an hour poring over it, I reckoned it would take me ten years of ten minutes a day for me to make any headway at all. However, like a child starting school, I was learning the letters. The metro station opposite Heidi's flat had a long name which began with a Russian K and ended with 'SKAYA'. I memorised it and, like Orpheus, descended deep into the underworld and boarded a train – no looking back. I realised after a few stops that most of the stations begin with K and all of them end in 'SKAYA' - the word for station. To make navigation even more difficult, most of the central metro stations had several names – a different one for each line that passed through it. The list of station names on the platform wasn't in any logical order and they all looked frighteningly similar. Lena had tried to persuade me not to even try to go anywhere on the Metro. She offered to drive me anywhere I wanted and was convinced I would be lost forever in the system. She hadn't been able to understand why I'd take the Metro when I could ride in a Chevvy with a chauffeuse like her. Too late, I realised that I should have asked her to make me a big label in Russian – 'PLEASE LOOK AFTER THIS BEAR' – before letting me leave the flat.

I'm glad I insisted on doing it. It was an unforgettable day underground. There were bronze sculptures, marble sculptures, crystal chandeliers, mosaic ceilings and floors, marble floors, murals, paintings, stained glass and art deco. As my confidence grew, I hopped off at any station which looked interesting. On closer inspection, many of them were blatant Communist propaganda – socialist realist statues of idealised workers and murals showing the USSR's prodigious military strength. It was all about power. I was roughly buffeted when I stopped to study the ceilings, which were largely unnoticed by the hurrying passengers, but to me they were a fair match for the Sistine Chapel. The platforms were so clean I could have thrown a banquet down there (I'm told Stalin did!). And one gilded, mirrored, pillared marble hall was as elaborate as our Guildhall in London. These temples to the arts were Stalin's gift to the people of Russia: they could enjoy them every day, regardless of social status.

At the end of the day, I emerged at my own station, proud and unscathed, if very weary. Lena was surprised when I rang her. 'I think I never see you again,' she scolded.

No chance!

When Lena wasn't working, and Heidi didn't want to drive, we had to find alternative methods of transportation.

'Is this a taxi?' I whispered to Heidi one evening as, having walked fearlessly out into the six-lane road, she flagged down a battered Lada.

'Nope,' Heidi replied casually.

She gave the driver the address and negotiated the fare in rapid Russian. He nodded and hurtled into the traffic.

'Do you know him?' I asked.

'Nope.'

'Isn't it sort of dangerous?'

'Everybody does it,' came the reply. 'He makes money. We have a cheap ride. It's the Russian economy. It's all right. Don't worry.'

I did worry. The car was a patchwork quilt of mismatched panels - it looked as though it had been stitched together – while the driver had graduated in the accelerator/break school of driving, which was disconcerting as he appeared to have no anticipation of lights, junctions, or slower moving traffic. And he had obviously never been acquainted with the theory of stopping distances – he swerved across lanes to avoid hitting the vehicle in front.

Luckily, I could walk to most places from Heidi's flat: Red Square and the Kremlin were just ten minutes away. On most days, I passed by Lenin's tomb, strolled by St Basil's Cathedral with its sugar-craft domes, and wandered through Gum - pronounced Goom – the famous Red Square department store and shopping arcade (there wasn't actually much to buy there in 1997 - I renamed it 'Gloom' in my head).

But to me a landmark as important as any of these was the green kiosk on the wide pavement outside Heidi's block. Like an ahead-of-its-time Tesco Express, it was stocked with smoked halibut, caviar, meats, cheese, fruit, sweets, chocolate, milk, bread and alcohol. The average office worker shopping there would need deep pockets – these were luxury goods in Moscow, one of the world's most expensive cities – but for me they were necessities: I hadn't come all this way to end up eating a Big Mac in one of the ubiquitous McDonalds.

The kiosk was manned by two smiling women who looked like mother and daughter. Taking pity on me, they allowed me to go round the back of the counter to see the pictures on the labels (if there were any), or pick up any other clues about what the packets and tins contained.

I sniffed, rattled and felt the items while they watched my every move with ill-concealed amusement. Each day I suspected they eagerly awaited the arrival of the comedy cabaret, their faces composed into a look of polite concentration when I burst through the door, and no doubt collapsing into unbridled laughter as soon as I left. I struggled; I mimed. I was like a student at RADA out to get an Equity Card. Strange mooing, grunting and baaing sounds were exchanged. But, amid lots of laughter and female bonding, I got what I needed – although admittedly not always what I wanted and not always what I thought I'd got.

***

We had saved St Petersburg and its *pièce de résistance*, the Hermitage, for the end of my Russian art tour. Heidi had taken time off work and so, having stocked up on caviar and vodka for our journey, we boarded the midnight sleeper from Leningradski Station as though in a black and white film. It was pure nostalgia, and feeling again as though I was acting the part of a spy in a novel, I kept looking round for Kim Philby and co.

When we were released into St Petersburg the following morning from our mobile prison - the unsmiling stewardess had locked us in our cabin – I was beginning to worry about the state of my liver. We made for the dome of St Isaac's magnificent cathedral, and from this vantage point Heidi and I surveyed the network of canals, onion domes and the series of bridges over the broad river Neva. These are dramatically raised at midnight every day, leaving 'forgetful' revellers on the wrong side until dawn, but Heidi and I had no time for high jinks. Scanning our guide book, we discovered that if we spent one minute in front of each of the Hermitage's three million exhibits, it would take us more than a decade to see everything. We had just one day. We would have to be very selective.

The building itself is a massive mint green and white confection - a palace crafted in icing sugar – and houses the collection of the Great Tsars. They were the ultimate collectors, trawling Europe for the best of everything: paintings, sculpture, ceramics, furniture, clocks, silver, porcelain, glass, jewels by the bucketload, skipload, lorry-load and more. Crazy shopaholics, they had strutted about, followed by a retinue of personal shoppers, grabbing the best of everything to show off in their huge palace, regardless of the near-starving populace outside. I could just picture the scene:

'Shall we have another Leonardo, love?'

'No, I prefer one of these golden peacocks. It'll look lovely at the top of the stairs and the kids will love it.'

'Well, let's take both, then!'

No wonder they met with a bad end.

I could have spent a week, maybe even a year, in the Hermitage and still only scratched the surface, but after a dozen or so overstuffed rooms, an overwhelming lethargy began to creep through my body, my brain. How much more treasure could a woman absorb?

'I've got cultural indigestion,' I said to Heidi. 'I need a toilet and a coffee, in that order.'

Heidi looked at her plan of the building. Her sense of direction was formidable.

'The toilets and cafés are on the ground floor.'

'How far?' I asked, like a petulant child. Heidi, being twenty years my junior and American, had a lot more tourist energy than me.

'Well, I guess we're above them now – but the staircase is

at the other end of the building. There must be an elevator though, in a place like this,' Heidi added quickly, seeing my dismay.

She stared at a heavy damask curtain. 'I wonder what's behind that... Hey, look at this..!'

She pulled it back with a flourish.

'That's lucky. Come on.'

The lift clanked and groaned like an arthritic gent with a zimmer frame but slowly moved downwards before juddering to a halt. We pulled back the criss-cross metal gate, pushed open the heavy door, groped through another heavy curtain – and we were right there: the toilets. The smell of stale urine and disinfectant permeated the area. It was a shock after the opulence of the building and its treasures, a bizarre sight. The whole place was tiled in marble, the effect of which was negated by the row of wooden stalls painted in Soviet green and the dim, low-wattage lightbulbs, unadorned by shades, which swung gently above them. The cubicle dividers were like stable doors, only reaching just above waist-height when you were seated, and as I scurried into a vacant stall I tried not to meet anyone's eye in case I was drawn into a conversation I couldn't deal with, having only reached page ten of *Russian in Ten Minutes a Day*.

After we had found the café and drunk the weak, muddy liquid that was sold as coffee, Heidi and I decided to return to the secret lift to resume our tour. I was amused at being able to dive behind a curtain and be transported clandestinely around this monumental building, and found myself wondering how Peter the Great had managed to get around. I was just imagining an anachronistic scene featuring roller blades or scooters when Heidi noticed the basement button.

'That's not on the plan. Wonder what it is?' she mused – and firmly pressed the '0'.

The lift moved slowly down before coming to a crashing, juddering halt.

Silence.

When we alighted it was into an underground storeroom, stark and gloomy. The only source of light came from isolated fluorescent tubes which flickered and buzzed. The air felt clammy and cold.

'We shouldn't be here,' I whispered. 'Let's go back.'

Ignoring my comment, Heidi edged forward out of the lift. I hung back, waiting for alarm bells to ring, CCTV cameras to frame us, and burly guards - ex-KGB men, of course - to carry us off to some dreadful Russian jail where we would languish for years. But nothing happened - nothing at all.

Heidi beckoned me out with a grin and I cautiously shuffled into a wonderland of storage cages, packing cases, racks stacked with paintings and shelves holding priceless porcelain, jade and a piece of glass like a Fabergé egg. This place was acres bigger than Ikea and just as confusing, except we had it to ourselves and there were no checkouts, queues or trolleys.

The silence was unnerving. I edged along behind Heidi like the back end of a pantomime horse, trying hard to remember long-ago history lessons. Were the Romanovs shot in the cellar of the Hermitage? No, of course not: they were taken east by train to Ekaterina. What about Rasputin, the Mad Monk? He had been a favourite of the Tsarina and was held prisoner and finally murdered after many futile attempts on his life, which had included poisoning, stabbing, and shooting. He'd finally died by drowning in the River Neva – or had he? Some considered him immortal. I couldn't remember the details. Was his ghost down here with us? I shivered. We could rot down here and never be discovered.

Heidi, however, was pioneering an onward route and I had no choice but to follow.

We ventured further through piles of boxes, debating in whispers what might be in them but not daring to touch. There was a thick layer of grey dust on everything and I had an overwhelming desire to write my name in it, just to prove my presence: 'Chris was here'.

Foolish.

'Why do they bother to light the place,' I asked, 'if nobody comes down here?'

'Well, two things,' Heidi answered, drawing on her knowledge of the workings of the Soviet engine.

'First, there's probably only one universal switch for the whole building so the lights'll stay on everywhere during opening hours until the comrade of the lights leaves at night. Secondly, I think the group entrance is somewhere at this level. I've seen coach parties draw up here and the passengers disappear down a ramp.'

Once again, I was impressed by Heidi's knowledge. She had only been to this Winter Palace once before, and then for a very quick visit between meetings.

'So could one come in as a tourist and hide in here until everyone had gone?' I speculated.

'No,' she replied. 'I bet the route is heavily cordoned off, and groups will be quickly marched through anyway. They are the people without visas who arrive on cruise ships. They are heavily supervised.'

Our confidence growing, we ventured deeper and deeper into the cellar. In one big section there were rows of wooden racks on pulleys which obviously held paintings, and I was itching to pull just one out. The light was too dim for Heidi to read the labels, but there could be a Picasso or priceless Kandinsky entombed among them – and what about all those boxes? There could be icons, gold, jade, diamonds or enamels lingering unseen. The squirrel curator inside me desperately wanted to get them out and look inside, to identify and hold the contents.

We had walked a long way and there was still no sign of any end to the place. The cellar probably stretched for miles - under the river Neva and beyond. We could be underwater by now. My fear of being discovered and arrested was replaced with a fear of being lost in that cold, dark catacomb for ever. I was wishing that, like Hansel and Gretel, we could mark our route so we could find the way back. I wished I had a ball of string, pebbles or something. I was tempted to trace arrows in the thick dust. The utter silence, broken only by the eerie puttering of the lights, was totally unnerving.

'Heidi, I want to go home,' I said pathetically, like a child. 'I think we're lost and I'm scared and cold.'

It was a relief to turn and follow her back to the security of our magic lift and escape from that eerie cellar. I hadn't realised that my new friend had an unerring sense of direction even in the dark.

We retired again to the cafeteria to recover and review our antics of the last few hours. It was patently obvious that, in a place that housed art worth billions, there was little in the way of security. I could have pocketed that small Fabergé egg I'd seen and no one would have been any the wiser. There had been no security searches on the way into the building and I doubted there'd be any on the way out.

'What would you choose to take from here if you could have just one thing?' I asked Heidi. 'This is purely hypothetical, of course.'

'A Matisse,' she replied immediately. 'Matisse's *Dance*.'

'Now that would be difficult,' I reflected. 'You would choose an extra large painting, wouldn't you? It wouldn't fit into your flat and it definitely wouldn't fit into your handbag. What about *Blue Pot and Lemon*? That would be easier to conceal under your coat.'

'Ah, you're talking *stealing*,' Heidi smiled. 'I'd be OK with the smaller one. And you?'

Despite being tempted by the Fabergé egg in the basement, I remembered a painting I'd seen for the first time a few hours earlier on the second floor. It was an early Picasso from his blue period: *Dance of the Veils*. Painted when he was just eighteen, it hinted at the heights he would achieve in the future. If he could paint with such maturity at such a tender age, it explained why he had felt a need to find a radical way of moving forward, pushing back boundaries, portraying what that newly invented art form, photography, couldn't.

'I've always wanted a Picasso,' I said to Heidi, laughing. How pretentious that sounded! But then it struck me: both 'our' paintings were on the same floor in adjoining rooms. If we'd been thieves – which we weren't, we were just playing a game – that would have been very handy.

'Why don't we...' I said mischievously, '...go and see what security is like on the second floor? Just out of interest, of course.'

'How would we do that?' Heidi asked.

'I don't know yet. Wait and see.'

It seemed strange, having come from a society obsessed with security, alarms, video cameras and X-ray machines, that the post-Communist regime should be so lax, but in the very first room we got to, security was a mere one-woman operation. She was sitting upright on a rigid wooden chair, her expression dour, her feet placed neatly together, her hands folded in her lap. A Soviet grey skirt, thick grey stockings and flat, black-laced shoes completed the look, while her hair was pulled tightly back from her stern face.

This was a room in which a re-hang was in progress, and in one corner I noticed an empty frame still hung on the wall. Curious, I drew close to try to figure out their hanging system. Were the frames on ordinary picture hooks? I could see no wires or security devices.

What would happen if I touched it? Surreptitiously, I stretched out my hand while I thought the attendant wasn't looking.

All hell broke loose.

The *babushka* leapt to her feet, screaming and yelling. Four attendants from the adjoining rooms immediately came running, as did Heidi who was in the room next door – which housed 'her' Matisse and 'my' Picasso. She stood watching the scene from the connecting doorway as I looked plaintively in her direction.

'It's an empty frame. I just wanted to see how it was hung. Tell them I'm English,' I begged, 'I have a gallery and I'm just interested in how they hang the paintings here.'

Heidi rapidly explained and calm was restored, although the four attendants stood in a little huddle for a while, discussing the incident and eyeing me suspiciously, watching my every move. I caught up with Heidi two rooms away among the modern Russian paintings.

'Wow! You caused a stir,' Heidi observed. 'Were there any devices behind that empty frame? Any sensors?'

'No, it was just hanging on an ordinary picture hook.'

'Well, it would be easy then,' she said. 'My Matisse and your Picasso.'

'Hardly: you saw what happened. I was immediately surrounded. There was no way I could have even got an empty picture frame out of that room. Look, they're still lurking over there, watching me.' There were all four of them, hanging about in the doorway.

'But I could have taken anything I wanted out of the other rooms,' Heidi smiled triumphantly. 'You were the decoy, weren't you? Everyone was looking at you and the other rooms were deserted. All the guards left their posts. I could have been in the lift going down to the basement, over the barrier and out of the group exit in two minutes.'

'Hmm,' I mused. 'I wonder if they ever do a stocktake..?'

***

Nine years later, in August 2006, a headline in the *Guardian* caught my eye: 'STAFF SUSPECTED OVER MISSING HERMITAGE TREASURES'.

The article went on to report that an audit of the Hermitage Palace in St Petersburg had just been completed, with alarming results. Silver, enamelware, icons and jewellery worth nearly

£2.7 million had disappeared. It was thought to be an inside job.

It wasn't my friend and I, milord. Honestly. We just thought about it. It was just a fantasy.

In a statement, the Hermitage's Director, Mikhail Pietrovsky, said: 'There is no doubt this could not have happened without the participation of the museum staff.' He went on to say that the items hadn't been insured because they were in storage: only exhibited artworks at the Hermitage are insured. Moreover, 90% of the three million items in its collection are in storage at any one time, kept in a giant labyrinth under the museum. This must have been the cellar Heidi and I had found, I realised.

There was more dramatic news: the curator in charge of the collection had suddenly died at her workplace when the inventory check began in October; her husband, meanwhile, was implicated in the disappearance of certain items. The head of the Federal Cultural Heritage Agency was quoted as saying that the theft was part of a larger trend of poor security and unscrupulous workers. Cataloguing was chaotic, he lamented, and he criticised the directors for not using modern technology to monitor the inventory. 'What happened at the Hermitage for us was not unexpected,' he concluded.

It wasn't unexpected as far as I was concerned, either.

Six months later, the case of the curator's husband, Nikolai Zavadskaya, came to court:

'January 24th 2007

HERMITAGE EMPLOYEE WALKED OFF WITH TSARIST TREASURES.

Husband sold off 77 items including gold salt cellar

Case highlights low wages and poor museum security.'

The *Guardian*'s Luke Harding covered the trial, and it was a desperately sad story. Nikolai Zavadskaya's wife was described by her many friends and colleagues as the perfect worker. She was polite and hardworking and had even volunteered to work at weekends (that ought to have aroused suspicion for a start!). She was a specialist in enamels and had simply walked out of the staff exit with the treasures she had selected, unchallenged by security guards. But she was also diabetic and, her husband explained, he had sold the pieces to antique dealers and pawnshops simply in order to buy insulin for his wife.

The court was told that the stolen items were worth seven and a half million roubles, but Mr Z strongly disputed this valuation. 'It isn't possible to sell these things in our country at these prices,' he said. Nevertheless, he was found guilty and sentenced to five years in prison, and ordered to pay the Hermitage damages of $283,000.

But if the case was a tragic one, it did at least focus attention on the low wages paid to Russian museum staff, and on the shambolic security arrangements used to protect one of the world's greatest collections. The audit had revealed that the artefacts stolen by the Zavadskayas were among more than two hundred silver and enamel pieces missing from the Hermitage and, after the trial, President Vladimir Putin ordered the country's museums to review their collections urgently.

**

Twelve years after that first visit, I landed once again at Domodedovo Airport - this time with my son Peter, his wife Janet, and their daughter Sylvie. Peter and Janet had studied Russian Economic and Political History at Manchester University, and were excited to be witnessing the emergence of a new state. Socialism had been replaced with capitalism: this was now a society based on wealth, shopping and celebrity.

After almost a week with Heidi in Moscow, we set off again, on the midnight train to St Petersburgh, a trip that filled me with déjà vu. We were going back to the Hermitage and Sylvie, who had heard about the Magic Lift in the Hermitage many times as a bedtime story, was literally shaking with excitement as we approached the magnificent building. It looked the part. She was expecting a Harry Potter experience, with the lift a Hogwarts Express to untold adventures. But the reality of the Hermitage in 2009 was disappointing; we found a tourist attraction with a two-hour queue and a computerised ticketing system. The modern toilets were conventionally western and spotlessly clean. Worst of all, our magic lift had been replaced with a fast, efficient, disabled–friendly steel elevator. There was no '0' basement button.

In the second floor galleries, the Picassos and Matisses were still on show, but although there were fewer guards, each room was now fitted with movement sensors and alarms. However, these were not the most striking additions.

The museum was closing for the evening and we were navigating our way to the exit when we passed through an ante-room where I noticed two large Renoir paintings which I'd never seen before. They were life-size portraits of a man and a woman and definitely hadn't been there on my last visit. Heidi – who had accompanied us - translated the explanation.

'These paintings and 23 other Renoirs which hang in the adjoining room were 'discovered' in a store room during an audit. No one knew of their existence before that. It is thought that they might have come from Germany during the Second World War.'

She and I looked at each other. They must have been in the basement – perhaps in the packing cases I had been itching to open. I had known there was something really important down there. I wonder what else they found.

I wonder where 'my' Fabergé egg is.

The Relief

It looks like a Nicholson.
It smells like a Nicholson.
It feels like a Nicholson.

I am staring hard at the grubby piece of card in my hand as though I've never seen it before. But I have seen it. I've had it for the last eighteen years but I've never looked at it properly. I've considered and accepted it within its context and assumed it's a Percy Kelly. Now I'm not so sure. This rather insignificant looking construction in dirty white card could have been made by one of Britain's best-known early pioneers of abstract art; the man who gathered together some of the towering figures of the first half of the twentieth century; the man who helped to found the St Ives group of artists, attracting them to him like bright, exotic butterflies to buddleia in the clear, translucent light of the northern coast of Cornwall.

Could this be an original Nicholson Relief?

'Hey!' I shouted as I stumbled my way across the damp garden from my studio. 'Guess what! I think I've found a Ben Nicholson!'

At this point I was so excited I dropped it. It landed butter-side-down on the wet grass and as I picked it up a small piece became detached – er, well it sort of fell off.

Michael, my partner (who confusingly bears the same Christian name as my late husband, and is thus sometimes referred to as 'Michael 2' - I did try to persuade him to change his name to Fred or Albert but sadly he declined), looked largely unimpressed as I put my find down on the kitchen table as reverently as a waiter presenting the main course in a Michelin-starred restaurant. I then carefully and ceremoniously placed the detached piece back on top.

'Why is that bit separate?' he asked. He notices everything. Why does he always ask difficult questions?

'Because I just dropped it! It'll easily stick together again. It's a relief.'

He sighed. 'Why? Why are you relieved to have dropped it?'

He's a patient and practical person most of the time – he has to be – but he just wasn't getting it, was he?

'Look: it's a relief! The piece of work. That's what it's called. It's made of layers of thick card built up into a relief.'

'Ah, yes I can see that now. But where has it appeared from and what makes you think it's a Nicholson? Calm down while I put the kettle on.'

This man is so sensible he makes me furious sometimes.

'So, where's it come from?' he asked as we sipped our tea, the relief between us on the table. 'These things don't just materialise in that studio of yours - or do they? You didn't make it yourself just to confuse me, did you? Is it a test – or a joke?'

'It came off the back of a lorry,' I said mischievously.

He didn't look convinced.

'Come on – be serious!'

'I am serious. Truly it did.'

I paused for effect. The drama queen inside me was fighting to get out.

'You know when Percy Kelly died and his effects came up to the gallery from his cottage in Norfolk? Well, there was a chaotic pile of stuff in the back of the van. You've no idea! It was stuffed to capacity. There were stacks of wooden bread trays overflowing with paintings, drawings and prints, but there were also documents, postcards and letters spanning the whole of Percy's life. There were telegrams from Cunard, Lord Eccles and Anthony Armstrong-Jones; documents from his schooldays, army days and college days; empty tea packets, paint tins, old brushes, marmalade recipes, plastic plates, shopping lists, tobacco tins, and budgie feathers. He'd hung on to everything.

'All these things were mixed together in the back of the

124

big transit van that delivered Kelly's estate to Castlegate House. The driver thought I'd go crazy at the mess he'd brought, and I too had my doubts until I reached into the back of the van and flicked through a few of the contents. There were paintings and drawings of a quality I'd dreamed of for many years. They were pure Kelly at his best. Just to see them, to touch them, reduced me to tears - which disconcerted the driver even more. He put an arm round my shoulders. "Don't cry, love. I knew you'd be upset at all this rubbish," he said. Then he helped me carry the rubbish up to the studio, looking puzzled.'

'Hold on,' Michael interrupted. 'Let's get back to the present. You've told me about all that before, but Percy died eighteen years ago. Are you trying to tell me there was an original Nicholson among his things? You've had it for eighteen years and you've only just noticed? You must be slipping!'

'Hey, you weren't around then – it was years before we met,' I replied defensively. 'There was so much all at once, I was overwhelmed.'

After I'd sorted it out into some sort of order - which took a while - I invited Brian, Percy's estranged son and heir, to come and see it and discuss options. I took him up to the studio on the top floor of Castlegate House and I showed him all the paintings, drawings and prints which I had carefully photographed, made into two sets of slides and catalogued. By the time we eventually got to the pile of personal stuff, he was bored.

I was disappointed and exasperated. This 46-year-old man's attention span was extremely short, especially as this was about his own dad. I showed him a sheaf of papers on which his father had made many abortive attempts to write about his life in the futile hope of getting on the Civil List. I dug further down the heap and showed him his father's school reports, college reports, his dissertation for his final exam, and his degree certificate. There were letters from people who had bought his work in the early days – including several from Melvyn Bragg – but it was all greeted with indifference. His son was totally apathetic.

'This is about your father's life, Brian,' I said, in the hope of drumming up some enthusiasm. 'Perhaps you'd like to take the box home and look through it? You never know, there might be something you want to keep.'

'That projector might come in handy,' he said.

'OK – but what do you want to do with the rest?'

'Oh, just chuck it out,' came the answer.

'May I have it for my archive?' I asked.

He nodded.

Brian left that day with a selection of photographs, the boxes of numbered slides and the projector. I couldn't even persuade him to choose a painting for his house – his sensible wife Doreen later chose a couple which I was glad to get framed for them.

'So,' I concluded as Michael poured us another cup of tea, 'I put all that stuff in a big plastic storage container – my Kelly archive box - for future reference. Which is now.'

'So what you're saying is that Percy had a Ben Nicholson original?' he replied. 'Come on, love - I think you're getting carried away. Where would he have got that, then? He didn't move in those kind of circles - did he? Did he ever meet Ben Nicholson?'

'Probably not,' I had to admit.

'So how did he get this?' he asked, turning the relief over. 'I think it's very unlikely to be a Nicholson. It isn't signed; it's also foxed and it's falling apart. You know as well as I do that provenance is everything and condition comes a close second. I think it's failed on both counts, don't you?'

Michael and I had been together for over ten years and we almost knew what the other was thinking. He had saved me from all sorts of disastrous situations where I'd been about to do something daft and impulsive without engaging brain first.

'Yes, of course I know all that,' I replied firmly. 'But I can explain. There is a link. The link is a woman called Helen Sutherland.'

Percy Kelly's acquaintance with Helen Sutherland, a P&O heiress, is well recorded. After meeting the acclaimed Cumbrian poet Norman Nicholson (no relation to Ben) at an exhibition of etchings in Maryport in 1958, Percy was fired up with enthusiasm by what he had seen. He wanted to learn how to make prints. Norman Nicholson gave Percy a letter of introduction to his friend Helen Sutherland, knowing that she would be interested. He was right. She invited Percy for lunch at her house at Cockley Moor near Ullswater, about 30 miles from where Percy lived.

He had never met anyone like her before. She was old, she was rich, she was elegant, she was passionate about the Arts and she was a collector. She had moved to Cumbria in 1939, 'downsizing' from Rock Hall, a large stately home near Alnwick in Northumberland where she had been a keen supporter of The Pitmen Painters of Ashington. She continued to support artists - particularly working class artists - from this remote farmhouse at Dockray. As Norman Nicholson had suspected, his friend Percy proved to be an ideal candidate for her attention.

When Percy told Miss Sutherland of his ambition to go to art college to learn printmaking, she helped and encouraged him to apply. It is highly probable - but not proven - that she contributed to his college fees when his application for a grant was turned down. She certainly followed Percy's progress with close interest through his four years at Carlisle College of Art. He visited her regularly and talked to her about the courses he was doing. Printmaking became his passion - particularly etching. He was at the college because he wanted to master the technical skills printmaking demanded.

'Bear with me,' I said, seeing Michael's raised eyebrow. I rushed back out to the studio, leaving him frowning and looking sceptically at the bit of dismembered card. I returned with a large loose-leaf, ringbound essay.

'I found the relief in here,' I explained. 'It was among Percy's things that came up from Norfolk on the van. It's his college dissertation.'

'Journey into Textile Design' was the title written in an elegant, simple, modern typeface on the grey hessian cover. It was somewhat battered by its 50 years' existence but still impressive. It bore the college exam label dated 1965 on the inside front cover. It was a beautiful piece of work: another demonstration of Percy's ability to get things aesthetically perfect.

The typewritten dissertation began with a description of Percy's first meeting with Helen Sutherland at Cockley Moor and it was here, Kelly wrote, that he first saw fabrics by Edinburgh Weavers.

'Listen to this,' I said to Michael and began to read aloud.

'After viewing and discussing the paintings, Miss Sutherland showed me some samples of prints and woven fabrics that she had just received from Edinburgh Weavers. It was a discovery and a very stimulating one. I felt how compatible they were with the refinement of Nicholson's paintings and especially the white plaster reliefs with their purity of form and design.'

Ha! That had caught Michael's attention.

Percy had been along to the design studio of Edinburgh Weavers, who were not based in Edinburgh as their name suggests, but in Nelson Street, Carlisle. In his dissertation, Percy had explored the origin of some of the fabrics which were based on the work of some distinguished artists. As Michael and I turned the pages of Percy's dissertation, there was sometimes a fabric sample and sometimes a little watercolour 'sketch' based on the work of some leading twentieth century contemporary artists: William Scott, Alan Reynolds, Humphrey Spender – and (oh joy!) Ben Nicholson. The Nicholson sample, which was titled *Relief Tapestry*, was a natural, textured fabric based on geometric shapes which were woven into the cloth, forming a relief. I turned to the next page, which was blank.

'Look,' I said, 'this is the page where Percy stuck the relief in. That's the sort of thing the designers based the fabric on.'

Underneath the old, dried-out glue, the typed label read: 'Ben Nicholson 1935 Relief'.

I picked the relief up from the table and looked at it again. It was almost 80 years old. Yes, it was now off-white and slightly foxed, but the date was right and the place was right. Helen Sutherland was an avid art collector and it is well known that she held the largest private collection of Nicholson's work at the time. She was also known to be generous, often giving away sketches and paintings. When Kelly wrote his dissertation she was in her 80s and planning to move away from Cumbria: Cockley Moor was too large and too remote for an elderly woman living alone. The winters were harsh. She was planning to spend some time in the kinder climate of Rome and would have been sorting through her many possessions. Had she given the relief to Percy as a gift? It was probable that Percy's choice of the Edinburgh Weavers as the subject of his dissertation had been suggested to him by her. Printed Textiles was his least favourite subject, but it was compulsory for all students at the college: Carlisle was a textile city and there was plenty of employment in the design studios for graduates. Percy didn't want a job and he hated all things commercial, but on his visits to Helen Sutherland he would have seen much of the Edinburgh Weavers' fabrics which she used liberally throughout her home. She admired and knew Alastair Morton, the company's founder and a Scottish genius of design, personally and Alastair was also a great friend of Ben Nicholson; in fact, he subsequently employed Nicholson's eldest son Jake as a designer.

All the links were in place. The evidence stacked up nicely. Ben Nicholson is one of the most important British artists of his time and I was so excited I was ready to catch the next London train to get the relief authenticated.

But hold on – Michael was right. I was getting carried away. I had to consider the counter argument. Ben Nicholson's reliefs were in plaster or wood: I'd never seen any in mount board. Maybe this was a Kelly imitation. But Kelly would have made his different in some way. He would certainly not have typed 'Ben Nicholson 1935 Relief' below it.

In 1935 Percy was a seventeen-year-old telegraph delivery boy in Kendal. He had joined Kendal Art Society but he had never seen a piece of abstract art and would not have been interested if he had: he was developing a pale watercolour technique. If he had made the relief 30 years later to illustrate his essay, he would have claimed it as his own work and dated it 1965. With his hubristic self-belief he would have been proud to put his own name to it.

I placed the relief down on the table and sighed. What a pity the top layer had come adrift. The glue underneath was dark yellowy-brown; dry and crackly with age. It could be important in dating the relief, but the detached section should really be stuck back in place to protect it if it was to have any credibility. But how could I do that and remain true to the original?

After some thought, I got some natural water from the stream that runs past my studio window, dampened the old glue carefully, and placed the whole thing in my book press. I was sure that a forensic examination of that original glue would show up as 1935 vintage. A few days later, I took it out of the press and propped it up on my desk to look at it while I typed. It was now happily restored to its original state.

I loved the relief, regardless of who had made it. I didn't care about its monetary value because I hadn't even considered selling it - but I did care about its provenance. I wanted to know for sure whether it was a Nicholson or a Kelly. As a collector of work by the St Ives School, I wanted to mount it on a white backboard in a simple white St Ives box frame, add it to my St Ives collection and enjoy it. But did I own it? Was it mine to keep? Brian was long since dead. He had given me the archive, but neither he nor I knew there was a potentially valuable piece of work among it at the time. But was it valuable? If it was a Kelly imitation of no value then it was definitely mine. If not, I assumed it belonged to the estate. It was now up to me to establish its provenance - for richer or poorer.

The rain was still sheeting down as I spotted Michael picking his way across the garden to the studio with a mug of steaming coffee to spur me on. Dashing out onto the sodden decking to take it from him quickly, I turned and stepped back inside only to skid on the polished, wooden-planked floor. The coffee flew up in the air in a great arc, splattering down onto my desk, papers, computer and... the relief. *Oh dear - forensics will have a great time if it ever comes to that*, I thought as I quickly mopped the coffee off it with a tissue and ruefully put it back into its portfolio for safety. It was certainly accident-prone - was it trying to tell me something? Percy might be pleased I'd mistaken his work for a Nicholson but he would be angry at my carelessness. And if Sotheby's did analyse the age of the glue, I would have to confess: Kenco Decaf c. 2011 would also show up in any analysis. But this is how history builds and misleads - each century, each decade adding its own imprint, another layer.

The morning after the coffee fiasco, I looked at the relief again in daylight. About ten inches square, it bore all the characteristics of a Nicholson: perfect circles cut out of rectangles mounted off-centre but in perfect balance. However, it was made from heavy whiteboard rather than plaster. It could be an experimental piece on which to base a plaster relief. It could even be the little macquette Ben had made for the designer at Edinburgh Weavers. Had he ever worked with card? I mused. Plausible - but I suspected, if I was brutally honest with myself, that I was probably looking at the work of a very clever Kelly, who had 'made' a Nicholson to illustrate his essay. It had been good to dream.

I returned the relief to the dark obscurity of the archive box - I was reluctant to put it in a frame for the time being. It was 'on hold', waiting for something to happen.

And something did.

Robert Adam and Carol Robertson - printmakers extraordinaire - of Graal Press in Edinburgh arrived at the gallery. They had been drawn by the magnetic force of Kelly's newly discovered etching plates. Robert had been excited when I told him I had found them in wooden boxes on the outhouse floor after Carlisle College of Art had taken Kelly's printing press away. He had immediately jumped in the car and sped down from Edinburgh, taken the plates away, cleaned them up, removed the rust and taken a pull from each one.

We were now meeting to discuss what to do about them. Robert confessed to being quite emotional about handling Kelly's plates - using them, trying to intuit Kelly's methods, the colour and amount of ink used. The emphasis he gave to each one had made him feel close to the artist. He was impressed at the different techniques Kelly had used making them. He was puzzled at how little they had been utilised, but pleased they were not clogged up with ink. We spent hours looking and planning and admiring the skill of this extraordinary artist. No wonder the college print lecturer had written 'Kelly has changed the face of printmaking at the college' in his final assessment.

Over lunch, we began to talk about Percy's college days, when most of the plates and etchings had been made.

'Hey, you should have been here a few months ago,' I said casually. 'Do you know what - I thought I'd found a Ben Nicholson relief among his college stuff.'

Carol and Robert sat up sharply. They demanded more information. I told them the story so far and they were riveted.

'Oh, I want to see this dissertation,' Carol said. 'Come on, Chris: where is it?'

I got it out, protesting and laughing about my misguided

excitement, my carelessness with the coffee, my foolishness in thinking it was a genuine Nicholson.

Carol turned the pages over carefully and stopped at the relief page. She looked at me wide-eyed.

'That is a Nicholson,' she stated firmly. 'I'm sure of it.'

'Why do you say that so confidently? Why are you so sure?' I challenged. 'He worked in plaster and wood. I've never seen any in mount board.'

'But I have!' She looked to Robert for confirmation. 'You have too, Robert. You know – when Willie showed us hers!'

I couldn't help giggling, but Carol gave me a stern look and explained. She had worked very closely with Wilhelmina Barns-Graham for several years on her *Millennium and Time* series of screen prints. Willie, as she was affectionately known to friends, had been a close friend of Ben Nicholson, Barbara Hepworth and the original St Ives group during and after the Second World War. She had her own studio in St Ives (as well as her native St Andrews) and had been awarded a CBE for services to the arts before her death, aged 92, in 2004. Carol and Willie had become very close when collaborating over the screenprints, and Carol had visited her Scottish studio many times. She had also seen her collection of small Nicholson reliefs – gifts from Ben himself. They had been mounted on the wall of her studio and were just like the one now lying on the table between us: experimental, unsigned pieces of a similar size and format to 'mine', to be used as a basis for larger works. I was stunned. Here was another piece of positive evidence to fit into the jigsaw.

There was more. As Robert and I continued to talk it over, Carol got up and walked over to a piece of Percy's calligraphy which was hanging in the kitchen. I had bought it at the first exhibition after his death in 1994. On a background of potassium-stained paper he had written in brown inks:

'Silent, dark and restless umber.
Green moving sedge
Stained ochre brown.'

It was a beautiful piece. Percy had written to a college friend about how he had seen the work of painter and modernist poet David Jones for the first time at Cockley Moor. He recounted in that letter that he had returned to his studio after that visit and made his own 'David Jones'. And this was it – now hanging on my kitchen wall.

'This could easily be mistaken for a David Jones, you know,' Carol said, pointing. 'But Kelly didn't try to pass it off as such, did he? Look, he signed it with a monogrammed 'PK' bottom right.'

She was right. I hadn't thought of that before.

'Look!' said Carol, pointing to the pulls from the etching plates which were strewn on the table. 'Look at Percy's work. He would never have just copied that relief. He would have done his own individual take on it. He would have played with the image. Then he would have signed it: he was a show-off. That isn't a Kelly - it's a Nicholson. I'm sure of it. I can feel it.'

It was what I'd felt, too.

Just like that, in the blink of a lunchtime, I was off on the detective trail again.

I drove to the village of Dockray the next day. I'd never been there before. It is well tucked away.

Turning right at the pub into the steep, narrow lane which stops abruptly when it reaches the moor and the dense wood just beyond, I found Helen Sutherland's house, Cockley Moor, set back from the road. It looked like any other traditional Cumbrian stone-built farmhouse, but the barn close to the road was familiar. Percy had made a beautiful abstract lithograph of it in the print room at Carlisle College, heavily criss-crossed with black tree shapes. His strong black lines and the abstract quality of design translated well into the medium. He had made it specifically to fit a page in the dissertation and titled it underneath – 'Helen Sutherland's Barn'.

Builders working on the roof of the barn told me that the owners of the house were away. When I briefly explained my connection, they were quite happy for me to snoop. As I walked through the gate, I stepped into the past. I imagined I was Kelly approaching the house on that first visit. I saw it through his eyes. In his dissertation, he had described how the front door had been opened by a uniformed maid who led him to Miss Sutherland – and Paradise. 'I stepped out of a grey January day into a different world,' he wrote. 'It was wonderland to me.'

The house that he found himself in was like no other house he had ever been in. It was light and bright, full of books and paintings, as well as Scandinavian furniture and furnishings. Miss Sutherland's magnificent collection of British and European art was hung or strewn casually everywhere. For Percy, who had grown up in a tiny, overcrowded terrace house with only religious tracts on the wall, it was astonishing. Many of the paintings were stacked against the walls or propped above the bookshelves.

After lunch, Miss Sutherland had showed him her treasures, producing two Picassos from a cupboard like a magician bringing doves out of a hat. They were hidden from view because she didn't like them very much - but she did recognise their future importance to twentieth century art. For Percy it was a revelation; an adventure in the history of modern art. She encouraged him to visit her again and use her library whenever he wanted. As an educator, she must have been thrilled to have found a naturally talented, intelligent pupil in Percy.

Thereafter, he made frequent visits to Cockley Moor; visits which he recorded in his letters and diaries. He and Miss Sutherland discussed her collection at length; pieces by Mondrian, Seurat, Boudin and Picasso were inspected, analysed and debated. Helen showed Percy pieces by Winifred and Ben Nicholson, Barbara Hepworth and David Jones, as well as poems by Kathleen Raine, all of whom were regular visitors to Cockley Moor, just as they had been to Rock Hall in the Thirties – which of course was when the Nicholson relief was made. Had Ben given it to Helen at some point as a kind of 'thank you for a nice weekend' card?

However, I had found no proof that Percy was ever invited to any of these house parties, and likewise no evidence of a meeting with Ben Nicholson. I feel sure if he had met him he would have recorded it in his diaries or in his letters. Evidence suggests that Helen Sutherland preferred a one-to-one friendship with Kelly: theirs was an educational relationship, not social.

I was thinking about this as I walked round to the other side of the locked, deserted house where Helen Sutherland had installed large floor-to-ceiling windows to maximise the view. I peered inside and imagined the weekend house parties, the chatter and exchange of ideas; the white grand piano, the white gramophone and the modern Swedish furniture. Looking at the large, split-level living room with its polished pale wood planked floor, I imagined the evacuees from the west end of Newcastle that she housed during the Second World War sitting round her on that floor while she taught them. An old man in the local pub in the village had earlier told me about the boys running riot through the village and fields.

I wondered whether the 'bidet thing' he said she had installed in her bathroom was still there. I could imagine her – an austere, single, independent woman dressed in beautiful pastel silk chiffon blouses in lilac, pale cream, blue and grey. They were always the same style, with covered buttons and tiny, pin-tuck pleats, and were tailor-made for her in London and sent up to Cumbria. No wonder Kelly was overwhelmed.

That garden was full of ghosts. I sat down on a bench on the back lawn enjoying the breathtaking views towards Ullswater and imagined it as it had been, with a foreground of a Barbara Hepworth bronze. I could see the sculptor's slight frame and high forehead as she directed the workmen on the positioning of her piece. I could see Ben Nicholson striking a pose, holding forth about abstraction. I could see his first wife, Winifred, with her children gathered around her or scampering around the garden. I could see Helen's friend Kathleen Raine writing another piece of verse quietly in a corner, and Welshman David Jones, head down, pacing the lawn fighting his recurring bouts of depression. Kelly, a carpenter's son, a twin in a family of eight who lived in that tiny two-bedroomed terrace house, must have sat here too, I thought. No wonder he was overwhelmed, excited and inspired.

***

The canopied entrance to Sotheby's is guarded by a modern Cerberus in fancy dress - an elaborately uniformed doorman who evaluates all who approach and springs to open the door for those he judges worthy. He opened the door for me and I was glad to slip inside, escaping from bustling Bond Street. I was clutching the portfolio containing Percy's dissertation: I bet neither Kelly nor his tutors at Carlisle College of Art ever thought it would enter the hallowed portals of such a prestigious place.

I was early for my appointment. Perched on a banquette in the reception hall while I waited, I watched a parade of well dressed, long-legged, designer-handbag-toting women stride through; intriguing men with foreign accents, distinguished-looking men with loud, stertorous voices of command, men in suits, men in red sailcloth trousers, young Cressidas and Fionas answering telephones in cut-glass tones, and scurrying staff. Meanwhile, a live sale was relayed onto large screens from one of the palatial auction rooms - all gilt chairs, numbered paddles, murmuring opulence.

The 20th Century Art department were intrigued, even impressed, with the dissertation. As I told my story again and stated my case, producing back catalogues of Kelly's exhibitions, I had an attentive audience. They loved Kelly's work and decided to keep the relief for a closer look by a Nicholson expert.

A few weeks of scrutiny later, the answer came back: it

couldn't definitely be confirmed as a Ben Nicholson but conversely it couldn't be totally ruled out. Auction houses are always circumspect in cases like this - they daren't risk a false description - but I think everyone was disappointed, most of all me! Back into the archive box it went once again…

***

A few months after my visit to Sotheby's, on a sunny autumn day, I made a visit to the Gallery of Modern Art in Edinburgh – always a pleasure.

The approach is dramatic: the front lawn is sculpted into a stepped mound – a modern version of a Stone Age earthworks – which is reflected in three crescent-shaped pools of water.

The massive sculptures by Tony Cragg sat well in this landscape. I spent a long time in his exhibition, which spread inside and out, intrigued and delighted by it. Then I slipped away to the permanent collection upstairs to see if Diana van de Lugt's bequest, the Winifred Nicholson *Moonshine*, was on display (it wasn't). Any thoughts of 'my Ben Nicholson' relief were absent. I had given up. It was filed and forgotten.

It was very peaceful on the top floor. I had the place to myself - all the action was downstairs with the Tony Cragg show. I wandered quietly from room to room. The St Ives Group was well represented, and there were letters from Naum Gabo to Ben Nicholson in a display case which particularly captured my attention. Then I turned a corner into the next room and stopped abruptly. There in front of me was a white relief in mount board very much like mine: same board, same shapes, same size, just configured slightly differently.

The legend to the left of it read: 'Ben Nicholson, White relief 1935 Oil on carved board'. It was in the same font – and had possibly come from the same typewriter - as the label in Kelly's dissertation.

Underneath the relief was this exposition:

'Ben Nicholson made his first carved relief during a trip to

Paris in 1933. While working on a painting, part of the thick white ground chipped off leaving two distinct layers. He exploited this accident in a series of white and coloured reliefs from the mid nineteen thirties and continued to produce such works for the rest of his career. Made by sticking layers of board on to one another and also by carving into the surface. These relate to the purity of Piet Mondrian's work. Ben Nicholson visited his Paris studio in 1934.

They also relate to contemporary international style buildings by architects such as Corbusier and Ben's brother Kit.

Also his friendship with Barbara Hepworth and Henry Moore may have prompted this move into three dimensional art.'

I was so excited I wanted to shout out but I didn't dare. Instead, I got out my mobile and took a picture before the nice young steward appeared, having heard the click, to warn me against taking photographs. I apologised as I stowed my phone away safely in my bag.

'I've just found one of these at home! That's why I'm so excited about it!' I cried.

'Found one of what?' He followed my eyes and frowned. 'Oh you mean you found a Nicholson, do you?' His voice was flat and sceptical. A Ben Nicholson isn't something you just come across while tidying your knicker drawer or broom cupboard. On the other hand, public art galleries do attract eccentrics and the slightly unbalanced. He must have met a few.

I explained more fully.

The steward was a bright young man and soon perked up. 'Have you a phone number?' he asked. 'Our curator might be interested in that.'

I handed him a card.

Alice Strang rang me the following day. She was definitely interested. She knew all about Helen Sutherland, of course:

they too had benefited from her will, gaining some interesting additions to their collections. She wanted to see the relief. She wanted to see the whole dissertation. The gallery also had a collection of fabrics by Edinburgh Weavers in their archive, and there were many intriguing connections - too many to ignore.

When I returned to the gallery to meet her, she greeted me warmly and first took me to the storeroom to see Diana's *Moonshine*, still sparkling as ever. She remembered how Diana had sponsored the *Winifred Nicholson in Scotland* exhibition over the road in the Dean Gallery.

Back in her office, she looked intently at my relief.

'So you catalogued the whole of Kelly's estate?'

I nodded.

'So you must be familiar with his work. Were there any other three-dimensional works among his effects; any similar reliefs?'

'The work left in his cottage when he died spanned more than 50 years and there was nothing like this,' I explained. 'Everything was on paper or board - often cheap scraps, lining paper or cereal boxes - all flat, two-dimensional pieces; no models, no reliefs. He made a model boat in wood once.'

Alice considered the case carefully but, like Sotheby's, was reluctant to commit. Her main argument against my find being a Nicholson was the same as theirs: it all came down to the cutting of the circle. It is very difficult to cut perfect geometric shapes out of thick board. The shapes before me looked perfect to my eyes, but apparently Nicholson was such a perfectionist that after cutting a circle he would always sand it down to make the edges super smooth. Under microscopic scrutiny, the edges of mine did not come up to the meticulous standard that Ben would work to. However, in Alice I'd at least made a new friend.

The following January, I went to an exhibition of Ben Nicholson and Mondrian at the Courtauld in London. Ben had gained a lot from the time he had spent in Mondrian's studio in Paris in the Thirties. Mondrian worked in a totally white studio and used just three primary colours consistently in his simple abstract works. He hated green. He was a purist and a minimalist – in tune with the things Nicholson was embracing at the time. Nicholson then reciprocated and found Mondrian a live-in studio in Hampstead near to the flat he shared with Barbara Hepworth. They were close.

I spent a long time in that exhibition looking at pieces created at the same time as my relief in 1935. Percy would have been seventeen then. He could not have made a Nicholson-type relief, I felt sure: he would have had no idea who Nicholson was. It wasn't until the late 50s that he moved from his conventional, tight watercolours of the Lakes landscape into strong charcoal drawings of industrial West Cumbria. But although it was a huge leap forward towards abstraction, they were still nothing like Nicholson's work. And then there was that label again: if Percy had made a copy of a relief he had seen at Cockley Moor in 1962, why had he dated it as being from 1935? I came away from that exhibition absolutely convinced I had a Nicholson... again.

But does it matter? My 'Nicholson' has now been restored: the foxing treated, it is beautifully mounted in a white frame with plenty of space to breathe. I doubt if I will ever be able to prove its authenticity as a Ben Nicholson and I'm not at all sure I want it to undergo the indignity of a DNA 'paternity' test. But why is that important? It is a beautiful piece of work. Surely art should be valued and appreciated for what it is - not for the signature on it.

Nevertheless, this relief will always be a Nicholson to me.

The Man Who Dreamt Horses

Why had I agreed to have breakfast with a man I'd never met before? I supposed I was here in this run-down café at the seedy end of Earl's Court because he had something I wanted - well, I hoped he had. I wasn't sure. I knew very little about him except his name, which was John. That was all: I had no idea what he looked like or how old he was. It wasn't a situation I was comfortable with.

When John had telephoned me unexpectedly a few days before, I had agreed to meet him to get him off the phone. It was late, I was in bed at the time, and my husband was semaphoring circular 'wind it up' signs at my side, but I'd kept going with the call because this man had told me he'd got some photographs I was eager to get hold of. It was tantalising, but it was also rather tenuous. He was possibly a press photographer, but everything was vague.

I sat idly watching the runnels of condensation creep down the window in a pinstripe pattern as I waited. The smell of dank, wet clothes melded with the welcome aroma of coffee. It was winter and early-morning-cold outside, but at least it was warm inside the café. Business was brisk. The intermittent scream, hiss and grind of the Gaggia coffee machine was deafening as two women in matching brown overalls skilfully manoeuvred their way round each other in a noisy rhythmic dance, banging out the spent grounds, grinding more beans, frothing up the milk. Smart-suited men and women rushed in and grabbed a coffee on the move, workmen in high-vis yellow jackets were demolishing bacon butties at an adjoining table, and a bag lady was huddled in a corner muttering to herself, her worldly possessions straining to escape from numerous bulging carrier bags.

I felt conspicuous. I didn't belong in this place. I was an incomer from the north who had landed in the capital on the Glasgow sleeper in the early hours. I looked around again. John was late. Maybe he wouldn't show up. I scanned every new entrant hopefully. How long should I give him? Perhaps I should drink up the coffee I was nursing and go on to my next appointment.

The door swung open yet again and a gust of chill air blew in as another customer entered. No, this wasn't my appointment either. It was a tall, thin, dishevelled man with white longish hair and a straggly beard. He was wearing denim jeans and a disgusting jumper that was unravelling at the elbows and quite holey everywhere else. *Moths,* I thought absently and looked away, fully expecting him to join the rummaging bag lady. But when I looked up again I was surprised to find him towering above me.

'Chris?' he said, stooping and holding out his hand. I recognised the soft, cultured voice from our one and only late night telephone conversation. This was my breakfast 'date'.

'You must be John.'

He sat down and, without saying anything, smoothed out the folded newspaper he was carrying. From between its pages, he extracted several very good black and white photographs of an astonishingly beautiful woman. Her eyes were heavy with kohl, Sixties style, and her skin was pale. She had high cheekbones, an elegant nose, and a dazzling smile for the photographer. She looked natural, sensitive, perfect.

'Didn't want to get them wet,' he began, gesturing at the newspaper. 'Are these what you want? I took them years ago for *Tatler*. She's as beautiful as ever. These are copies. You can have them if you like.'

Yes, I certainly did like. Photographs of the artist Sheila Fell were hard to come by. Her death in 1979, at the age of just 48, was tragic. Her physical beauty was legendary. Allegedly every man she met fell in love with her, and all of them extolled her beauty, her voice, her manner. She appeared to be an amalgam of Circe, Cleopatra, Helen of Troy and Delilah - not to mention Scilla, who tempted sailors onto the rocks and into her thrall. A lot of men had ended up shipwrecked.

Meanwhile, John had caught the attention of one of the overalled women and hot coffee and croissants were swiftly delivered to our table. 'Thank you, Pat,' he said to the waitress, turning on the charm. He was very attractive when he smiled - if you liked the lean and hungry look.

'I come in here a lot,' he said, turning back to me. 'My digs are just round the corner – bed and breakfast.'

My mind was still on the photographs. In one, Sheila was reclining on a chaise longue in a dramatic striped skirt, her dark eyes alluring and full of promise. These weren't just snaps for a magazine – they were too intimate. It was obvious the man behind the camera had a personal relationship with his subject.

'How did you know Sheila?' I asked.

'I was in love with her,' he said, his eyes becoming glassy, his voice softening. 'We met in The French Pub in Soho in the late 50s when she was an art student at St Martins. She was working behind the bar. She needed the money: her family up north were poor. Her dad was a coal miner, but he'd been injured in a pit accident and was unable to work.'

I listened as John described how the pub had been a happening place at that time - Francis Bacon, Lucien Freud, Jeffrey Bernard, George Melly, Maggi Hambling, Vivienne Westwood and numerous others had all gathered there.

'It was a mad, arty, unconventional, drunken crowd,' he continued. 'I loved it. Their behaviour was outrageous. They lived to shock. And there were always men around Sheila.'

His eyes rested on the pictures again. 'Our love affair lasted for years on and off. It continued after she left college - after she became more successful and her work was widely collected. Her work became as desirable as she was.'

As he talked, tears welled up and began to trickle down one cheek. The coffee-making women glanced over and nudged each other. By now I was getting some hard looks from the regulars. We had unwittingly become the centre of attention and I could almost see the question marks above their heads: Who is this strange woman who has made John cry? Has she brought bad news? Are they lovers who have had a disagreement? Are they splitting up? Is she dumping him?

He remained oblivious to the interest we were attracting.

'She was going to marry me,' he continued. 'She came to stay at my house in Ireland. She brought her daughter. Not many people knew she had a daughter: by a Greek sculptor. Can't remember his name - not important. She didn't marry him either.'

'So when you say you *nearly* married her..?' I prompted, now as curious about John's story as I was about him. If he was Irish, his accent certainly didn't give any hint of it...

'She invited me to meet her parents. She had an exhibition at the Stone Gallery in Newcastle, and we arranged to meet at the opening and then travel afterwards to Cumberland to stay at her parents' house. I'd proposed to her. She hadn't said no.'

As John continued to talk, I was busily making notes. I was gathering material to write a biography of Sheila Fell and had done a lot of research into her background. I had been following up links and carefully writing down any new information I picked up from the many visitors to the gallery: Aspatria, the mining town where Sheila had been born in 1931, was not far from Castlegate House. I also knew that only a select few of her men friends had enjoyed the privilege of meeting her parents, which was why John felt so sure of her more serious affections. Sheila's mother was puritanical, teetotal, and fiercely proud of her talented only child - but she was ashamed that her daughter had presented her with a grandchild: 'born out of wedlock' were the whispered words used. This was a stigma in the Sixties, and doubly unacceptable in the small, close-knit community where the Fells lived. Sheila's mother desperately wanted her daughter to marry, and that made Sheila cautious about introducing her to men friends: she didn't see marriage as an option. Why would she? She was a modern, independent woman, and after she moved to London in 1950, her talent as a painter was being recognised. Art was her passion - domesticity would not fit in with it. She didn't want the hard life her mother had as a seamstress and the wife of a miner who was now unemployed (like so many of the men in the area).

In 1958 Sheila made two sombre paintings, both entitled *Wedding in Aspatria*. They are dark, mysterious, and are unlike any other of her paintings. They both demand close scrutiny over a period of time. The more you study them, the more they reveal. These paintings tell a story - but what is that story? Did this tableau, depicted in different ways but with the same characters, really happen or is this a dream? Or maybe a nightmare? The landscape is dominated by two features; the first is a pit on a hill above a village with the pithead and wheel standing white in the foreground. The second is the large church with a few terrace houses clustered around it. The wedding in the foreground seems to have been almost irrelevant. It is taking place among the gravestones. The bride and groom are sad and faceless and are only half formed. Their bodies are falling out of the bottom of the picture. Maybe it is a wedding which never took place. A woman in white is sitting to one side by a gravestone. She looks like an angel in despair and the graveyard is haunted by dark, indistinct figures, maybe one of them is a priest. A white gravestone in the foreground repeats the shape of the pithead wheel. It is so dark it is hard to work out what is happening without strong lighting. Maybe she didn't want us to even try to interpret it. Figures loom out of the darkness, then recede. There is an atmosphere of doom. This is not a happy event. One feels that this is a comment on marriage, on her parents, and on life in Aspatria.

From the start of her career, Sheila - who was also highly talented in music and dance - chose a future in art. In 1947, when she took up her place at Carlisle College of Art, sexism was the norm. Carlisle was a textile town and I had listened to the complaints of many women students of that era - and later - who were pushed into the design and printing department of the college - the men were given more choice and allowed to do

Fine Art if they wished. Sheila wanted to paint, but the college insisted she do textiles instead and arranged for her to be taken on at Morton Sundour, a well-known textile firm who were based in the city, in the belief that this would lead to a precious job. But Sheila hated it, and after two years of misery and protest she successfully applied for a place at Central St Martins to study painting. She never lived in Cumberland again.

Post-war London was a sophisticated, exciting place, full of change and new ideas, and Sheila's voice became low and cultured – almost too 'posh' - to fit in with the cosmopolitan society she mixed with, and in a piece of film made by a youthful Melvyn Bragg mostly in Cumberland in 1961, Sheila is seen with her mother in Aspatria speaking without a trace of her northern accent. Many of us northern lasses - Barbara Hepworth and Joan Bakewell among others - 'lost' our northern accents when we moved south. We conformed in order to fit in and get on.

In every other way, however, Sheila was steadfastly loyal to the north. An only child, she remained devoted to her parents and was well aware of the sacrifices they had made to send her to college. One of the first things she did when she was financially stable was purchase their rented house in Aspatria for them. She used the time on her frequent visits home to make sketches - often in the company of Lowry – and these became the basis of the gritty, atmospheric, dark oils which she painted in her London studio. The landscapes of her childhood defined her. You could still feel the wind and rain in her work, with the heavy mountains looming oppressively over all - as W.E. Johnson wrote in the *Guardian* in 1962: 'She carries Cumberland with her wherever she goes, not so much in her pocket as in her blood.'

Because Sheila made the oils far away from their source she could concentrate on the bones of the landscape rather than topographical accuracy. In London, she was unencumbered by unimportant detail, and when she went back to Aspatria for two

147

or three days, it seemed dull and lacklustre by comparison. Maybe she felt oppressed by life as it was played out up there, in those little tight-knit villages where nothing was private; where people tilled the heavy earth above ground or else hacked a dangerous living deep underneath it.

I brought my attention back to the present as John resumed his story. Having proposed to Sheila many times in the ten years he had known her, he set off for the Stone Gallery in Newcastle in 1967, sure that this time she would agree to marry him. But his confidence was misplaced. She didn't turn up at the opening of her exhibition. There was no message, no apology, nothing. He was devastated. She had stood him up and all his future hopes were dashed. He never got to her home, never met her parents, and he never got over it. He returned to London from Newcastle alone and frustrated – yet, undaunted, he carried on with his suit and pursuit for the rest of Sheila's short life. I could see that John was still a man obsessed. He couldn't let go; he was continually telling me how much he loved her in the present tense.

'After the "no show" at the opening,' he continued, 'the Marshalls were furious - they owned the Stone Gallery. Lowry, who had come to support her, wasn't best pleased either – but he was a grumpy old fellow at the best of times.'

Tears were now running openly down John's face. Another coffee arrived with a look of sympathy for him and a glare in my direction.

'Lowry helped Sheila a lot,' I said, hoping to draw John out further. 'Particularly in her early days after leaving college. He admired her too, you know. He said she was the greatest landscape painter of the twentieth century and it was he who was responsible for getting her into the Royal Academy. What was their relationship? Do you know?'

John stiffened. I had clearly opened up a sensitive subject – maybe I'd pushed it too far.

'He was an old man,' he said, sharply. 'Sheila assured me

it was a platonic relationship; it was based on art. There wasn't anything sexual between them - but he didn't like me. He didn't like any of her men friends. He expected a one-to-one friendship. He bought two of her paintings at the first exhibition she had after leaving St Martin's. It was at the Beaux Arts gallery in Mayfair and Lowry asked the owner to arrange a meeting with her afterwards. He realised she was struggling and offered her an allowance there and then to keep her painting.'

John paused.

'He was invited to Aspatria many times,' he continued bitterly. 'Sheila used to give up her bedroom for him, and went to sleep in the attic loft. Lowry got on very well with her father – well he would, wouldn't he? They would be a similar age and background, I guess. As her patron, he then thought he was entitled to her undivided attention.'

I reflected on how Lowry must have been delighted to discover that his protégée had working class roots in the north, yet he could still meet up with her and follow her progress in London. John, however, was absorbed in his own train of thought.

'Sheila had a top floor flat and studio in Chelsea, in Redcliffe Square,' he went on. 'Lowry turned up unexpectedly one afternoon and rang the doorbell. I was there at the time, and we were in bed. Sheila got up to see who it was – she could see him from behind the curtain, pacing up and down the drive. He rang the bell many times and wouldn't go away. He seemed to sense she was in and with somebody. She told me they'd had a row about it afterwards. He felt entitled to her full attention – and of course, he really hated Bruno.'

This was an interesting development. I knew Sheila had had a boyfriend of that name, and that he was an architect who worked for a practice involved with the Festival of Britain on the South Bank. But I didn't know much else about him and was keen to find out more.

'Tell me about Bruno?' I prompted.

'Bruno Damaan - a German architect, damn him! He bullied her. He and Sheila used to fight – and I mean physically. I hate to think about it: she was so small and fragile.'

John began to recount an occasion not long before Sheila died. I could hear the jealousy in his voice. 'All three of us were in a cab and a huge row broke out between Sheila and Bruno. It got so loud that I stopped the taxi, got out and walked home. I couldn't bear any more. Bruno was the last person to have seen her alive.'

Bruno and Sheila were intending to buy a flat together in Central London: both of them were doing well and had a bright future ahead of them. They must have been a golden couple. The day before, a Saturday, they had been at a friend's wedding together. Sheila had had a lot to drink and when they returned to her flat, Bruno had left to give her time to sober up. When he came back the next morning, he found her lying on the floor. The cause of her death was alcohol poisoning. She was only 48. What a tragedy for her daughter, for Bruno, her friends, her family, her admirers, and what a loss for Art. She had given an interview to Hunter Davies for the *Sunday Times* just a few days earlier in which she said that she intended to live to 104 because she had so many paintings still left in her head. The newspaper hit the stands on Sunday 16th December 1979, the morning Sheila's body was discovered.

I tried to imagine all those paintings that the world would never see.

I glanced at my watch. It was almost ten o'clock - I had to go. I always packed in as much as I could on my visits to London to make the long journey worthwhile.

John was lost in his memories. I gently broke the silence.

'I'm afraid I have to go now. May I take these?' I picked up the photographs. 'I'm building up an archive with the intention of writing Sheila's biography – very little has ever been written about her and we mustn't let her memory die, must we? She deserves better.'

Mopping his face with his handkerchief, John sadly nodded agreement.

'How much do you want for them?'

'Nothing. Please take them.'

It wasn't the response I was expecting. John didn't look as if he had any money. He'd told me he was in cheap digs, but when I'd tried to cut our late night phone conversation short - 'Better ring off - your phone bill will be enormous' - he'd said he didn't have to pay. I had wondered then whether he still worked freelance as a photographer for one of the papers - or maybe he was a British Telecom employee on night shift. But now I'd met him, it seemed unlikely. He looked too old.

Thanking him, I asked if he intended to see the Royal Academy exhibition of Sheila's work which was due to open in a few weeks' time. It would mark the tenth anniversary of her death. 'I'm covering it for *Art Review* and have an invitation to the reception and private viewing. Would you like to come with me?'

'I'd love to,' he said. 'Is it really ten years? I still can't believe she's gone, you know.'

Time was now shooting past and I, already late for my next meeting, stood up and gently offered to pay for breakfast. He too stood up, protesting. Perhaps it was the look on my face that made him realise how he must appear – an impoverished Irishman; a shabby old hack; a retired press photographer lodging in a B&B. He pulled me back down into my seat and faced me intently across the stained table top.

'This Earls Court hotel is just temporary,' he said. 'I *am* looking for a place to buy in London: I need to be nearer the House.'

He stood up again and moved proudly to the counter to settle the bill, leaving my inquisitive mind working overtime. That last word had been said with a significant Capital Letter. There's only one House in London, isn't there? Maybe two if you count the Lords. So who had I just breakfasted with? Was he an MP or a peer of the realm? Looking at the tall, lean figure standing stooped and lined at the counter, the latter seemed the most likely. This John was a tad unkempt to be part of that great band of 'men in suits and old school ties'; he was more the eccentric aristocrat. But it seemed impertinent to ask outright, so we just shook hands.

'It's been lovely to be able to talk to someone about Sheila – someone who understands,' he said as we parted. 'Oh, I nearly forgot. Perhaps you'd like this as well.' He handed me an old copy of *Tatler* magazine he'd fished out from somewhere inside his newspaper. 'My pics are in there but I wrote the feature article as well.' Glancing at it quickly, I saw his name at the bottom: John Kilbracken.

Back in Cumbria, I nipped down to the local library straight away and grabbed *Who's Who* off the shelf. I eagerly flicked through the pages, sure that John would be there - and he was.

The man I had just met was John Kilbracken, journalist and author, who had succeeded to the title 'Lord Kilbracken of Killegar DSC' at the age of 32, when his father died in 1952. Educated at Eton and Balliol College, Oxford, he been married and divorced twice. During the Second World War he had been a Spitfire pilot, and after that he had worked as a freelance contributor to the *Daily Mirror*, *Sunday Express*, *Punch*, *Vogue*, *The New Yorker*, *Time Life*, *Tatler* and the *Evening Standard*.

Gosh. What an intriguing and diverse set of achievements.

John and I met again as planned a few weeks later, at the opening of the Royal Academy retrospective. I was relieved to see that John had scrubbed up well and was much tidier than he had been at our previous meeting. His grey suit was somewhat crumpled, but he now looked sad and distinguished rather than sad and dishevelled.

We dined together afterwards in the heart of Soho, in a small, informal bistro that John knew, close to Carnaby Street.

I had a strong feeling he had been there with Sheila - The French Pub, where they had first met, was just a few streets away. I insisted on picking up the bill this time, and John told me a little more about himself under my gentle questioning, filling in the gaps in the abbreviated *Who's Who* entry.

He was funny and self-deprecating, enjoyed telling stories against himself, and confessed he was hopeless with money. He told me that in 1952, when he inherited his family's estate, its sole stock consisted of a single, aged cow. The house was damp, dilapidated and sorely neglected and in order to try and raise money for death duties, he had launched himself into a range of unsuccessful enterprises. At one point he had tried selling square yards of Irish bog to Americans for a nickel apiece. That sounded like a good wheeze to me, but he told me ruefully that he failed to make any money from it as the cost of sending a receipt for each nickel was two nickels. Clearly he was not a businessman. We laughed a lot about that.

John had led an interesting life but among all his many adventures and projects one thing particularly fascinated me. When he was at Eton he had been one of those rare children who had dreams which predicted the future. I suspect many of his school friends dreamed of being Prime Minister, Chancellor of the Exchequer, or even Lord Mayor of London - not John Kilbracken, though. A typical Irishman, he had always been, and still was, interested in horse racing, and claimed that he could 'dream winners'. This made him a popular figure at school with both pupils and masters, especially before big races. His success rate was quite high by his own account - and he was demonstrably a modest man so I believed him.

Although John talked more about himself this time, it was Sheila who was once again the centre of attention for most of the evening. Her presence at our little round table was palpable. I had brought along the *Tatler* magazine he had given me and we discussed it at length. The waiter quietly worked around it as it lay between us on the cloth, delivering and clearing dishes of which I now have no memory. I saw myself as the host, entertaining two lovers. Sheila had never married Bruno or any of her many other admirers, but John still truly believed he was her favourite. It sounded very much the other way round to me, and in the light of her premature death, it was an unbearably poignant night.

We were the last people to leave the restaurant.

**

Fifteen years later, in 2005, I fulfilled a long-held ambition. I mounted a major exhibition of Sheila Fell's work at Castlegate House – the first since the Royal Academy's 1990 retrospective and the first commercial exhibition since her death. I was thrilled that it was taking place in her native Cumbria, just a few miles from her home town.

When I opened Castlegate House as a gallery in 1987, Sheila had been in danger of being forgotten, but I'd been determined not to let that happen. However, it had taken me twenty years to build up the contacts I needed for the exhibition – the names of the people who would trust me enough to lend their own paintings for it; the people who would be willing to allow me to remove a work from their wall at their home for six weeks, probably leaving faded wallpaper and a terrible, empty space behind.

In addition, I had to have enough of Sheila's work in stock to sell in order to cover the considerable cost of the show – the insurance alone was astronomic. Because Sheila's life had been so short, her total output of work was quite small, so her paintings rarely came up at auction. It had taken me most of the latter part of that twenty years and a lot of capital to build up a collection of sixteen paintings for sale and I would have to sell most of them to make the exhibition financially viable.

As the opening approached, excitement mounted: this exhibition was going to make waves.

Invitations had been posted, press releases had gone out,

publicity had been done. All that was left was the hang, which Angie and I had been looking forward to for some time. We did enjoy a good hanging!

The thinking stage is the most important part of a successful hanging. First we decided on the mantelpiece paintings: there were three rooms in the gallery, and three mantelpieces. We chose the three biggest and best paintings for them, and worked from there outwards. Paintings were spread on the floor around the wide entrance hall and then sorted into harmonious groups according to chronology, size or subject matter, colour harmony, or even style of frames and mounts. We then allocated them to the different rooms and it was quite tense until it was right: there was a lot of passing from room to room, making adjustments. Not a single painting could be hung until it was in the correct position.

Angie and I would have a little game, choosing our favourite work – one piece each - and allocating them to one of the gallery's two 'magic' spots. I'm definitely not going to tell you where those magic places were, but whatever we hung in them almost always sold first.

Once it was all done to our mutual satisfaction, we could do the easy bit – the actual physical hanging of works on the wall – before relaxing with a well-earned coffee.

We were still at the thinking stage of the Fell hang when the telephone rang. It broke the silence – and our concentration – intrusively.

'I'm sorry. I should have put the answer machine on, shouldn't I?' said Angie

'Possibly, but don't beat yourself up about it. This exhibition is rather special and we don't want to miss important calls so close to the opening, do we? It might be a London critic.'

We laughed. Critics rarely came north - they regarded it as provincial.

Angie disappeared down the hall to answer the phone. She returned a few minutes later.

'It was someone called Gabriella Filippo for you,' she said.

'Who? Never heard of her. What did she want? If she's trying to sell us something, she can go away.'

'I don't think she was, but she wouldn't say. She just said it was very important and concerned the Fell exhibition. I told her we're busy and asked her to ring later on.'

We were quickly back at work, and I was soon lost in admiration at the paintings we were hanging. *Mechi Farm*, a bright oil of the first mechanised farm in Cumbria, was my favourite. In the foreground were fields full of golden corn stooks, roughly worked with a palette knife, while in the background were farm buildings and a characteristic tall clock tower so that the workers always knew the time. That farm and its clock tower still stood and were just a few miles from the gallery, but you wouldn't have recognised them. This wasn't a literal painting, but it was a delight: many of Fell's works were dark and heavily varnished, but here yellow ochre had replaced her usual burnt sienna, chrome yellow her dark umber.

'Shall I put this in your magic spot?' Angie teased. 'After all, it nearly got you arrested.'

'Yes, of course, but I'll do it,' I replied, laughing. 'It will give me a lot of pleasure.'

Every painting holds a story and this one had been hard won. It had happened like this:

I had bought the painting via a telephone bid at Christie's, paying for it by BACS straight after the auction, informing Christie's that Michael and I would pick it up when we were next in London. I was longing to see it in the flesh and, when I did, I was not disappointed: it needed a good clean but it met my expectations. Obviously, Michael and I didn't want to keep such a valuable work in our hotel room, so we handed it back to the man in charge of collecting at Christie's, telling him that we'd be back on Thursday at 5.00 p.m. to pick it up before we got on the train home. We duly arrived at the appointed hour, and Michael went off to pick it up and start wrapping it while I went to Accounts to get the vital chitty.

Accounts denied any payment had been made.

I knew it had gone through instantly. Back and forth we went while time moved on. Finally, we reached deadlock. I gave up and rushed into the packing room, which was humming with people as it was the end of a big sale and it was close to closing time. I told Michael what the problem was.

'We're going to miss the train,' he said. We looked at each other. We looked at the painting. And then we picked it up and fled.

There was a number 14 bus just coming round the corner and we jumped on.

'You know what,' Michael said when we were going round Hyde Park Corner, 'we'll be on CCTV. We're going to look very suspicious.'

'But we've paid for it!' I exclaimed. 'And, besides, they do know us – we have an account. We're not stealing: this is definitely ours. I'll ring them tomorrow.'

'You might find Interpol waiting at Penrith,' Michael replied.

'Or MI5 at Euston,' I jested.

Nevertheless, I did keep glancing behind to see if there was a police car closing in on the number 14.

We made it to our train with two minutes to spare but by the time we reached Watford, Angie had phoned to tell me Christie's were trying to get in touch – they thought that someone had collected my Fell under false pretences. They had given her a description which sounded a bit like us, she said.

I rang first thing the next morning and they were relieved to know we had got our painting. They apologised for the cashier's mistake, all was now well.

I was standing back admiring the work when Gabriella Filippo rang back.

'I'm a researcher for *Woman's Hour* on Radio Four,' she said. 'I hear you have a Sheila Fell exhibition starting soon. I wonder if you would come and do an interview about the artist? Can you tell me a little about her?'

'I certainly can,' I replied eagerly, 'and I can send you a catalogue which will fill you in with the details a bit more. Where shall I send it?'

She ignored this and carried on asking me a few irrelevant questions.

She's probably testing me for sound and reaction in an interview, I thought, and I appeared to have passed - Gabriella wanted me to be live on air on Radio 4 on Friday.

'Which Friday?' I asked.

'Tomorrow,' she replied.

'Oh, I'm sorry,' I said. 'Tomorrow is impossible. It's the opening day of the exhibition and it's going to be really hectic here.'

'That's all right,' she said. 'You can do it from your local studio. We don't do telephone interviews: the quality isn't good enough for *Woman's Hour*. We're talking national radio, you know.'

'Yes, I realise that,' I said, feeling patronised. 'But where is the local studio?'

'I'll find out and ring you back. Where are you again? Is it Wales?'

She obviously didn't have a clue where Cumbria was and sounded very dubious about Cockermouth. I had to spell it out several times. When she did ring back, however, it was to ask if Carlisle would be all right.

'I don't want to be awkward,' I said, 'but Carlisle is a 60-mile round trip from the gallery and I just won't have the time tomorrow. The first day of any exhibition, particularly this one, is really important. It's a viewing day and I have the local press and a television crew coming round at 11.30. May I do the interview next week?'

'No, it has got to be this Friday. It's been scheduled in. I'll see if there is anywhere else where you can go to record it.' She paused. 'Is there a city closer to you than Carlisle?'

I wearily told her we don't do cities very much up here –

Carlisle has a cathedral, but otherwise we just have towns, villages, hamlets...

'I'll ring you back,' she said, yet again.

Angie had hung the rest of the show by this time and I was feeling a bit guilty when Gabriella called with her next offer.

'You can do the interview at Whitehaven or Keswick - your choice.' She pronounced Keswick with a hard W, as in candlewick.

'Where in Keswick?' I asked.

'Oh, I don't know – I'll find out.'

This woman didn't seem to know much, despite being a BBC researcher. Why was she so insistent the interview had to be tomorrow? *Woman's Hour* goes out every weekday. The Fell exhibition continued for six weeks. There was something strange going on. It all seemed wrong somehow, but she quickly came back with the information.

'Right. You have to go to a place called the Skiddaw Hotel. It's in Kes Wick. Do you know it?'

'Yes, I know the Skiddaw Hotel. It's in the precinct in the centre of the town.'

'You need to get there about ten o'clock and you must ask at the reception for the key. OK?'

'So they have a recording studio in the Skiddaw Hotel?' I was sceptical.

'Yes, they must have,' she said vaguely. 'Good luck!'

And she rang off abruptly before I could ask anything else – anything useful like her contact number. I was confused and uncertain. None of this made sense. I'd have put money on the Skiddaw Hotel not having such a thing as a recording studio. To increase my disquiet, I met a friend later that day who had lived in Keswick for years, and when I asked her if she knew about a secret BBC recording studio, she laughed.

'You know what day it is tomorrow, don't you?' she said, after some thought. 'It's April the First.'

Oh dear, what a fool I'd been. It was obvious now that I'd been set up.

I worked very late that evening so that everything was ready for the next morning's pre-opening press conference, and in the small hours of a restless night, my crossword addict's brain played around with Gabriella Filippo's name. *Big April Fool* emerged on the scribble pad, give or take the odd letter. What was I to do? Why hadn't I realised I was opening an exhibition on April Fools' Day? Was one of my friends – or enemies – playing tricks on me? *Not funny,* I thought. Tomorrow was one of the most important days in the life of the gallery and I was tempted to give the interview a miss - but what if the call was genuine? *Woman's Hour* was a coveted slot. I couldn't afford to lose that opportunity.

April 1st was bitterly cold with a deep frost. Skiddaw was shimmering white above the town. Even though I didn't intend to hang about, I dressed up warm - a challenge because I needed to look decent for the television interview at the gallery afterwards. I went for serious layering: I didn't want to get a chill before such an important exhibition.

Promptly at ten o'clock, and looking a bit like the Michelin Man, I presented myself at the reception desk of the Skiddaw Hotel in Keswick's Market Place.

'Good morning,' I said brightly, trying to sound confident, 'I've come to use your recording studio. I've been told you have a key.'

The receptionist looked at me blankly. 'What did you say you wanted? What's your room number? Have you lost your room key?'

I felt stupid. My worst fears were being realised. I was so foolish falling for this silly joke.

The receptionist sent for the manager and he also looked at me quizzically.

'I've been sent here by the BBC to use your recording studio,' I explained again, embarrassed.

If he gives me the same blank look as her then I'll be off without hesitation, I thought: *nobody is going to take me for a ride*. But the manager disappeared below the counter and scrabbled around like a demented hamster for some time. He eventually surfaced holding a large, unlabelled key. Tentatively, I enquired where I might find the door to which the key might fit.

'Ah,' he said. 'Go to the town hall and it's the blue one at the back.'

'Where's the town hall?' I asked, feeling really ignorant.

'Opposite the police station,' he said – and with a shrug he went off to do whatever hotel managers do when not dealing with the overdressed mentally fragile.

Out in the precinct I had to ask a local-looking passerby – i.e. one not decked out in full hiking gear - where the town hall or police station were. It turned out I'd passed both of them many times but never clocked them. Once in the know, I saw the town hall was a prominent building – a big, Victorian edifice on a busy corner where drivers have to concentrate to avoid annihilating jay-walking tourists.

Oh joy, there was a blue door at the side - but the key didn't fit. I walked round the back where I found a small yard and three doors – but all of them were painted blue! I felt like Alice in Wonderland. The first blue door was a broom cupboard. The second was an outside lavatory but, abracadabra, the third door opened to reveal a very small room with a chair, a telephone and a switchboard which looked like my gran's old radio set with the back off. Everywhere there were multi-coloured wires, valves, switches and coloured bulbs.

Eureka! Success at last. My spirits rose. Perhaps this wasn't a trick.

I sat down and got my bearings. Besides the switchboard, the room's dominant feature was an old-fashioned radiator which was kicking out kilowatts like we were in the Arctic. A card of instructions which lay on the table ordered me to shut the door firmly and lock it – which I did – then to sit down and await a call. Already I was perspiring. I removed my fleece,

161

woolly hat, scarf and gloves and still I was way too hot. I thought I was going to pass out - and what would happen then, eh?

At that moment the phone rang shrilly, making me jump in surprise. I picked it up, half expecting a voice to say 'Big April fool!' but no, it was an engineer doing a voice test.

'You'll be live in two minutes,' he said.

By now I was running a serious temperature so I shed a thermal vest and a few more woollies. Perspiration trickled slowly down my back. I was now down to my underwear and considering doing the interview naked – well, it was radio – when the phone rang again. It was Martha Kearney and we were away.

Mercifully, the interview was a short one, or I would have been a melted heap of lard on the floor. Having re-dressed, locked up and returned the key to the apathetic girl at the hotel, I roared off back to the gallery to open the exhibition. It was just 10.45.

Thanks to all the publicity the exhibition had attracted, people poured in. Because so few of Sheila's paintings had been available to buy in the past there was a high demand and *Mechi Farm*, placed in my magic spot, was the first to sell. I was pleased to see it was going to a good home and even more so when the new owner whispered that she intended to will it to a prominent public gallery on the south coast. Another painting, an exquisite small snowscape, meanwhile became the scene of a bidding war between a medical man who was on holiday in the West Indies and an accountant who was present in the gallery. The doctor was on his mobile and the accountant was pacing the room as they placed their counter-bids, with the doctor winning in the end. It was surreal selling a snowscape to a man on a tropical beach on the opposite side of the world.

To accompany the exhibition, I had produced a catalogue which included the superb photographs John Kilbracken had taken of Sheila in happier times. He had also given me permission to reproduce his Tatler article, *WITH DREAMY EYE AND MAGIC BRUSH*.

The piece began:

'I first met Sheila Fell fifteen years ago when she was a beautiful waif of twenty two, in the crowded bar of the French pub in Dean Street. To say I instantly fell in love with her would be hyperbole, but it wouldn't have been difficult; her wonderful physical features (long dark hair, classical profile, long-legged boy-girl body) were combined with a total personal integrity and utter devotion to her business which was painting. At this time she had never sold a picture; she was living on an allowance of £100 a year, of which thirty shillings a week went on the exiguous disordered flat in Hampstead where she lived and worked, leaving less than ten bob to cover everything else.'

It ended:

'Although she has lived in London ever since, her heart and her work have always remained in Cumberland. I have hardly seen one of her paintings – those sombre brown, brooding canvases – that did not depict a scene from her own county even though it may have been painted in London. She is totally independent of outside influence and can only work when the time is right and on the thoughts she finds in her head. Shy and quiet spoken she is often withdrawn almost totally from the world, the telephone and doorbell disconnected, going softly from room to room playing Mozart at the upright piano not dealing with bills and correspondence, completely involved in her own introspection. She still teaches two days a week at the Chelsea School of Art because it provides security; though two large canvases of hers would more than pay her year's salary. The great bursts of creative energy simply come when they come and then there is no stopping them.

They will go on coming for ever. Totally committed as she is to her life as a painter which comes before all else and to the exclusion if need be of easy joys, she will grow in stature from

163

decade to decade as I have seen her grow for those fifteen years since that far away moment in the French pub till she belongs among the greats.'

John was too old and frail to make the journey across the Irish Sea to visit the exhibition himself, but I rang him a few times to tell him how it was going; since our breakfast in Earls Court we had kept in touch and he had rung from time to time when he felt the need to talk about Sheila.

One of these calls happened to be on the day of the Grand National and Ailsa, my Saturday assistant, always keen on the gee-gees, stood close by my shoulder, holding her breath as I asked John if he still dreamt winners. There was a long pause.

'I'm so sorry, Chris,' he said at last. 'I just don't dream any more. I've lost the magic.'

Ailsa and I backed a loser that day.

The following year, John Kilbracken died, aged 86. The many obituaries confirmed everything he had told me about his remarkable life that evening at dinner. He was a lovely, modest man and I shall always remember him with affection. After his death I wrote to his son, Christopher, about any letters that might come to light referring to Sheila Fell. John's ex-wife, Sue, called me back a few weeks later to say they had found an oil painting of Killegar that might be by Sheila, but it wasn't signed and she hoped I might be able to authenticate it.

She told me that the house was still falling apart, with insufficient money to make it comfortable: the painting, she hoped, might raise some money to contribute to essential repairs. I suggested the selling of the peat bog to Americans scheme and she laughed. She'd heard that one too.

I must go to Killegar and see that painting...

Footloose in Japan

I once held a tea bowl made by a Japanese potter, Shoji Hamada. The reverence and awe I felt at holding that exquisite object, feeling the hands of the potter beneath mine, is something I've never forgotten. It seemed as though I was holding the secret of life itself. As I turned his small pot in my hand, I realised how little I knew about ceramics. Hamada is the doyenne of potters. It was he who helped Bernard Leach set up his St Ives pottery in 1920. He had met Leach in Tokyo and found they had much in common and a lot to learn from each other. Leach invited Hamada to England, where he stayed for four years. In 1955 he was the first person in Japan to be given the title 'Living National Treasure' – the equivalent of a knighthood. Hamada died in 1978 but I wanted to make a pilgrimage to Mashiko, the town in Japan where he had lived and made these exquisite pots. I wanted to breathe the air he breathed and see what he saw. It went on my travel wish list (although in the 'difficult without a guide' section).

Many of the potters I showed at Castlegate House followed the Japanese method and style, which is revered around the world. Japanese potters are recognised as masters of glazes and oxides, form and design. 'It's all in the foot,' one of my potters, William Plumptre, said to me one day as he picked up a bowl, turned it over and pointed out the ring of clay on the bottom on which it stood.

I was fortunate that three of the best potters in England were living and working on my doorstep, William among them. After studying ceramic design at Chelsea School of Art, he had spent two years studying in Japan - one of them in Hamada's town, Mashiko - under another National Treasure, Tatsuko Shimaoka. He had learned to build and use a climbing kiln, to use woodash glazes, and to perfect the distinctive rope decoration technique before returning to Cumbria to set up his own successful pottery.

Edward Hughes was born in Cheshire but studied ceramics at the Art School in Kyoto. He lived and worked in Japan for many years before returning to England with his Japanese wife Shizuko, setting up a workshop just a few miles from the gallery. In his studio one day I picked up a simple, square, black lidded box. It was perfection. The lid effortlessly guided itself back with a whisper as I replaced it. How I regret not buying it: I didn't know it was my last chance. Edward tragically died, aged 52, on the Ennerdale Fells in 2006, at the peak of his career.

Edward's pots are quiet and unsophisticated. He believed that they should be used and he told me how many were bought by housewives in Japan for daily use. Michael, my partner, gained his approval because he bought a small bowl which he uses for incense sticks as he meditates. I have a deep brown, irregular faceted pot which I use for white lilies. It is one of my most valued possessions.

When we first visited him, Edward told us that he exported 90% of his pots to Japan and they commanded significantly higher prices there. (He is still better known in Japan). People in the UK just aren't prepared to spend such large amounts on a pot.

The first potter I ever showed, Jim Malone, also lived close by (as I was overjoyed to discover). One of our most well-respected British potters, he follows the Japanese method punctiliously, making his own glazes to Japanese recipes and digging and sourcing his materials locally so that they carry the colours and textures of the landscape. He works in silence in an isolated studio with a church-like atmosphere of serenity. He is a purist – no compromises, no short cuts.

The opportunity to cross Japan off my wish list finally came in 1999 when my Japanese friend Etsu Peascod, knowing of my interest in Japanese pottery, offered to be my guide and mentor in the country of her birth. I first met Etsu in January 1986 when planning the move to Cumbria. She was selling her house on the northern slopes of Skiddaw, one of the highest mountains in England. She was the young widow of the climber and painter Bill Peascod, who had died tragically on a mountain a few months previously, leaving her with a remote house and a small child. We lost touch when we didn't manage to buy her house, even though we all wanted it to happen. We renewed contact with her in Edinburgh a year after buying Castlegate House when I was planning a retrospective of Bill's work at the gallery, and again in 1994 when Etsu was living in Australia and needed another exhibition of his work. Now, five years later, she was living in Japan again.

I knew Etsu would be the perfect guide, not only because she straddled East and West, but because she had studied art in Kyoto and understood what I was looking for. She had worked out an interesting itinerary for us using her local knowledge and contacts, and planned our stay in temples, traditional Ryokans, and at the houses of her artist friends. She also assured me that Hamada's town of Mashiko was included in our tour. It sounded good. I eagerly accepted her invitation.

Japan is the most strange and unpredictable place I have ever visited.

I was quite relaxed as the plane landed smoothly at Osaka, but my troubles began before I even disembarked. Osaka was the stopover between Bangkok and San Francisco and the cabin crew were convinced that I was trying to get off too soon.

'Madam, madam,' the hostess shouted after me. 'Come back. You not there yet! This is Osaka.'

I turned and smiled. 'That's where I'm going.'

And I carried on walking.

On my way out, several people helpfully tried to turn me back. I didn't fit the pattern: I was not Japanese, I was travelling alone, and I was female. Politely shrugging off all offers of assistance, I strode confidently through to Baggage Reclaim and out through Customs, where I had arranged to meet Etsu. I was looking forward to meeting up with her again, smiling to myself and rehearsing our reunion. So I was surprised when the uniformed official at Customs took me and my luggage to one side, summoning a woman colleague.

Never mind, I consoled myself. *It's only because I look different from everyone else here.*

They went through my hand luggage and then started on my suitcase. They took everything out and spread it on the counter. It was not very pretty. I'd been travelling for almost two weeks.

'You come from Bangkok?' the first official said.

It was a rhetorical question.

'Why you stop in Bangkok?'

This was not a rhetorical question. He wanted an answer.

'For a holiday.'

'Why you come here to Osaka from Bangkok?'

There was an uncomfortable silence. I was trying to frame the truth in words that would sound plausible and convincing.

'I have an art gallery in England and I have come to study Japanese pottery.'

'Where you going to study? Which school?'

'Erm, not at a school actually. A Japanese friend is meeting me here. She's an expert in ceramics. We will travel together to visit potters. I hope to set up an exhibition of Japanese ceramics in England next year.'

'Why to Osaka?'

'This is where I have arranged to meet my friend.'

'What your friend's name?'

'Etsu, Etsu Peascod.'

'Peascod. That not Japanese name. Where she live?'

'Er, somewhere near Kyoto, I think.'

'You not know? Why you not know? If you stay with her you must know address. How you get there then if you not know?'

'Erm,' I hesitated. This was difficult. 'Erm, I won't be staying at her home. She is living in her father's house at the moment until she finds a place of her own. This is my first visit to Japan and she is meeting me here with a car and we will be travelling together. We are going to be staying in hotels,' I added, lamely. 'We always email each other and I've never asked her for an address. She has just moved here from Australia. I have her former address in Sydney...'

'Where you go to see these potters then?'

'Er, I don't know yet. My friend has worked out the itinerary.'

I tried to remember the name of the town where Hamada worked but even Mashiko evaded me under this aggressive interrogation.

'She will be my guide. She is waiting for me out there in Arrivals.'

I looked at my watch. It was late. Time moves at a different speed in airports. It was now double-quick.

'She will be worried about me. She might think I have missed my flight.'

The officials now abruptly changed tack.

'Where your husband?' the uniformed woman asked, my passport in her hand. Her voice was becoming shrill.

I was taken aback. 'I don't have a husband,' I said coldly.

'Yes you do,' came the sharp reply. 'You missus. It say here.' She tapped the page hard.

'I am a widow,' I said quietly. 'My husband is dead.'

'He not dead,' she came back vehemently. 'He in Bangkok!'

I was astounded. 'No, he is dead,' I said, carefully and clearly enunciating my words. 'He died five years ago.'

Michael 1 had died of cancer in 1994, soon after our return visit from Australia to arrange the exhibition of Etsu's late husband's paintings, which made all this even more disturbing. How I wished he really was in Bangkok, even if it got me into more trouble than I was in now.

'You lie. He in Bangkok! If he not in Bangkok then why you stop there?'

She was staring straight into my eyes. I was uncomfortable

in the extreme. I repeated my denial.

'So why you go to Bangkok then? You tell me that.' We were eyeball to eyeball now. 'You fly Manchestair to Osaka but you stop in Bangkok. Why?'

I was already regretting my little holiday in the sun. I didn't realise how it would be seen.

'Japan is cold this time of the year and so is England.' I tried to smile a bit. It made no difference. 'I wanted to have a break in a warm climate. When I looked at flight options from Britain, Bangkok came up, so I booked it and spent two weeks travelling in Thailand.'

'You stop Bangkok to see your husband,' she persisted. Her voice now had an underlying hint of hysteria. This was getting out of hand. My journey and I now sounded suspect. I was actually beginning to suspect myself. I glanced at the wall clock. It was well over an hour since I had landed. Michael had been dead five years and no, I don't carry his death certificate around with me.

'You got drugs in Bangkok?'

What could I say to convince these people that I was not an international drug smuggler?

'No, I certainly did not.' I wished I wasn't getting flustered. I took a deep breath and exhaled slowly.

Meanwhile, the woman began to pick through my things. She ripped open my first aid kit and triumphantly extracted the pristine hypodermic syringe in sealed packaging that I always carry in Africa and Asia in case of accident. It was embarrassing. Not as embarrassing, though, as stripping to my underwear in the side room and being scrutinised and handled in a non-sympathetic way. I was terrified and bracing myself for the rubber glove's appearance – but fortunately it didn't come to that. However, it was long after midnight when, feeling ruffled, dirty and shredded, I walked out into an immaculate and cavernous arrivals hall. There was not a scrap of litter anywhere.

I'd never experienced a totally empty airport before. It was unnerving. The highly polished marble floor echoed eerily with my footsteps and I looked around, unsure what to do next. The check-in desks were all closed. The Arrivals and Departures boards were an empty black. Blinds were pulled down at the shops and metal bars covered the bureau de change. Etsu didn't have a mobile phone and nor did I. There was no way I could travel in this crazy country without her. I had nowhere to stay and no language in which to find a hotel. I couldn't even read any signs. There was no tourist office. Everything was closed. Where would I go?

I wondered where Etsu was and what she must be thinking. She would have seen that my flight had landed hours ago. She would have watched passengers come through and waited a while - maybe an hour - but after that..? Would she have given up and gone home to bed?

I needn't have worried. My elegant friend was asleep and lying as still as a sphinx on a marble bench, designer handbag under her head, arms folded on her chest. I gently woke her up.

My induction in Japan and its potters began in Kyoto the next day.

'We are going to a special temple first today,' Etsu said. 'We will meditate there before we go to see some pots.'

The temple was situated in the middle of a tranquil garden, surrounded by little paths, pergolas and bridges, just like a willow pattern plate. I watched and followed as Etsu slipped out of her shoes and mounted a raised wooden platform in the temple which overlooked a rectangular area of small white stones bounded by trees. Several dark rocks appeared to spring out of this sea of pebbles and a pattern of lines swirled around them.

After Etsu and I had been meditating for a while, a monk appeared with a wide wooden rake and began to re-emphasise the lines and whorls in the gravel. It was clear that only perfection would do.

I glanced at Etsu. Her eyes were glassy bright. I realised

that she had brought me to the garden that had inspired her husband Bill, so many years before. I had one of his paintings at the gallery called *Raked Garden* - a minimal, all-white work, textured with combed lines created while the paint was wet – and I realised that its lines were the same as those the monk had made.

As Etsu and I sat side by side, I knew we were both thinking about him; a Maryport man who had begun his working life as a miner aged fourteen and who had grown to become a famous climber and artist. She had met him here in Kyoto many years ago when he was lecturing at the art college where she was a student. She was eighteen and he was older than her father, but they fell in love, married against her parents' wishes and, after a spell in Australia, came to live in Bill's native Cumbria when he reached retirement age. Tragically, he only enjoyed a few years back in the place he loved best, doing what he wanted to do – painting and rock climbing – before he died of a heart attack on a mountain in Wales.

We left the raked garden feeling uplifted, pensive and sad. Thoughtfully, we made our way through the improbably bright green moss gardens and orange-leafed acers to our temple hotel rooms, where we scrubbed ourselves clean until our skin glowed scarlet, before we could soothe it back to pink in the thermal baths. I had never before, and have never since, experienced that level of cleanliness of body and mind.

***

Everyone in this country appeared to be crazy about pots. Everywhere I went, the emphasis was primarily on ceramics, with lacquer work and textiles close behind. There were huge, supermarket-type warehouses everywhere – even in small towns or out in open country - with pots piled up on tables and shelves. Stock ranged from normal, everyday production pottery to fine studio pots costing thousands of yen, yet these places were always busy with people scurrying about, filling baskets. What did they do with all the pots? Did they carelessly break and replace them? I think not. European potters grumble that their work fetches so much less than paintings, despite the heavy production costs, time and skill involved in producing it. In Japan the few painters I met complained in just the same way: they felt undervalued and I'm not surprised.

The first potters Etsu took me to see had invited us to stay overnight in a remote country village outside Kyoto. We arrived in heavy snow to see icicles hanging from the roof, guttering and trees. The walls of this couple's house were made of paper panels and there were more icicles inside, dripping gently in the feeble heat put out by the ancient stove. They served a delicious meal from their iridescent hand-thrown, oven-to-table dishes, and we ate sitting on the floor at a low table, with our legs folded to one side.

This is an excruciating position for a Westerner to maintain for any length of time. I am convinced you have to be born to it. Shivering with the cold from the fierce draughts that were sweeping through gaps under and around the doors, I had to keep changing position to avoid cramp, even kneeling for a while until they finally took pity on me and allowed me to stretch my legs out in front of me under cover of the heavy table cloth (in Japan it is considered rude to point your feet at anyone). There was a heater under the table, which was bliss, and I eventually got my feet warm by bedtime - just as well because the bedroom was also icy. I went to bed with all my clothes on.

We looked at our hosts' showroom the next morning before leaving. I loved their pots but they were prohibitively expensive by our standards. I thought of the Japanese housewives Edward Hughes had told me about who used his pots every day. A simple, earthenware casserole was considerably more than double the price of a Le Creuset cast iron pot. I would be scared to use them at all at that price.

For the next leg of our tour, Etsu had booked us into a series of traditional inns, called Ryokans. Unlike the big multinational hotels in the cities - the Hyatts and Sofitels where Europeans were catered for, where you could sit on a chair at a table, eat with cutlery, and pretend you were anywhere in the world - these hotels had a strict code of behaviour laid down and developed over centuries. There was no tolerance here, no allowances made. I had to learn and conform – fast.

On arrival at a Ryokan, the whole complement of staff would come out to greet us like a scene in *The Mikado*. The hostess, Mama-San, would be controlling the pageant; she and the staff, arms folded into their kimono sleeves, would line up on the platform and all would bow deeply. We would be expected to bow less deeply in return, and then the performance would begin. We had to get to their level.

Two pairs of slippers awaited us, facing helpfully away from us. The platform was about two feet higher than the ground, which made changing shoes a tricky operation. Etsu, without a word, demonstrated the correct way to manage the manoeuvre elegantly. She slipped one foot out of her shoe and lifted it into the slipper on the dais, then she transferred her weight onto the slippered foot while deftly stepping out of the other shoe and placing her foot into the second slipper. Mission accomplished, a member of staff quickly stooped down from the platform, took Etsu's shoes, and placed them neatly in a shoe rack at one side. At no point did outside shoes encounter interior floor. Conversely, no inside slippers ever touched the outside floor. I watched intently. Now it was my turn. I was the only outsider now and I had to become an insider without falling over and making a fool of myself.

My biggest mistake was to have brought laced shoes and zipped boots to Japan - slip-ons would have solved a lot of problems. I had watched Etsu carefully but it was impossible for me to match her smooth elegance. I could sense her anxiety as I loosened the laces of my shoes as much as I could. I knew she was silently cheering me on. I wobbled on one leg for ages, managed to haul myself on to the platform, but couldn't get my boot off the other foot despite shaking it about a lot. In the end Etsu had to lean down from the edge of the dais and pull it off, then haul me up to join her.

'Why can't I just sit on the step and change my shoes?' I asked Etsu petulantly later.

'Because you can't,' she snapped.

It was final. I respected her too much to argue. I did improve with practice, though I never got it totally perfect

My feet were a constant embarrassment in Japan – my Achilles heel. A few days later I unwittingly did the worst thing ever, which wiped out all the intensive etiquette training.

When we reached our room in the Ryokan, we had to remove our clothes, shower, then have a bath and change into the kimono provided. The kimonos were beautiful, comfortable, and solved the problem of deciding what to wear. They were also a great leveller as every guest had been issued with an identical garment.

Etsu and I had dined privately in our room at first while I adapted to the uncomfortable sitting position and mastered the chopsticks. This was essential if I wasn't to starve: there were no concessions to Western ways, and definitely no spoons or forks. I practised hard until Etsu finally decided I could manage this difficult art and that the time had come to unleash me on the wider world. We went down to the dining room in our slippers and kimonos. This was my coming out. What a debut!

We were led to our table at the far end of the room through an avenue of low tables where groups of people in kimonos just like ours were eating. I was beginning to get the hang of the Japanese small step shuffle, feeling quite proud of myself, when the world almost came to an end. Everyone had stopped eating. Everyone was staring at me. The room had gone absolutely silent. The waiters stopped and stood still as statues. I stopped. Etsu stopped.

'What's the matter?' I muttered to Etsu.

She looked down at my feet. That was where everyone else was looking, too.

'Oh my God,' she exclaimed. 'Get out. Get out now. Come on.'

She grabbed my arm and marched me out swiftly. She was red-faced with embarrassment.

In the corridor I turned, totally shaken. Etsu was furious.

'Do you know what you've done?'

'No.'

'You've come down in your toilet slippers!'

'What?'

'Get upstairs and change them immediately. You can only wear those in the toilet.'

'How do you all know they are toilet slippers?' I asked like a sullen teenager.

'Because it says so on the front: look.'

I looked down. There was simply a black squiggle design on the top of the white slipper. Apparently it said 'toilet' in Japanese, and toilet slippers in an eating place are beyond forgiveness...

It wasn't just shoes that caused me embarrassment. My first lunch in Japan was in a Kyoto noodle shop with Etsu and her brother. I went to the toilet while our meal was being prepared and found the facility clean, beautiful and simple - like most things Japanese. The gently heated seat was an unexpected luxury that made me sigh audibly with pleasure. There was no visible flush and no toilet paper, but to my right was a control panel with a battery of knobs and push-buttons and diagrammatic instructions. The first was for a front spray, the second a back spray, the third a blow dry, the fourth a flush. I pushed each of them in turn, an experience that made me giggle and then laugh out loud. It was ingenious. I wanted one of these at home. I emerged into the crowded café smiling broadly.

'Hey,' I said as I sat back down at the table, 'You know that toilet...'

I tailed off.

'Yes, we do know,' said Etsu drily. 'We heard you. So did everyone else in here.'

'What?'

'We heard everything. The walls are only paper, you know.'

I subsequently found heated seats everywhere: on trains and buses, in waiting rooms and offices. This was before we in Britain had even thought of heated car seats, so it was a novelty. I loved it. It was my favourite thing.

***

In Shiga Province, a short drive from Kyoto, Etsu and I visited the studio workshop of Yasuhiro Kohara, whose irregular-shaped bowls were beautiful and practical, followed by the studio of Sawa Kiyotsugo, whose pieces, by contrast, were works of art. Unlike most of the pots we had seen so far, which were beautiful and functional, these ceramic pieces were purely aesthetic: to be looked at and enjoyed rather than used. They were sculptures. Many had been deliberately distorted in the kiln, and some had great cracks and folds.

Sawa handed me this statement in English: 'As I try to create the images I have in my mind, I am captivated by the sensual, yet rough beauty of Shigaraki clay. I am inspired by the challenge of expressing myself through clay. As I fire my just completed pieces, I am already thinking of what to make next.'

This lovely man told me he had shown his work in America, New Zealand and England, and had another exhibition planned soon for New York. He was eager to have an exhibition at Castlegate House. This was promising, I thought, until I saw the prices in his back catalogues and thought about the logistics: transport, shipping, what to do with the unsold pieces. Sawa also said he would like to come to

England for the exhibition, and I realised it would all be too expensive. His previous international exhibitions, I noticed from his CV, had all been in embassies or arranged by the British Council: they would have raised grants to cover the costs. Nevertheless, I went through the ritual handing-over of my business card and Sawa reciprocated, also giving me a printed invitation to the opening of his next exhibition in a department store in Tokyo the following week. His best work had already gone there. By sheer coincidence, Etsu and I would be in Tokyo at the same time and we agreed to go.

Before we left Sawa's studio, he handed me a poem written by a well-known Japanese poet, Hideo Mori. Written after Mori had seen Sawa's pots, it epitomises the artist's philosophy. I still have it in translation.

> *Twenty years of making pots*
> *Contorted, cracked, uneven glazes, stone burst surfaces.*
> *How different from the flawless perfection*
> *Of Copenhagen or Wedgewood.*
> *Some the fire totally transforms.*
> *No matter – their shapes have beauty too.*
> *The potter can make but not control.*
> *With a prayer he lights the fire.*
> *The gods of the kiln decide the rest.*
> *Who knows how future ages will judge*
> *these works?*
> *I think the peasant potters of Korea,*
> *Could they have guessed that the tea master*
> *Sen No Rikyu would one day prize their*
> *Humble bowls?*
> *Wabi Sabi the aesthete of quiet beauty still*
> *Holds sway in the world of Japanese ceramics.*
> *Tradition strengthens, yet confines*
> *So what will Sawa do next?*
> *What new endeavours will the winds of New York*
> *Carry him to?*

178

***

One of the most enjoyable things about my Japanese adventure was bathing in various hot springs. First, I had to sit stark naked on a little wooden stool by a tap and scrub myself thoroughly until I had changed to the colour of a freshly cooked lobster. Only when most of my skin had disappeared down the plughole was I allowed to get into the hot, open-air mineral bath.

At one hotel in the mountains, the bath was outside on the roof. The temperature was sub-zero and the twinkling of the lights in the valley and the shimmering of snow on the mountains made a beautiful picture. The cloudless skies were full of stars and a full moon – the same moon and stars that would be shining over the Lake District in a few hours. It made me feel a little homesick.

Surprisingly, I was not homesick for English food, although the food in Japan was the strangest I had ever had. Breakfast included green soya gloop and hot Wasabi gunge that hit my sinuses and then the back of my eyes; there was raw fish so fresh that it almost swam to the plate, and lots of unrecognisable things displayed as art on beautiful, hand-thrown platters. It seemed sacrilege to disturb it. I wanted to paint it rather than eat it. Most of the time, I had no idea what I was putting in my mouth - which was possibly just as well, although there was nothing I didn't like. I asked about one dish, *taikoyaki*, and was told it was octopus balls. I didn't question further: I just ate them. I was never hungry, yet I lost weight – although that could have been due to all the effort required to actually get any food to my mouth with the chopsticks.

Another important Japanese custom that I found myself required to master - after sitting, eating, exchanging business cards and shoe-changing – was the Art of Bowing. In the West a simple handshake is enough for a new or business acquaintance. In Japan the protocol of greeting by bowing is much more complex.

179

Think of the Ronnie Barker sketch with three men in a row: 'I look up to him,' says the middle one, 'because he is upper class and he is better than me. I am middle class. And I look down on him because he is lower class.'

'I look down on him,' says the tall man on the left, 'because I am upper class.' And so it continues until the small man on the right says: 'I know my place!'

I had to know my place here in Japan - but where was it? In any encounter an instant assessment had to be made as to whether the person being greeted was worthy of more or less respect than me. If the person was providing a service – in a hotel, shop or gallery - then an incline of the head would be enough, and would be met with a bow from the waist. If the person was a friend or relative of my host, a deeper bow was required. This was mutual and simultaneous. It required quick decision-making and perfect appraisal of their social status. If the person I was greeting was a distinguished potter, then my bow of respect would have to be much lower than his. The Japanese learn this from birth.

'But how do I know the status of all I meet?' I asked Etsu.

'Just watch what I do and follow,' my patient guru replied. I was being schooled - again.

The following Sunday morning found us in the mountains that surrounded the large town of Nagano. I woke up on my futon on the floor of my tissue paper-walled hotel room to see thick snow and receive a seriously strict lecture from Etsu.

'This is an important day,' she said solemnly. 'We are going to visit a sword-maker. He is the son of Yukihara Miyairi, who was a National Living Treasure.'

I didn't like to point out I don't do swords. I was becoming polite and biddable with all Etsu's instruction and etiquette. I didn't recognise myself any more.

Kozaemon Miyairi had decided to become a sword-maker just months before the death of his father in 1978 and, after a long and arduous training, he was now a Master in his own right. A sword-making license in Japan is hard-earned (and rightly so).

Etsu schooled me thoroughly before the visit and I paid close attention. I must not upset a swordsman - the consequences could be dire.

'You must remove your shoes *gracefully* at the door, and put on slippers,' she said, giving me a hard stare. 'Then we will be led to an audience with the great man.'

I felt confident. I was getting better at the shoe pirouette.

'Sword-makers are greatly respected in Japan and we must bow low – very low. And you must stay down a long time.'

I had to forget any thought of political correctness and just get on with the bowing as low as I could go. The principle, as explained by Etsu, is that he who bows lowest and stays down longest gets maximum points. We practised several times until I'd cracked it. I demonstrated the lowness of my bow and received the Etsu nod of approval. I felt like a good pupil. I was determined to make up for my earlier mistakes. I respected my friend and I desperately wanted to please her.

Kozaemon Miyairi lived in a simple wooden house with a sloping, tiled roof and paper-thin walls. We were greeted at the door by an apprentice who led us through the building to a stark, minimalist room. There was a line of rope above the door from which metal strips - possibly swords in their first, raw state, hung like icicles. Etsu and I stood shoulder to shoulder like soldiers on parade in front of the simple table in the centre of the room. Then the apprentice solemnly carried in a long, lacquered, ornately decorated box which he placed ceremoniously on the table. This was followed by two more boxes. Then Kozaemon Miyairi made his entrance. He was dressed all in white, his loose, Judo top and trousers protected by an apron knotted with white string round his waist. He stood before us rather like a high priest and inclined his head slightly. He had a presence.

Etsu and I went into the full bow: legs straight, the crowns of our heads close to the floor, our hair grazing our feet. We stayed there for a long time. I was determined to be last up and kept flicking a glance sideways surreptitiously, to see if Etsu had come up. It was an embarrassingly long time before she unfolded her body slowly and I followed. I was proud to have won but Etsu was scowling at me as the apprentice opened one of the boxes and unwrapped the murderously long, thin sword from its soft white cotton covering.

As the sword-maker explained his art in Japanese, I understood nothing of what was said, but watched in horror as he demonstrated the sharpness of the Katana swords. Kozaemon placed one into my hands very carefully, having explained in grotesque mime that if I touched the blade it would take my finger off. As for what would happen if I dropped it...

The sword and handle were all one piece, but the handle was scored and rounded with Japanese characters etched down the length of it. I'd no idea what the inscription said, but Etsu told me afterward that Kozaemon had said it had been commissioned by a ruler in the Middle East. I shuddered at the power it might yield. It can take more than a year to make a sword and they are now sold for millions of yen. I hoped it was just a collector's piece, but these swords were made for fighting and execution. I felt I was hovering on the edge of an alien and dangerous world: a mediaeval world.

Etsu and I were not allowed into Kozaemon's forge as women are considered bad luck, but we were introduced to his children and served tea ceremoniously by his wife. When we took our leave it was amid much more bowing, but not so low this time as his wife apparently commanded much less respect. I was tempted to go lower but... no, I must conform to society's rules. Especially in a sword-maker's house.

As soon as we were back in the car, I was in trouble. I thought I had done so well I couldn't help crowing about it a bit. That was a mistake.

'Hey, I was last up,' I said.

Etsu tossed me a withering look.

'You were terrible,' she said. 'I don't know what he must have thought.'

'Hey, wait a minute! What did I do wrong? You're saying that because I won.'

I grinned as I said this. I was teasing her. Another mistake.

'Nobody won! This isn't a game. You are NOT supposed to peep sideways,' she said sternly. 'You're supposed to keep your head down straight.'

'But I did,' I protested. 'I only moved my eyes sideways. He couldn't see that!'

She ignored this. 'I showed you how to do it. It is a very bad thing to keep looking.'

I was chastened. We went off silently into Nagano town to see a kimono designer and maker. I promised to try to behave better.

The kimono-maker lived in a tiny flat in a large block, and we were warmly welcomed. In marked contrast to our reception at the sword-maker's, he and his wife bowed much more deeply than we did. He then showed us several beautiful garments that had been hand-sewn and printed. The kimono that he was making for Etsu, the purpose of our visit, was pale, heavy silk, with a minimal black stem curling round it and matching precisely at all the seams. It is no mean feat to print a very long piece of fabric and gauge where it will match up when wound around the body. Etsu tried it on with the traditional wide belt and the wooden platform shoes which required special white socks to fit the big toe and go round the thong in the sole. They were rather like flip flops, but I didn't mention that or I guessed I'd be in trouble again. Nor did I dare ask the price of the garment, but guessed it was several thousand pounds. It looked like a difficult and uncomfortable item to wear, but very glamorous. It suited Etsu's colouring and her petite frame perfectly.

There was one last stop on our itinerary before Tokyo: Mashiko, the home of Shoji Hamada, the initial inspiration for my trip. In reality, Mashiko was simply a long street lined with a succession of ceramic shops - I lost count at 50 - which led up to Hamada's compound. Inside were his thatched house, his workshop with his wheel still in working order just as he left it when he died in 1978, and his climbing kiln with its rounded chambers creeping up the slope like a giant caterpillar. The museum which housed Hamada's personal collection offered no possibility of my holding one of his pots again – everything was beautifully displayed and protected in glass showcases - but I felt I could relate to him in a different way having been to the place where he had lived and worked.

The bullet train got us back smoothly into Tokyo in two hours - Etsu explained proudly that the average delay on this miraculous transport system was six seconds – and we were soon back among the department stores of the big cities. These were vast emporia, often spanning several streets linked with fly-overs, and it was easy to get disoriented. I got lost several times; in the store where Sawa Kiyotsugu's exhibition was, I was also delayed at the chocolate counter for some time – they were handing out irresistible samples.

'You just take one,' Etsu admonished as if I were a naughty child. 'And you don't keep going back.'

The gallery covered the whole of the top floor - a vast space - and was full of Sawa's beautiful, misshapen pots. He immediately came over to greet me and led me round the exhibition. It was crowded. Red spots were going on everything. I studied the buyers: they looked very ordinary, but I noticed that a woman in a shabby brown coat had just bought a small pot at more than 150,000 yen – over a thousand pounds. I was impressed but sorry I was unable to communicate with her.

'Can you ask her why she has chosen it and what she's going to do with it?' I asked Etsu. 'Ask her if she's bought it to display and enjoy, or if it's an investment. Or is it both?'

'I can't translate that,' Etsu said. 'It's too impertinent.'

I was inclined to agree with her, so I will never know. Sawa led me to a group of sofas where his mates, all potters, all men, were gathered drinking tea. I was privileged to be invited to join them as an honorary male. Etsu watched uneasily from a safe distance, like a chaperone watching their debutante come out at the palace. Meanwhile, I was introduced as a gallery owner from England and all the business cards came out, accompanied by much bowing. I was really enjoying this now that I'd had some practice.

I stowed away all the business cards I had accumulated on this trip in a small bag I'd bought for the purpose and which was now bulging. The potters were a lovely bunch of people and I felt very comfortable with them, even though we didn't understand a word we were saying to each other. Fifteen years later, I still receive Christmas cards from some of them.

I would have liked to have bought some of Sawa's pots, but they were seriously out of my price range and wouldn't fit in my hand luggage. Besides which, I'd had so much hassle getting into this strange country that I didn't dare contemplate trying to get out with a huge misshapen pot worth several thousand pounds.

There was no way I could have done this trip without Etsu, to whom I will be forever grateful. I was not always a very good pupil and I think I presented her with far too many problems and embarrassments with which she dealt with great restraint and respect. Thanks to her, I gained a far greater insight into Japanese pottery and Japanese protocol.

As my leaving day approached, I began to worry about the airport: I was having flashbacks to my arrival in Osaka. I took leave of my marvellously patient friend and guide, caught the airport bus, and faced up to it. I'd made sure I had on my best matching underwear this time as well – just in case. At the airport, head held high, shoulders back, my fears became reality when I was asked to stand to one side with my luggage before I had even reached the check-in queue. I was in the naughty corner yet again. I was once more being singled out. I could see no other Westerners anywhere. I cringed as an officious-looking woman in severe grey uniform approached. I felt victimised. This was abuse and discrimination, I thought, feeling extremely indignant. She asked to see my tickets and passport, which she silently scrutinised for some time.

'Wait there please,' she said, giving me a grim look before marching away with my documents. Nobody else was being treated like this – but then they were all Japanese, weren't they?

Uh-oh, I thought, *here it comes,* as she returned some time later with an expressionless face. *I am never, ever coming to this mad country again.*

She handed me my passport and a boarding pass with two hands as though they were very precious, bowing from the waist as she did so.

'Would you mind very much if we upgrade you to First Class, Madam?' she asked, dipping her head again respectfully.

I was tempted to reciprocate with my full bow, but resisted. I *had* learned something about manners and protocol in my two weeks in Japan. I inclined my head and smiled. I would not spoil my chances now of wallowing in First Class luxury.

The Box

To: charlesoakley@cloud9.com
From: chris@castlegate.co.uk
Date: November 3rd 2009
Subject: Memories

Dear Charles,

I doubt you will get this message as I don't have a forwarding address, but I'm sending it anyway and hope it will reach you. We've lost touch, as they say, and I am missing dropping in for a small G&T on my way back from the Arts Council board meetings in Newcastle - sadly a lot more T than G as I'd be driving! You always took a vicarious pleasure in the art news and the gossip – you were hungry for it. Your tired eyes always brightened in welcome, especially when I came in and said 'You'll never guess what's happened now!'

I've been to see Anne since you left. That beautiful house on The Wall is redolent with your presence still. Your paintings are everywhere on the pale cream walls - they sing out - and your studio is exactly as you left it: the books and tools, the model aircraft flying across the wall like ducks, the ships suspended from the dado, the glass domes protecting interesting curiosities - and of course your boxes: each one a little theatre of ideas. The front covers of the New Yorker are still pasted up, edge to edge, on the downstairs toilet walls. Nothing has changed - except you are not there.

Miss you.
Chris

To: charlesoakley@cloud9.com
From: chris@castlegate.co.uk
Date: November 10th 2009
Subject: Memories

Dear Charles,

Do you remember the first time I came to see you, twenty odd years ago? Perhaps you don't, but I remember it vividly. There was a dead crow hanging on a thread inside your studio window – shades of Damian, but he hadn't invented himself then. Was it intended for maggot cultivation or was it a bird scarer? Either of these was hard to believe, because the house and your studio were immaculately clean and tidy. You never told me what that crow was about. I asked, but got just an enigmatic smile in return.

It was the late Eighties and I had only just opened the gallery and I was looking for artists. (I still am – I am always looking for artists.) You generously agreed to see me, though it was a busy time for you. The work I saw that day was impressive: detailed watercolours and exquisite three-dimensional hinged boxes which opened out slowly to reveal incidents from history or clever takes on famous artists. Ordinarily I don't go for meticulous work, preferring some things to be left to the imagination, but you always left enough unsaid – almost too much, sometimes. Mysteries attracted you and your work was full of them: you based several boxes on the 1924 Mallory/Irvine Everest expedition, drawn by the puzzle of whether they died before or after reaching the summit. There was a personal connection, too: Mallory and Irvine once lived near your grandmother in Birkenhead, and during your army career you were posted to Darjeeling: you could see Everest on a clear day from the top of Tiger Hill, you said.

Nothing was what it seemed in your work, and it often wasn't clear what was painted and what was a carefully placed three-dimensional model. You would sit there on your grandfather's sea chest and watch me struggle to work things out. You always made me do the work: bet you don't know how many times I made a diversion to the reference library in Carlisle on the way back from your house to follow up a clue. If only Google had been invented at the beginning of our business relationship - it would have made my life so much easier.

As we talked that day, I was aware that Anne was quietly packing for a trip. You showed me two open-ended first class air tickets to Chicago, which had been sent to you by a mysterious multi-millionaire called Fred who was a collector of your work. I could hardly believe that – nor could you. His invitation had come totally out of nowhere. You said you'd only met him once for about 30 seconds at an opening at your London dealer's, and now he'd commissioned you to do three works based on three Chicago houses (well, one was an apartment). You didn't look like the sort of artist who would paint to commission, but Fred had arranged everything - even a chauffeur and housekeeper to look after you in his town house. It sounded to me suspiciously like the beginning of a Sarah Paretsky crime novel and I was slightly worried for you, but Anne's quiet efficiency and your calm insouciance reassured me. I was happy for you and curious about the trip. What if the houses were boring suburban houses? Would the housekeeper be a Mrs Danvers? Would Fred turn out to be a mad control freak? I left you with my imagination running riot, wondering if I'd ever see you again.

As I left that first day you promised to contact me when you got back from Chicago. I knew you would. By now I was desperate to know more about you and your work and the mysterious Fred. I also wanted an Oakley exhibition. I think you knew that, but you wanted to make me earn it - not in a malicious way: I don't think you have a malicious thought in you – but as a challenge. I had to prove myself to get it.

Yours,
Chris

To: charlesoakley@cloud9.com
From: chris@castlegate.co.uk
Date: December 4th 2009
Subject: Anne

Dear Charles,

Called in to see Anne yesterday on my way back from Newcastle. We were talking about you, of course. She was trying to remember details of that wonderful trip to Chicago. I bet you remember it well.

I told her how excited I was to be invited for lunch after you'd recovered from jet lag – also relieved that you were back and it wasn't a scam. She told me what a success the trip had been. Everything had come to pass as the prophets - and Fred - had foretold, but in a way that exceeded all expectations. A chauffeur-driven limo was waiting for you at O'Hare and Fred's town house was right on the Chicago waterfront, within walking distance of the city centre. Donna, the young housekeeper, was friendly and looked after both you and Anne very well, and you soon began work on your boxes. The town house was easy because you were living in it. The apartment was the most difficult of the three - tricky because it had to be done secretly. All you knew was that it was a surprise gift for the occupants: a couple whose very young baby made their movements unpredictable. A clandestine commission was perfect for you, though, and Sam the chauffeur kept watch to allow you to take photographs before the owners returned. You never met them. You never met Fred. His country house was in the leafy, affluent suburbs and was very grand, but he was away in Europe at the time of your visit. It must have been weird to have such an elusive client - but I suppose it was an advantage to be left completely free to do as you wished. In any case, it all sounded unbelievably fascinating and romantic.

After lunch, you showed me the finished commissions before they were couriered to Fred. I was astonished. The craftsmanship and imagination were superb: three little boxes each depicting the exterior of a house, each standing on a beautifully crafted easel, each opening up on tiny hinges to reveal hidden treasures inside. The town house, with its canopied front door, opened to reveal a black-and-white tiled hall like the one you have used so often in your Vermeer studies. The curved staircase, the paintings on the wall showing other rooms in the house, the bronze lurchers guarding a door at the end of the hallway; all were so well conceived. It made me want to pass the canine sentries, open the door and see what was beyond.

The box of the country house was even more imposing, with its sweeping drive and classical portico. Inside, miniature paintings on the walls showed the interiors of other rooms. You hadn't forgotten the back of the box, either: if you lifted it from its easel and turned it over, you found a fountain in the moonlight on the back. Gosh you were clever. But the clandestine apartment box was the cleverest of all, with a scale model of an antique baby carriage standing at the front on the balcony - a gift to the young owners from Fred and his wife (although Anne and I agreed it looked very uncomfortable for a newborn...) the French windows opening to reveal a painting of the room within.

All three called for close scrutiny. You noticed things – small things – and everywhere there were witty references to the owners: things you had picked up on in your brief time inside each place. Your attention to detail was impeccable... as ever.

Yours,
Chris

To: charlesoakley@cloud9.com
From: chris@castlegate.co.uk
Date: 2nd January 2010
Subject: Stop press news

Dear Charles,
Exciting news. Michael and I just made a serious New Year resolution to go to Chicago. I've wanted to go ever since you told me about your mystery trip all those years ago, and Michael is crazy about minimalism, modern architecture and

jazz (but that's why you two got on so well). It's his sixtieth birthday in May, so that seemed a good excuse for a visit to a city renowned for all three.

There is a new spirit of urgency these days. You felt this, I know. You wisely told me to do everything - take every opportunity before the energy was sapped out and I was too old to do it. The years are passing quickly, so I've got on with it. We've done lots of research; looked at plans of the city, located the architectural gems we want to see and investigated hotels and transport. I was just about to book the flights when I remembered Fred and your commission. More than twenty years on, things must have changed. I'm wondering if he still lives in Chicago and whether he still has your boxes. Does he still own those houses? I'd love to find them. I have no idea what age he will be. I called and asked Anne but she has no idea. Of course she hasn't – she never met him. I'm wondering how I can locate him - Fred the invisible man.

I'm going to try. You've taught me how to research and not give up until I have the answers.

Thank you Charles. Wish me luck.
Chris

To: charlesoakley@cloud9.com
From: chris@castlegate.co.uk
Date: January 11th 2010
Subject: The detective

Dear Charles,
I reckon you'll be proud of me: I have begun the detective work systematically as though I am researching one of your paintings. All I have to work with is a man called Fred who once had a house on the Chicago waterfront, together with my twenty-year-old memories of three boxes of three houses. Of all the mysteries you have confronted me with, this is the most challenging. I've spent ages on Google Earth which shows me

miles and miles of Chicago waterfront. There are only a few houses – it is all skyscrapers along the lakeside. I know what the front door of the house looks like from the photograph of your box, but that is too long a shot. I can't get a view of front doors on Google amid the forest of tall buildings.

I'll keep going. No worries.
Chris

To: charlesoakley@cloud9.com
From: chris@castlegate.co.uk
Date: January 20th 2010
Subject: Fred

Dear Charles,
Just got back from London and the opening of a Percy Kelly exhibition at Messum's in Cork Street. (80% sold on the opening night!). It was the London Art Fair in Islington, too – a bit hit-and-miss, as usual - but I also managed to see a couple of good exhibitions. I'm still on the Chicago case, of course.
A few weeks ago, I wrote to your toffee-nosed Mayfair dealers. I explained about my connection to you. They must have known about your exhibitions at Castlegate House. All I asked was for my enclosed letter (unsealed, so they could check it out) to be forwarded on to Fred if he was still around. They haven't bothered to reply. I bet they would have replied if I'd been intending to buy some expensive piece of art. I usually get on OK with fellow dealers but I think yours feel they are superior to a small northern gallery... So I called in person. It's a very discreet place, isn't it? I pressed the buzzer for entry. The receptionist stared at me through the glass door with distaste. She was looking me over to see if I was worth admitting to the holy ground. She hesitated too long. I stared her out. She eventually pushed the button when she realised that I wasn't going to admit defeat and wander off. Once inside, she was totally negative. The boss appeared at my

insistence, but he wouldn't tell me anything. They refused to tell me if Fred was still alive, nor would they tell me his surname or even forward on a letter. They had some interesting pieces on the walls by John Hoyland, a Royal Academician friend, and I would have liked to spend a little time with them, but I was quickly shown the door - literally. I felt like a bag lady. Guess they thought I couldn't afford a Hoyland - and they're probably right: some of his command six-figure sums now. Dream on!

Anyway, I'm not giving up on Fred. We have time. I will do some detective work and try to crack it. It would be a pity to be in Chicago and not follow up your work.

I'll keep you posted.
Chris

P.S. If you think of Fred's surname, try to get a message to me somehow.

To: charlesoakley@cloud9.com
From: chris@castlegate.co.uk
Date: February 3rd 2010
Subject: Success

Dear Charles,
I'm so excited I'm beside myself. I've done it! I've found Fred. I can't tell you how but it is through friendly contacts in the London art scene who are not as precious as your dealers. They didn't hand over any information, of course, but they kindly forwarded my letter telling Fred of our connection and asking him if he still has your boxes. To my delight, an enthusiastic email has just dropped into my inbox from Fred, assuring me that he is still in Chicago, that all the houses are still standing, and that he and his wife still treasure all your works: 'Charles' work is wonderful and deserves to be remembered. If we can help in any way please let us know.'

Hey, there's an accolade for you. He sounds really nice.

I have replied immediately telling him we will be visiting Chicago in the spring to look at Art and Architecture, and asking if it will be possible to meet him and see your boxes.

Fingers crossed, eh?
Chris

To: charlesoakley@cloud9.com
From: chris@castlegate.co.uk
Date: February 6th 2010
Subject: Chicago

Dear Charles,
What news! I am so excited I can hardly type this. Fred replied to my email straight away. He is enthusiastic and wants to know the dates when we are visiting: he has suggested late spring when the weather will not be too extreme. He's hoping we can find the time to meet up and look at his paintings and boxes.

We're now madly finding flights and looking for hotels: we want to stay somewhere nice and central as it's a special birthday celebration after all. I also need to arrange cover for the gallery - wonder if we can manage two weeks away..?

This is so exciting.
Chris

To: charlesoakley@cloud9.com
From: chris@castlegate.co.uk
Date: February 10th 2010
Subject: Unbelievable

Dear Charles,
Just got an email from Fred. You will not believe this. He says that early May will be good – the cold winter will be over

but it will not be too hot – and he has offered us his town house. The town house, Charles! The one on the waterfront where you stayed! This is unbelievable. He has no idea who we are. He has never met us. What generosity! Of course, it's our connection with you that has worked the magic. Thank you so much. We'll be celebrating Michael's birthday in Chicago!

I've booked our flights and I'll keep you posted.
Chris

To: charlesoakley@cloud9.com
From: chris@castlegate.co.uk
Date: May 5th 2010
Subject: From the waterfront house

Dear Charles,

Hope you can do email where you are. Do you have broadband? Hope so. Bet you get better speeds than us in rural Cumbria – it's pathetically slow!

Guess what? You won't believe this, but I am writing from Fred's house on North Lake Shore Drive, Chicago. I am in the sitting room, in one of the elegant, pale green chairs which I am certain you will have occupied. (Michael's already had it upside down and says it's a genuine Chippendale.) We are living in one of your boxes!

We landed at O'Hare yesterday and I admit I was feeling a little uncertain. It was just like a dream – I kept thinking it might be. All I had was the address and telephone number that Fred had given me. I asked the surly cab driver if he knew North Lake Shore Drive and he gave me a killer glance, yawned, scratched his belly and asked what number. Then, without a word, he shot off at speed through acres of suburban grot – shabby industrial estates, rundown shopping centres, abandoned wastelands - all unimpressive. Dusk was falling as we hit the city. Michael sat up smartly and nudged me as we got our first glimpse of the skyscrapers silhouetted against the

darkening evening sky. He soon picked out the Sears Tower -
now the Willis Tower – and the John Hancock Tower looming
black behind it. His Mastermind specialist subject would be
iconic buildings. We were pressing our faces to the cab
window, cricking our necks to look up to them – it was like
being at the bottom of a Grand Canyon of buildings – when
suddenly we emerged from the tunnel of concrete and glass out
into fading light and the shore of the lake. I couldn't see the
other side: it makes our English lakes look like dew ponds. I'm
going to love this city even more than New York, I think.

Anyway, heading north on the expressway by the lakeside
we abruptly pulled off onto a slip road and screeched to a halt
on the forecourt of a skyscraper apartment block with a really
fancy entrance: liveried doorman, concierge, corporate
sculpture.

'This isn't it,' I whispered to Michael.

I leaned forward and showed the bit of paper with the
address on to the driver.

'That's it, lady,' said the cab driver, nodding across the
side road.

I followed his gesture. I was astonished. You didn't
prepare me for this, Charles. You never told me Fred's house
was a four-storey, double-fronted mansion. But I knew it was
the right place because I recognised the front door with the
porte cochère canopy from your box. We paid off the taciturn
cab driver, who was disgruntled because the size of our tip was
not commensurate with our assumed billionaire status - but
then, we figured that everything disgruntled him - and made
our way to the door, where the housekeeper welcomed us
inside.

'Hi,' she said with a big smile. 'Welcome. My name's
Donna.'

Yes, Charles: Donna, twenty-something years older. She
remembered you and Anne well.

What a funny feeling it was to go inside: just like walking
into one of your boxes. The bronze dogs, the black-and-white

check tiles, the elegant, pale yellow chaise longue - all were the same. The colours were identical, too.

I still wonder how you did that. You always said colour blindness was an advantage to a painter: you painted what you saw, and if it wasn't what other people saw – well, was that important? We all see colour in different ways, you said. But that left so many questions unanswered. You told me you blagged your way through the army tests, but how did you get into the Slade? How did you teach those generations of students? More of your mysteries.

As Donna made us tea, I asked where the nearest supermarket was. She just smiled and shrugged and showed us the well-stocked fridge and drinks cupboard. (It turns out there's one on every floor.) She told us we'd just to tell her what we wanted and she would get it - Fred had said we must just help ourselves.

Michael and I were a little anxious about managing all the stairs with our luggage, but a door in the hall disguised a beautiful antique elevator complete with zigzag metal concertina gate, brass fittings and mahogany panels – a real period piece. You must have used that lift.

I've got to send this right now. I'm falling asleep as I type. Jet lag has caught up.

Chris

To: charlesoakley@cloud9.com
From: chris@castlegate.co.uk
Date: May 6th 2010
Subject: Day one. Time 18.30

Dear Charles,
Did you and Anne sleep in the four-poster bed with the yellow, flower-sprigged silk drapes? Between the finest Egyptian cotton sheets, and on the softest goose-down pillows? Did you wake up to a pink sunrise over the lake this morning as

we did? The sense of unreality deepened until I saw the untidy heap of clothes that we had left strewn across the yellow silk chaise longue last night before falling into bed. This isn't a dream. I really am here in Chicago, staying in the house of a rich American I've never met.

We've just had breakfast on the roof terrace (there's a fridge up here as well!). It's like sitting in the Gods at the theatre. Joggers with bobbing ponytails go up and down on the lakeside track, keeping to their appointed lane, while cyclists and dog walkers do likewise. A day of luxury, comfort and interest lies before us. I could easily get used to the millionaire lifestyle.

Chris

To: charlesoakley@cloud9.com
From: chris@castlegate.co.uk
Date: May 7th 2010
Subject: happy birthday

Dear Charles,

I think we've found Fred! We've met the family, anyway – can't miss them. They inhabit every surface in this house: they stand on the table by our bed, on the window ledges and mantelpieces - they even watch us in the bathrooms. They are a handsome bunch, archetypal Americans – small children engaged in sporting activities and parties, lovely brides, tall men, and slender, elegant, well-groomed women. It's a dynasty - like Bill Gates meets the Kennedys.

On a round Sheraton table in the library there are sporting photographs and, oh joy, in the middle is one of your boxes. It's one I've never seen. It is a simple, hinged box in the shape of a boat, resting on an exquisitely fashioned miniature easel. When the box is closed, it shows a life buoy in jaunty red and white with the boat's name – INSATIABLE - mounted on wooden boards. On opening, a fully-rigged sailing boat is

199

revealed. It seems to be competing in a race, and a man I assume to be Fred stands in the foreground, dressed in yellow oilskins.

Charles, you would be proud of me! After some time browsing among the bookshelves in the library, I have discovered that in 1987 Insatiable *won the Newport Regatta and went on to represent America in the Admiral's Cup. So Michael and I are now scouring the bookshelves to fit the rest of the family jigsaw together. It's strange to be living in the house of someone you don't know.*

Perhaps when we meet Fred we will find out more - I will keep you posted.

Gotta dash – we're going out to a wine bar we've spotted a few blocks away in Schiller Street for a birthday dinner. They've got free Wifi so I can send this.

Chris

To: charlesoakley@cloud9.com
From: chris@castlegate.co.uk
Date: May 8th 2010
Subject: Train

Dear Charles,
Me again. I may have solved another of the mysteries you left with me. This morning I asked Donna - the fount of all knowledge - if there was a broadband connection in the house.
'You'll have to ask Train for the pass code,' she said.
'Train?'
'Ah, Train lives in the basement flat. He's at school here. He's Fred's nephew. Just go down the back stairs and knock on his door. I think he'll be there now.'
Train is a dark, handsome young man of about twenty. When he told me the access code, I couldn't help asking about his unusual name. You know what I'm like.
'Is Train your nickname?'

'No. It's my real name. I was christened Night Train, in fact.'

He saw my brain working the possibilities over – was he conceived on a train, perhaps? - and he smiled a charming smile.

'I'm named after a legendary baseball player: Night Train. And Fred's my uncle – my dad's brother.'

Another clue to the family tree. For a baseball virgin it meant nothing, but later I began to speculate. I wonder if this young man was the baby in the pram in your second Chicago box? His age fits. I didn't go back and disturb him again, though.

I'll get this sent before we set off to explore.

Best
Chris

To: charlesoakley@cloud9.com
From: chris@castlegate.co.uk
Date: May 9th 2010
Subject: Oak Park

Dear Charles,
Guess what? Just had a telephone call from Fred's secretary. We're not going to meet him. Now that's a surprise. He's in Europe on business and we'll be gone when he gets back. He sends his apologies. He sure is elusive.

She enquired how we are getting on, and then asked if we had any free days. Well, our diary isn't fixed – it's just a tick list of things we want to do once we've oriented ourselves. Apparently, all your paintings are in the country house, and she wondered when we'd like Sam to come and take us there to see them.

'Oh,' she went on, 'Fred says that as you are interested in architecture, would you like Sam to take you to Oak Park to see the Frank Lloyd Wright houses? If you have time?'

Well you can imagine my reply. I think we can find the time, don't you? Sam is coming tomorrow at 9.00 a.m. We're off to climb some skyscrapers now to get our bearings.

Chris

To: charlesoakley@cloud9.com
From: chris@castlegate.co.uk
Date: May 10th 2010
Subject: Oak Park continued

Dear Charles,
Me again. The big black limo pulled up outside at 8.55 a.m. and waited in Goethe (rhymes with 'hurt her') Street at the side of the house. Did you notice that all the streets in this area are named after philosophers? A walk to the wine bar a few blocks away is an adventure in nineteenth-century philosophy.

Did you and Anne go to Oak Park? I don't suppose so, because if you had there would have been another box: the Frank Lloyd Wright story is full of drama and disaster – just your bag. FLW was a brilliant avant-garde architect. He built in Oak Park in 1889 for himself and his family, and constructed it around a large oak tree.

Young, forward-looking, 'modern' couples then rushed to commission him to build their houses: practical, workable homes full of light and beauty, each individually designed to meet their lifestyles.

They are liberally dotted about this suburban area, all within walking distance of each other. Together they formed a community which centred on the man himself, who lived and worked among them. He caused a scandal, though, when he fell in love with one of his Oak Park clients, leading ultimately to divorce, tragedy and exile with an ultra-dramatic finale of murder, arson and bankruptcy. You could make a marvellous box about that.

Sam is taking us to the country house tomorrow.
Good night my friend. Sleep well.
Chris

To: charlesoakley@cloud9.com
From: chris@castlegate.co.uk
Date: May 11th 2010
Subject: A day In the country

Dear Charles,
After speeding along suburban expressways, we walked into another of your boxes today. That beautiful country house is something else, isn't it? The limo drew in under a magnificent, classical-columned portico and we mounted the steps to another impressive front door. This house dwarfs our town mansion. Set in many acres of ornamental gardens, in a leafy, exclusive country park, it is a delight. I think Fred has bought the house next door and demolished it to make more garden since you were there. An elderly Irish terrier was enjoying the sunshine on the immaculate striped lawn, nestled contentedly in a designer dog basket from Saks. It is an enviable dog's life! Gardeners, painters, and house maintenance people were all busy around the place.
The housekeeper who greeted us pointed out the pieces you had made, Charles: a box of the Florida house, one of the Irish house, and one commemorating a trip to Russia. You are a dark horse, Charles Oakley. I bet you have photographs of paintings that you've never shown me. And then there was the box of 'our' waterfront house, in the sun lounge. It was far more exquisite than I ever remembered and means so much more now we are living in it. I can see that very little has changed since you made it, although I do now know that it's a breakfast room and snug which lies behind the half-opened door that had intrigued me when I first saw it. They were your trademark, those doors standing slightly ajar: another mystery.
I hadn't seen the box since that luncheon at your house in

1989 - more than twenty years ago, Charles – and it sent shivers up my back. I desperately wanted to talk to you about it. Your presence was palpable in this house. I thought I caught sight of you wandering through the oval dining room, which is currently being redecorated (hand-painted murals in the arches). Was that you on the ornate staircase which curls up above the grand piano? Or on the terrace by the pool, sketch book in hand? I imagined you turning towards me, one eyebrow raised, smiling approval. You were there in spirit – whatever that means.

What a time we are having. And all thanks to you.
Chris

To: charlesoakley@cloud9.com
From: chris@castlegate.co.uk
Date: May 13th 2010
Subject: Lake Shore Drive

Dear Charles,
Just a snippet while I think of it – it will amuse you. We did the John Hancock Tower today. This solid, looming black edifice has gone up since you were here - in fact, I suspect the nearby Gallery of Modern Art is post-Oakley too. The John Hancock Tower is almost as high as the Sears, but not quite. There's an audio guide in the Observatory at the top and a glass platform you can step out onto. The thought of it sets my stomach into a spin.

Of course, we immediately made for the north side and after much squinting through the telescope we could just make out our own 'little' house among the giant towers. The roof garden where we had just breakfasted is best seen from here. It is a microscopic dot in a sea of skyscrapers, even when magnified. The audio tour informed us: 'You are now looking north along Lake Shore Drive. This is Chicago's Gold Coast and Lake Shore Drive is the fanciest address in Chicago.'

Michael and I are staying in the finest house at the fanciest address in Chicago. We had a private giggle about that. What a place to use as a base to explore the galleries and parks, the architecture and shops. We feel we are the luckiest people on earth at this moment.

Chris

To: charlesoakley@cloud9.com
From: chris@castlegate.co.uk
Date: May 19th 2010
Subject: Home again

Dear Charles,
We are now back in Cumbria. What an experience. It has been good to share it with you, as only you can fully understand what it was all like.

I have a last piece of gossip. North Lake Shore Drive is on the market. At $5.5million. We have the sales brochure. What a shame we are just a few million short of the asking price. Never mind, we now know what it feels like to live like millionaires.

I'll leave you in peace now. Hope you enjoyed my letters.

Catch up with you sometime.
Chris

To: charlesoakley@cloud9.com
From: chris@thepinkegg.co.uk
Date: May 13th 2015
Subject: Vermeer

Dear Charles,
Sorry it's been so long: life has been rather hectic the last five years since I wrote to you.

Do you remember the first exhibition you had at Castlegate House in 1991? I coveted a box in that show -

Vermeer's Floor - *but I couldn't afford it then and I sold it to someone else. I felt quite jealous when it was collected at the end of the exhibition.*

Well, it's just come up for auction. I really don't need another piece of art, but I couldn't let it slip through my fingers again. I put in a bid, and I've just collected it from the local auction room.

I'm looking at it now as it sits on my desk in front of me, and I feel as though I'm looking into a room in a Vermeer dolls' house. As an artist, he fascinated you because he's a mystery man like you. He only completed 40 paintings in his lifetime and his house in Delft no longer exists. So you studied all his paintings and made a reconstruction of it, drawing on the research you did when you took your students to Holland to study the Dutch masters every year.

This room has a chequered tile floor and a black timbered ceiling, and a skirting board of blue-and-white Delft tiles. The perspective is so clever that it looks three-dimensional, but the painting is flat and stands out against the black surround. And, just as with Vermeer's work, there are paintings within the painting.

There is an exquisite miniature copy of The Music Lesson, *and through a painted doorway, a glimpse of* View of Delft from the Rotterdam Canal. *The painting on the right wall of the box is a puzzle - it isn't a Vermeer but after a morning's research I've identified it as* The Procuress; *a painting by his contemporary Dirck van Baburen. It was owned by Maria Thins, Vermeer's mother-in-law, who lived with her daughter and son-in-law – it also appears hanging behind the piano in Vermeer's* The Concert. *It gave me a frisson of excitement when I found that link. So there's a painting within a painting again.*

More soon,
Chris

To: charlesoakley@cloud9.com
From: chris@thepinkegg.co.uk
Date: May 25th 2015
Subject: Vermeer again

Dear Charles,

So far so good, but your box has left me with one more mystery to solve. Through a painted doorway to the left, there's a grim-faced woman lurking behind a curtain, her arms folded. She is dressed in a plain grey dress with a white puritan collar piece. Who is she? Is this Maria Thins, the dreaded mother-in-law, or is she a servant? Is she eavesdropping on The Music Lesson? You never put anything into your works that weren't of significance. I'd love to be able to drop in at your house on Hadrian's Wall, sip a G & T, and persuade you to give me another clue. Until then I just want to tell you how much I cherish this beautiful box.

Many thanks, Charles, for your friendship, generosity, and all the things you taught me.

Chris

Postscript: Charles Oakley 1925-2008

Charles Oakley's last box was the one at his funeral. An anagram of 'funeral' is 'real fun', and his was just that.

We entered the crematorium to the music of Chris Barber's jazz band and Ottilie Patterson's lush voice, and we marched out to a rousing Colonel Bogey. It was impossible not to smile, seeing everyone fall in step to the rhythm. Charles welcomed the unexpected, and the quietly delivered eulogy was a revelation. His modesty astounded me: he had achieved so much that I knew nothing about – the awards he had garnered as a star pupil at the Slade, and his exhibition at the Crane Calman Gallery which had been opened by Lowry. In 1999,

Charles won the Singer Friedlander/*Sunday Times* Watercolour Prize – I wish I'd asked him more about all these things when I had the chance. He will always be the Mystery Man to me now. And I'll never know now why there was a dead crow hanging in the window that first time I set foot in his studio. Perhaps it was a bird scarer – but that would have been disappointingly simple for Charles.

Adam and Eve

'Art colleges are a playground for ideas'
Grayson Perry Reith Lecture.

Degree shows are a must for finding fresh talent but need to be approached with caution. Prepare to be surprised, frustrated, stimulated and annoyed. Art students, on the whole, have no sense of the commercial, no sense of urgency, and no sense of time. But why should they? Art colleges are a playground for ideas, even if many of those ideas are impractical and non-commercial. However, if you have the stamina to fight your way through the grunge, they can be happy hunting grounds if you're a gallerist in search of hidden treasure.

There was a big queue outside Edinburgh College of Art when I arrived for the opening evening of their degree show. As I waited for admittance, I glanced along the chattering line. Some of these people would be friends and family of the students; others would be collectors or gallery owners hoping to spot the next big thing. This historic place had seen many of the top Scottish artists through its impressive porticos. The trick was to find the future stars before they became such and get them before anyone else.

I had an assignation with a young Japanese painter whose work I had noticed a month previously through the floor-to-ceiling glass doors of a commercial office block in Edinburgh. Her large, minimal abstract canvas was a focal point in the reception area.

I went inside to enquire further and the surprised receptionist told me the architect or estate agent had plundered the art college just a few blocks away for large pieces of art to brighten the place up and make it more attractive to potential tenants. I got in touch with the artist straight away. We spoke on the telephone. She was delighted that I had noticed her work and invited me to her final degree show. She was enthusiastic about her upcoming display and I was really looking forward to meeting her and seeing more of her work. She was a final year student so I thought I might be able to persuade her to give me an exhibition.

Once inside the palatial marble hall of the college, I immediately found her stand. It was in pole position, facing the entrance – one of the first you'd see on entering. I could see why she'd been allocated that space. Her clean, minimal acrylics on canvas stood out among the classical iconic columns. This was sheer quality. But there was no sign of the artist herself, despite my firm appointment. I hung around in hope for quite a while.

'I think she's round the pub,' a student at a neighbouring stand told me at last. 'You can leave a message if you like.'

I didn't like but I did leave my mobile number and a message in case she happened to remember and extricate herself from the celebrations. It was short, sharp and to the point. Then with a shrug I went off to look for fresh talent elsewhere. I battled through rooms of flickering videos, inscrutable mixed media creations and installations that would have confused the college cleaners: to bin or not to bin, that must have been their question. Frustrated, I felt like going to the pub as well, but I carried on stoically and was rewarded. I found eager, fresh-faced graduate Sarah Carrington that evening and I immediately offered her a show at Castlegate the following year. Her paintings shone out from an obscure corner of the MA exhibition room. Her seascapes were spectacular. I asked her if she exhibited her work anywhere.

'Oh yes, it's showing at The Elephant House at the moment,' she said.

'At the zoo?' I questioned with raised eyebrows. 'Won't they get trampled?'

She laughed. 'No – The Elephant House is a café in the old town near the uni and the Museum of Scotland.'

'Do you sell much there?'

'Not really,' she answered. 'Well, nothing so far - but fingers crossed.'

We met there the next day for coffee and I discovered a new delight. The café served great food and a vast array of speciality teas and coffees. It was to become even more special a few years later when J. K. Rowling revealed she had written the first Harry Potter book at one of the rough wooden tables. These days it is so busy it is hard to get in. I wonder whether she had been there, scribbling away in a corner, on the day that I met Sarah.

It was clearly a good place for literary inspiration but not for a gallery. Paintings don't sell themselves, they need human intervention. Sarah's paintings were hung so high and so close together they were seen as part of the décor, the majority of which was student posters.

In time, Sarah's work hit Glasgow and then London; however, throughout the many years of our relationship, she always kept her loyalty to Castlegate House.

Sarah wasn't my only discovery that evening at the college. I'd bagged a painter but my trawl of the sculpture department had yielded nothing suitable, as usual. Videos, yes. Installations, yes. Sculpture – no. Wandering in and out of depressing, confusing, interconnecting rooms, I reached the dead end of a dark corridor. There were just rows of lockers beyond, ending with a closed double door. *This'll be locked,* I thought as I casually pushed it. It resisted, so I pushed harder. Success.

I peered round the door and there before me was a flock of grazing sheep. They were life-size, luminous white and they were all giving me a stony look. It was disconcerting: their eyes seemed to follow me as I skirted the room sheepdog-fashion. Above them, the walls were hung with good sheep drawings – good drawings being a rare thing in art colleges these days. This student understood sheep; their anatomy, stance, habits. After a diligent search I discovered the artist was a mature student called Angela Hunter.

Angela was not in the pub – on the contrary, she was on the premises and keen.

'I like your flock,' I said, handing her a card. 'Do you think they'd like to graze in the gallery garden this summer?'

'Erm, thank you,' she replied, grinning, 'but I'll have to get my recipe right first.'

'What? Have you got sheep cookbooks then?'

'Sort of,' she said. 'These are mainly cast in concrete and they're very heavy – much too heavy to lift. I've learned that the hard way and hurt my back. Also I don't think they're frost-proof – they might crack. I daren't actually sell any until I've solved those problems. I'm currently experimenting with a fibreglass mixture. Look, that one there is fibreglass.'

She walked over and picked it up fairly easily. I liked this woman. She was positive. She was a problem solver and she had integrity.

'I can wait,' I said.

Months later, Angela invited me to her studio. She'd been experimenting with materials and was now ready to deliver a whole flock of mixed origins. The fibreglass really worked. We fixed an exhibition date.

'How will we get them to the gallery?' I asked with some trepidation. This was my habitual query.

'No problem. My husband has a garage and low loader.'

Hallelujah! This was good news – delivery problems solved.

A few weeks later, Angela and her husband left Edinburgh at midday to drive south. The sixteen sheep stood on the low loader two-abreast and were covered with a tarpaulin that had been firmly tied down. Unfortunately, it was a windy day and the ropes gradually loosened, unnoticed. The tarpaulin blew off as the cavalcade passed Gretna on the A74, north of Carlisle. They pulled off the road and decided to pack up the covering and carry on without it. Exposed to full view, the sheep looked so realistic that in Carlisle they brought traffic to a halt as they glided through the city centre on the dual carriageway. We're used to seeing sheep on the move up here on fellsides – grazing in fields, transported in trucks - but never standing on an open low loader. What a sensational sight they made as they came through Cockermouth: glistening white, immobile. We hauled them into the garden and they seemed to be grazing naturally under the trees. The Campbells from the nearby Sheep and Wool Centre came round with their trained sheepdog for a press photo shoot. The poor thing became confused by the animals' lack of response and I fear may have needed canine therapy after the experience.

All Angela's sheep sold. I bought one of them – I couldn't resist it. It stood in the garden for years and startled many a sheep farmer with its realism until first its ears and then its legs fell off - but that took many years of exposure to the weather, and there's a lot of weather about up here.

Angela and Sarah were the exceptions. Most students, I discovered, had no idea how galleries worked or had even begun to understand how to earn a living.

At the Carlisle College of Art degree show the following year I thought I'd struck gold again. Do I never learn? Towards the end of my trawl (which had yielded nothing), I came upon a heap of massive tree trunks casually arranged teepee-style in the middle of a studio floor. The carving on them was primitive and simple. These semi-supine figures had faces, genitals, and not much else. But they had the potential to be powerful and interesting: like the Moai figures which stand guard on the coast of Easter Island in the Pacific Ocean. I circled them several times. I imagined a line of them on the big lawn. They were probably not saleable as they stood – because standing was what they didn't do, and that was the problem. But they'd look good in the garden, providing our gardener didn't put them on the bonfire.

Their student maker wasn't there. I wasn't surprised.

Students spend three or four years on an art course culminating in an exhibition to show what they have achieved in that time but some of them, rather than engage in a dialogue with those who have come to the opening of said exhibition, go off to the pub with friends to celebrate. If only they could hang on a little longer, they might find they really have something to drink to.

I left a note along with a gallery card which said:

'I like your primitive people very much. I'd like to purchase two or three. How much are you asking for them? Give me a ring.
Chris'.

Some time later, he did.

'Er... hello. You left me a note – at the college.'

'Ah, yes. You must be the man with the trees. Am I right?'

'Er... yes.

'Well, thank you for ringing. I really do like your figures. Did you sell any at the show?'

'Er... no.'

'How much are they?'

'Er... I don't know.'

'Are they for sale? I didn't see a price list. Can I buy two of them?'

'Er... no. I've sold them.'

Hang on, this wasn't making any sense. I was confused. I started again.

'You've sold them? All of them?'

'Yes.'

'How much for?'

'Well, I've sold them to my father in lieu of my student loan,' the voice at the other end of the line confessed.

'Did your father want them?'

'Er... I suppose so.'

'You suppose? Where are they now?'

'In the college where you saw them.'

'Where's your father?'

'In Northumberland.'

214

'Does he really want them? Wouldn't he rather have the money?'

'Er, I don't know. I've got to get them out of the college by the end of this week.'

'Right. So how will you get them to Northumberland?'

'I don't know. My father will probably get them moved.'

'Do they stand upright?'

'No, they fall over. That's why they were lying on the floor. I intended them to stand upright when I made them but they won't.'

He seemed to be blaming the felled trees for their perversity in not conforming to his intentions. I felt like screaming: 'Problem solving – it's part of the course! Make it work!' But I didn't.

'Shall I come back and meet you at the college and we can talk about it? I can possibly get them moved.'

Why oh why did I persist?

'I'm working all this week,' he said.

'Where do you work, then?'

He mentioned a Carlisle restaurant where he had a job as a waiter.

'Look, why don't you come and see me at the gallery when you get some time off? Have you been to Castlegate House Gallery in Cockermouth?'

'No.'

'Do you know where it is?'

'No.'

He didn't even follow up with the obvious question. He was devoid of curiosity. I was fast losing interest in the face of this negativity. Surely an art student in Carlisle ought to know about commercial art galleries nearby, especially one as high profile as Castlegate? I rang off thinking I would never see the artist or his work again, and that I really didn't care any more.

A week later I was impressed when the artist and his girlfriend turned up unannounced in a borrowed, battered car. He told me

215

that his father had just collected the sculptures from the college. I asked him whether he had told his father about my offer and he admitted rather shamefacedly that he hadn't. I didn't understand what was going on at all. I showed him round the garden and asked if he could make any more pieces. I wasn't hopeful. He prevaricated. I asked what he was going to do now he had graduated. He told me he was now working in a different Carlisle restaurant as a chef!

'Is that a promotion then?' I asked.

He shrugged.

'Do you like the job?'

'Not really, but it's a job.'

'Are you a good chef?'

'Dunno.'

'Is it well paid?'

I knew the answer to that: the catering trade was synonymous with long hours, poor pay and little reward. At this point, I wanted to slap him, but restrained myself, not only because he was a lot bigger than me but also because I was beginning to feel - and sound - like his mother. There was absolutely no future in this for me. I was wasting my time and his. Giving up, I put both him and his tree trunks out of my mind.

A good six months later, I arrived home late one evening, drove into the car park and froze. My headlights had caught something horrible in the corner. My heart was thumping. I switched my headlights to full beam, leaned forward and peered through the windscreen. Two twelve-foot-tall giants were leaning nonchalantly against the garden wall. They were blocking the gate. The taller of the two had glaring eyes and a long, dangling penis; his missus looked less fierce but with genitals clearly delineated. She was in need of a good bra.

Good God, I thought, *it's that student. He's delivered. Only six months late!*

There was no note with the figures, no address, no

telephone number, nothing. They couldn't stay where they were as they were blocking access into the garden. They wouldn't be stolen – they were far too unwieldy - but they would frighten people. A lot.

They were carved from the trunks of two mature elms with a diameter of about two foot. With a team of volunteers we moved them with difficulty into the garden where the next problem confronted me: they still had no means of support. The student had passed on his problem for me to solve. I couldn't just prop them up: Health and Safety wouldn't allow it. Each one weighed tons.

I visualised small children being crushed by them, arms and legs sticking out from underneath a fallen trunk. Quentin Blake's superb but frightening illustrations of Roald Dahl's books came to mind. We hauled them into the back yard, out of the public area, propped them up against the wash house wall and waited... and waited... and waited for the artist to get in touch. There was no communication at all. When I next went to Carlisle I peered into a few restaurants but I didn't see him. I even poked my nose into a few back kitchens, but by I'd now forgotten his name.

For months we all ducked and dodged between these two totems on our way to the coal shed. We held one-sided conversations with them – they were as forthcoming as their maker. I enquired at the college but they had no idea what had happened to him, nor did they care. They were on to the next intake now.

Time passed until one day I was startled by a familiar booming voice coming from the garden.

'Hey, what do you want for Adam and Eve?'

I went to the garden door. It was Tony Thursz, formerly one of the best gynaecologists in the country. Now retired, he lived in the farmhouse over at Ennerdale that he and his wife Josephine had owned for decades.

'What are you on about, Tony? Adam and Eve? I know

this garden's lovely but you're not in the Garden of Eden, you know.'

'I've just seen them through the gate into the yard,' he said, gesturing at the tree trunk figures. 'I think they'd look a lot better on our hillside than leaning against your wash house wall, don't you? They'd be perfect.'

'Oh, those! No, they're not perfect, Tony. They've been hanging about here, loitering without any intent and getting in the way of everybody for two years.'

'Yes, but I'd still like to buy them,' he persisted. 'What will you take for them?'

I explained how an ex-art student had dumped them in the car park one dark night, frightened me to death, and run away.

'I've forgotten his name - if I ever knew it - I don't have an address for him and I don't know how much he wants for them. Apart from that, they're yours. If he happens to turn up, I'll point him in your direction and you can sort it out between you.'

'I've got just the place for them,' Tony said again, apparently not in the least discouraged. 'Adam and Eve can stand guard by our new, small coppice. They'd love the sweeping view down the valley to the Irish Sea - if you'll let me have them.'

I knew that view down Tony's valley. Alfred Wainwright, the 'Patron Saint' of all the Lakeland fells, had described it as the most beautiful valley in the Lake District and not without justification.

'But Tony, they haven't stood since they were trees. This couple are in recline!'

'Bet I can make 'em stand up,' he laughed. 'I'll take 'em! Thank you so much.'

'You're welcome!'

The following day Tony and his woodman, Hicks, arrived to load the trunks onto a trailer. Side by side, Adam and Eve looked like a pair of recumbent mediaeval effigies as they were driven away.

The next time I had cause to drive over Cold Fell, I pulled off the road by the big boulder that marked the turn to the Thursz house and drove gingerly down the steep, rough track. Below me I could see the flight of ponds that Tony and his wife Jo had created as havens for wildlife. The first one had been dug as a birthday present for Jo. It would have turned out cheaper to have bought her a JCB because other ponds had followed to mark various birthdays and anniversaries. These were not insignificant garden pools, they were more like mini-lakes, but everything the Thurszes did was on a big scale. They had stocked the ponds with fish again and again; herons and otters plundered them at the same rate.

Trees that the couple had planted decades ago were coming into maturity, a red squirrel shot up a tree as I passed, and a large hare bounded across and away in front of me. The Thurszes' white farmhouse and barns sat comfortably on what was fast becoming a nature reserve.

As I drove along the bumpy track to their farmhouse, I noticed Adam and Eve leaning indolently against the barn wall in the yard. I had to smile.

'Still hanging about, then – these two wasters?' I teased Tony when he appeared.

'Just you wait,' he said quickly. 'I have a plan.' He showed me some very strong, large-diameter plastic piping he had found.

'They'll each fit into a ring,' he said.

'What, white plastic? It'll look terrible, Tony.'

'Come for lunch next Thursday,' he said. 'Trust me. You'll get a surprise.'

A week later, I was on my way to the Thurszes' again. After passing the landmark stone circle on top of the fell at the side of the road and hitting the farm track, I saw them, Adam and Eve, standing side by side and gazing down the valley. I stopped and blinked several times. This was the first time I'd ever seen them in a fully upright position. They were impressive. Tony was right: they fitted into the landscape perfectly with a copse of young birch saplings forming a perfect backdrop. There wasn't a hint of white plastic: Hicks the woodman had drilled and inserted a pole into the bottom of each tree trunk, painted them with preservative, fitted them into the loose plastic tubing, stood them upright, and poured cement in around them. He'd then placed stones round the plastic tubing; perfect camouflage. First Eve and then Adam had risen, standing for the first time since they had been felled. They looked proud and weathered. They looked as though they had stood in the same spot for centuries. They belonged.

That was twenty years ago and they are still there, still looking as prehistoric as the standing stones on the fell above them. The wood has grown up behind them – but of the artist there is still no sign.

Magic Knickers

'You know these magic knickers..?' she said.
I shook my head.

'You've not heard about them?'

'No, I haven't.'

She was astonished.

'Where are they?' I asked. 'These magic knickers? Are they at the McLellan Gallery?'

She looked puzzled.

'No of course not, they're at Marks and Spencer! It's just a few doors down from the gallery. As we're going that way I thought we could nip in. They're fabulous. They'll take you down a dress size, at least.'

She gave me a perceptive look. I was tucking into a beautifully arranged still life of neatly-sliced exotic tropical fruit, topped with pomegranate seeds, double cream and shavings of dark Belgian chocolate. I immediately put the spoon down.

You had to be sharp to pick up the thread of artist Enid Foote Watts' lively chatter, liable as it was to encompass high art, low art, lots of gossip, food and fashion tips and now, apparently, knickers. It all poured out in random order, stream-of-consciousness style. I loved it. She was like a walking, talking Sunday colour supplement.

It was always like this when I called to pick up more of her paintings. Whatever time of day I arrived, she would have some little delicacy waiting for me, and would always instruct me to sit in the window of her tiny second-floor flat, ostensibly to keep an eye on my car. It was a bright yellow Vauxhall Astra Estate and Enid loved it: she called it a boy racer's dream and warned me that there was still a need for vigilance.

Enid lived in what was once the notorious Gorbals area of Glasgow: on the south bank of the Clyde, it had once been described as the most dangerous place in Britain, home to the Razor Gang and with drunkenness and crime rampant among the tenements. But whenever I looked out of her window down to the street below it was always deserted and peaceful. I could even catch glimpses of the river, although in the 1930s the view would have been blocked by rows of depressing slum tenements, some of them twenty storeys high. The area had since been cleaned up and transformed beyond any recognition. The overcrowded Basil Spence tenements were demolished in 1993, flattened and replaced by modern housing and the industrial workshops and factories that crouch under the broad M8 flyover.

I could hear the motorway's background noise as it snaked its way above the city centre, growling like the bad reputation of the area which still hung on in the minds of Glaswegians.

Enid's flat was small and overflowing with stuff which often spilled over onto the landing outside her front door. The neighbours didn't mind. Like her, they were gregarious and unfazed by anything. They recognised her as a fellow Glaswegian, born and bred in the East End, south of the river. They all looked out for each other, poking their heads round their doors as I clattered up the stairs, nodding as I passed and checking me out as I carried Enid's paintings down to the car.

Enid's home was also her studio and paintings were stacked against the wall of every room. Her use of colour was masterful and the landscapes she painted danced with jabs of chrome yellow and palette knife swipes of Alizarin crimson. Who else could paint the sky purple, the grass vermillion, and get away with it convincingly? But the flat was also crammed full of Enid's exuberant personality. She was a beautiful woman whose excitement about her work and life just tippled out and filled every space.

Like her paintings, everything about Enid was bright. Her most startling feature was her bouffant blonde wig, which topped her short, round frame in a perfect bob and never moved or changed.

It symbolised her ongoing battle with cancer, to which she

never made reference. She didn't have time for such a thing. She needed to get on.

After I'd eaten my welcome treat of artistically-presented tasty morsels, Enid and I would look at her work and begin the selection process based on what she decided I could or could not take away with me to hang in the gallery. This was governed to some extent by her other commitments, which were many – her work always sold well – as well as by my immediate past record of sales and how well I was dressed and behaving on the day. The outrageous got the most marks and therefore the most paintings. I worked hard at this, choosing my maddest patterned tights, a flamboyant neckpiece or craziest earrings whenever I visited, but I never came anywhere close to Enid's colourful eccentricities.

An interesting commentary on the making of each painting always ran in parallel with suggestions for lunch - my treat, her choice of venue - and a post-prandial offering of culture - her treat, my choice (in theory, anyway). As Glasgow is a City of Culture there was always plenty on offer, and it was usually within walking distance of her flat.

We had begun this tradition on my first visit many years before when I realised that if I wanted Enid's work I would have to go and get it. She had been determined to educate a mere Sassenach with what her home city had to offer.

'Have you ever been to Scotland Street School?' she demanded on that first occasion. She'd always dive straight in: it was never 'How are you?', or 'How was the journey?'; never the weather or the state of the roads. No, nothing mundane like that.

'The Scotland Street School? No – where is it?' I asked. I was cautious and defensive. I'd come to collect paintings, not go to school!

'Just round the corner, under the motorway – other side. Do you want to go and see it?'

I was hesitant before committing to anything that first

time. Later, I would be up for whatever she suggested, knowing it would be interesting.

'What's so special about this school?' I asked.

Seeing my blank face, Enid decided to help me. 'You do know about it, don't you? It was Charles Rennie Mackintosh's last main commission.'

The school just happened to be a short walk away from Enid's flat and, even better, close to an astonishingly good small Italian restaurant where she knew everybody and they her. And thus the pattern of subsequent visits was set.

Since then we had explored the magnificent Mac (Glasgow School of Art), the Willow Tearooms in Sauchiehall Street, The Burrell Collection up the road in Pollockshaws, the Gallery of Modern Art, Kelvingrove and Mackintosh's well-preserved house, the Glasgow Art Fair in George Square, and most of the commercial galleries and big exhibitions. Nothing on the cultural scene in Glasgow escaped Enid and a guided tour would always be a unique experience.

I had already picked up that today we would also be going to the prestigious annual exhibition of the RGI - the Royal Glasgow Institute - at the McLellan Galleries. Lunch would be at a hotel close by, and now it appeared that Magic Knickers were on the menu as an additional delight. As Enid pointed out, Marks and Spencer was sited conveniently between the hotel and the gallery. It was planned beautifully.

After a decent lunch - accompanied by a commentary on the state of our fellow diners - we headed to M&S and made our way to the lingerie through the maze of departments. Enid steered us briskly along and I followed as she shimmied past stacks of tights and stands of swimming costumes.

'Here!' Enid cried from behind a trembling display of bras. 'Look! These things are fabulous. I've got a few pairs now. They're so good.'

The elasticated instruments of torture she was holding were among the most unromantic items of underwear I'd ever

224

encountered. I would not want to be run over by a bus in them. I would be too embarrassed.

Enid carried on undaunted.

'Now, what size are you? I've got some of these with the long legs. They do wonders for my thighs.'

She thrust a long, black tube at me which I judged would surely pull up to my armpits; the legs would reach my knees. The middle bum and belly section was reinforced with stronger elastic. There would be no movement possible in this garment. It was built like a straitjacket: I would be as limited as an Egyptian mummy, the baby Jesus in swaddling clothes, or Houdini demonstrating his seemingly impossible feats of escapology. In this garment there would be no wobbly bits. They wouldn't dare to try to make an appearance. Enid drew my attention to the label which claimed that the knickers would take at least two inches off everywhere. So where would those inches of blubber go? They had to go somewhere, didn't they? They probably oozed over the top or were extruded onto the knees. They couldn't disappear. They would just be redistributed.

'Hey, you don't let your lover see you in these, though,' Enid cried, seeing the look on my face. 'Just remember to take 'em off in the bathroom. Come on. You'll feel a million dollars in them.'

Reader, I confess. Under great duress, I bought a pair. It's just one of those sacrifices you have to make in the name of art. Those buying Enid's work will never know or appreciate the hardship I have gone through to acquire it. To my great surprise, though, the knickers really were magic. They worked, even if getting into them was a gymnastic exercise and, once on, breathing was difficult and movement slightly curtailed.

The McLellan Galleries are just a few doors away from M&S on Sauchiehall Street and situated just two blocks below Mackintosh's famous School of Art. They had undergone a big restoration project after a fire in 1980 but had recently been upstaged by the opening of the magnificent Gallery of Modern Art in Royal Exchange Square. This classical, porticoed edifice was fast becoming Glasgow's most controversial art gallery under the leadership of the charismatic, outspoken Julian Spalding (Spalding's worst attribute, according to Enid, was the fact that he was an Englishman. Fee fie fo fum - why should Scottish art be in the hands of an Englishman?). By comparison, the McLellan was a shy contender with a low-profile frontage, but once inside, a magnificent double staircase rose up into a succession of light, airy, interconnected exhibition rooms.

A sandwich board on the pavement outside the building quietly announced the 'RGI ANNUAL EXHIBITION'. The RGI is a prestigious art society. Scotland has a history of producing a disproportionate number of exceptional artists: think of the Colourists, The Glasgow Boys and Eardley, Peploe, Blackadder, Bellany and many other Scottish luminaries. Competition for election to the Institute is fierce.

The RGI Annual Exhibition is an open exhibition, similar in format to the Royal Academy's Summer Exhibition, with works chosen by a committee of members. Enid was herself a member of the selection committee and as soon as we began in Room One, she became even more animated, telling me about the portraits and all the gossip attached to them.

'She's the mistress of the president,' she said, giggling mischievously as she pointed out a handsome middle-aged woman dressed in pearls. 'Not many people know that. And those are her paintings over there. I'm sure I don't know how she became selected!'

Nor did I. Maybe... no, I mustn't encourage her.

We carried on. There was no one about. The stewards must have been on a tea break, or maybe we looked harmless. Anyway, we had the place to ourselves. Thanks to Enid, the secrets of the mighty RGI were revealed at every turn and I learned a lot about the criteria they applied in making their selection. There were huge pieces by Alan Davie, John

Bellany, Victoria Crowe and David M. Martin to be picked over, while the big, fleshy nude models who sat for Jenny Saville looked as though they should have been introduced to Magic Knickers. With their many dimples and folds they were virtually oozing off their canvases.

Enid made a good critic and talked me through many works. There were justifications or damnations of other artists as well as the titillating snippets of gossip, and I also found a few promising names that I might like to show at Castlegate House (if they were willing to cross the border).

We carried on amiably until we reached Room Three, which was also lined with paintings but with a focus on three-dimensional pieces. It was dominated by an installation Enid hadn't seen before – a perfect, eight-foot-high pyramid of sand. Placed in prime position in the middle of the room, it was directly below the central glass cupola so that the facets of sand twinkled as they caught the light.

The pyramid was cordoned off with heavy metal chains and I carefully tiptoed up to it, frightened I might disturb it. I was impressed. How on earth did the artist make it keep its perfect shape? It defied gravity.

'It's very clever, isn't it?' I commented to Enid.

'Ach, it's been done before with sweets in wrappers,' she snorted. 'Trouble was the public kept eating it. But I know how he's done this one. It's not all solid sand, you know. That's not possible. It's stuck on a cardboard template.'

'No! I can't believe that,' I protested. 'It looks too natural. You can see it move when you walk past it.'

I gave a little, cautious jump - nothing more than a lifting of the heels - and a slight quiver vibrated through the pyramid.

'Oh yes it is,' Enid insisted. 'It's stuck on. Look!' And before I could grab her she glanced quickly round the empty room, stepped over the little fence - which was obviously not fit for purpose - and prodded the side of the pyramid with her index finger.

It began imperceptibly - the slight movement of sand. Just

a few grains, trickling down and gaining momentum as they went. Enid was already stepping back over the barrier, looking very pleased with herself, as I pointed in speechless horror at the place where her finger had been. By the time she turned round, the sand was moving with the regulated flow of an egg timer. The base of the pyramid was broadening slightly. Its apex was losing its sharp profile. We were both open-mouthed, transfixed by terror, but the flow of sand increased even as we stared. It had escaped beyond its bounds. My shoes were crunching on the wooden floor. Everything was slowly on the move.

Frantically, Enid began to scoop up the shifting grains in an attempt to build the pyramid back into shape. She gathered up handfuls of it, vainly trying to persuade it to go back from whence it had come, but without success. This impressive, dominating piece was shrinking and spreading fast. It was now an avalanche of sand.

I looked around wildly.

There was only one thing to do – escape!

'Come on Enid,' I said. 'You can't do it, love. Time to go!'

And I went.

I hadn't experienced this guilty, panicked feeling since I was eight, stole some matches from our house and lit a fire on Brightside Common, which subsequently got out of hand. Then, I had taken my coat off and begun beating at the flames, only to see that I was making the fire worse. I had given up, hidden in some bushes, and watched the fire engine arrive to come and put it out. This time I did not want to be the voyeur. I wanted out.

Call me a coward. Call me what you will. I really didn't feel good about myself. But I knew that things were only going to get worse: you can't put a genie back in the lamp, they say, and you can't rebuild a pyramid of fine, artistically arranged sand in five minutes either.

I legged it through the labyrinth of interconnecting rooms, past several lethargic attendants, down the stairs and out of the door. I swiftly crossed the precinct into a posh bathroom shop and examined the taps closely, keeping my eye on the gallery door opposite as I got my breath back and calmed down. Enid soon emerged, beaming. I waved. She joined me. We wandered off, arm in arm, to the Willow Tearooms down the street, and left the havoc she'd wreaked behind us.

The McLellan Galleries are now closed through lack of funding. I don't know what happened to the pyramid of sand, but Enid and I never spoke of it again. The Magic Knickers are now worn out. I have not replaced them.

Cancer eventually caught up with dear Enid and she died in 2003. She taught me a lot about life and art, generosity, tolerance, and good humour. She made me laugh. My visits to Glasgow are now so much duller. I miss her.

Bottle Tops

It was an inauspicious arrival. Cork Street was blocked by the dustcart. I could either abandon the black cab at the bottom of the street or sit and watch the clock ticking. Being a thrifty northern woman, I got out, picked my way through the refuse bags, and stopped abruptly on the pavement opposite Messum's Gallery. From the window, black-headed Swaledale sheep were staring out, flanked by the well-clipped bay trees which stood in fashionable metal pots on the pavement.

The painting on display was by my protégée, Karen Wallbank. *Gathering III, oil on canvas* had a large red spot on it, signifying that it had sold already. My heart sang. Karen had made it: she had successfully negotiated the journey from the remote farm on the moors at the meeting of three northern counties - Cumbria, Lancashire and Yorkshire - to Cork Street, the epicentre of twentieth century art in London.

I looked at my watch. Karen and her husband George would be on the train now - if they'd managed to get out of their snowed-in farm. There was no sign of snow in London. It was early January, but in London it is easy to forget the month or even the season. I hoped Karen would make it to the opening party that night. What would she say when she saw her work in the window? I took a photograph and stepped into the rarefied yet friendly atmosphere of the gallery, thinking as I did how it couldn't be further from the sheep pens and cow byres of hill farming in rural Cumbria.

When David Messum had ventured north the previous summer looking for new northern artists, I had conflicting feelings about his visit. He asked me to get some work together for him to select for this show. I had thought about this seriously. Did I really want to share my hard-sought-out and well-nurtured artists with a London gallery? They were like my family now. I was thinking of farmer Karen Wallbank and quiet Michael Bennett: I could sell all I could get of their work. It didn't make economic sense. What if David Messum wanted a Percy Kelly exhibition? People will queue all night to possess a Kelly. What was in this for me?

But hold on a minute, I reminded myself, this wasn't about me. It was about the artists and my pledge to do my very best for them. This would be a marvellous opportunity for them to broaden out - hit the capital. So I agreed.

David Messum came, he saw, and he selected. Running your own gallery is a lonely path and an isolated one - you live or die by your own judgement – and it was an affirmation of my choice of artists. He chose several oils by Sheila Fell, 25 Percy Kellys, and twenty unframed paintings from the hill farm by Karen Wallbank. He took them there and then.

After he left, I rang Karen. I told her she'd been talent-spotted.

'It's a good opportunity, Karen,' I said. 'But do you want to do it? It's your decision. It's your work.'

'What? Me? Showing in London? Next year? I can't believe it.'

'There'll be an opening and a catalogue so you'd better start to get some good work together.'

'Well, George'll have to get his teeth done now,' she responded obliquely, befitting her usual manner. 'His front palate's gone and he reckons he's too old to bother with it. Dentist told him it'd be about 800 pund. That's probably got summat to do with it. I'll tell him he's not cummin to Cork Street with me unless he gets it done. That'll sort him out.'

I took this to mean she was up for it.

When the catalogue arrived some months later, it was thick, glossy and expensive. There was a photograph of Karen riding her horse on the fells beyond the farm and, inside, her story: the woman who gave up an art career to marry a farmer. Her paintings looked great, and I was still flicking through when her email arrived.

Karen and I have always exchanged zany emails (or at least since I convinced her I wasn't a conwoman and that her work was valuable and worth showing). Hers to me have often made me laugh out loud because I can hear her talking in them. She has a unique and irreverent sense of humour, and her ability to laugh at herself as well keeps her firmly grounded. She is a very practical woman and an inspiration to all of us who might sometimes feel hard done by or sorry for ourselves. She is the antithesis of those of us who think they are special or possessed of an extraordinary talent.

From: Karen@wallbank.com
To: chris@castlegate.com
Subject: OMG

Dear Chris

Oh my Gawd, I just received the Bottle Top catalogue and I feel quite "humble". Talk about the best of the best in there. However I feel I own my spot, it looks good, I had a gulp at the price list. I hope I get at least one sold. However, there is no place like Castlegate and I am already working towards a smashing show with you later this year. (well I think you invited me – did you?). Don't worry you will always come first. You were the one who found me.

Wouldn't my dad just have loved this? It would have taken him three days to pick his clothes to come down with me and see the exhibition!! It's strange but I couldn't sleep last night and was thinking back to the time I got an acceptance from Goldsmiths College in London. I was in George's father's old kitchen, and my dad rang with the news. The letter had arrived at home and I'd told him to open it and read it out to me. I burst into tears and then cried again when I turned the place down. No regrets really, but you always wonder what if.

Anyhow I ain't done bad! So here's to a new year, our friendship and anything else we can dream up!

Love Karen xxxxxxxxxxxxx

I was so happy for her and glad I'd persevered all those years ago: tracked her down and persuaded her to trust me. She had been born and brought up in Leeds and when she left school at sixteen had been torn between a veterinary course and art. She had chosen art. She did a Foundation Course at art college in Leeds and had met George up on the fells while on a field course studying vernacular architecture. Up on those isolated moors she had become involved with farming and again had to make a choice. She had turned down the place she was offered at Goldsmiths and married George instead.

From: chris@castlegate.com
To: Karen@wallbank.com
Subject: Bottle tops?

Dear Karen
Glad you liked the catalogue. (Why bottle tops Karen? Am I missing something?)
They've done you proud gal. You're right - your dad would have burst with pride. I can see the smile on his face now. What a lovely man he was. You've come such a long way - and what a journey - and never mind Goldsmiths - you've done it with everything stacked against you. I don't know how you've brought up Hannah and the boys and looked after the farm and everything and still produced all these brilliant paintings.
Keep going
Love Chris

Her reply to my question was terse.

From: Karen@wallbank.com
To: chris@castlegate.com
Subject: Bottle tops?
Bottle tops - Cork Street. Kx

Of course. Why on earth didn't I think of that!

Karen was determined not to miss her London debut, as was George – he'd shelled out the '800 pund', had his teeth done and, requiring a return on his money, was giving them an outing. Tom, the Wallbanks' eldest son, had pulled their snow-bound car out of the yard with the tractor early that morning, towed it along the potholed track and down the narrow icy tarmac road to the main road which had been gritted. Virgin took over at Lancaster Station. After dropping their bags at the Mayfair apartment she had booked online, Karen couldn't resist a surreptitious peep at the gallery prior to the opening; she was also worried they'd get lost later in the dark of the evening and not be able to find it. They'd never been to Cork Street before, and rarely to London. The last time was in 1990 when Karen won the National Laing Painting Competition. She and George had an all-expenses paid trip and a chauffeur-driven car to the opening in the Mall Galleries. That was when I overheard her telling the Director of the Laing Construction Company that I did the paintings, not her. He looked disconcerted and I was horrified, until Karen quickly added: 'Chris stretches the canvases and gets 'em framed. She titles 'em, prices 'em and sells 'em. I just paint 'em.'

This time, Karen wisely purchased an *A to Z* and soon found the Royal Academy. 'We'll go back tomorrer and have a look what's on there,' she told me later. She also found posh Burlington Arcade with its thick red carpet and liveried footmen at each end.

'George didn't want to go through it at first,' she confided. 'He thought it was private - not for the likes of us. Then he thought we might have to pay, but I told him not to be daft. We're as good as anybody else and if we had to pay we could afford it.'

Once inside, however, George hadn't wanted to leave.

'I couldn't get him past the expensive watch shops. He'd always fancied a Rolex, but now he's thinking about the Jaeger Le Coutres – said they were less showy. Then he found the shoe shine in the middle. I had to stop him getting his shoes cleaned even though they weren't as mucky as they usually are.'

Finally, they'd got to Cork Street and Karen saw her painting in Messum's window. Even George and his new teeth were impressed by that.

'I couldn't believe it. I lost me cool - I think I had a bit of a screech,' Karen laughed. 'George told me to shut up 'cos people were looking. Well, it was such a surprise, wasn't it? Anyway, I daren't go in - it's ever so posh – I needed to get used to the idea. So we wandered back to the flat and picked up stuff for breakfast at the Tesco Express. Fancy that. Tesco in Mayfair.'

Trust Karen to have found one.

That evening the heady smell of exotic, expensive flowers permeated the whole room. The lavish sculptural arrangements were artworks in themselves. Exquisite canapés and wine in sparkling glasses were handed round on silver salvers. This was a London opening in a long established, family-owned gallery and it was smooth, elegant and sophisticated. The place was buzzing with well dressed, well heeled clientele when Karen and George arrived. I had been nervously keeping watch for them as I wanted to be a familiar face in case they were feeling shy about coming in. I needn't have worried.

It was an ice-cold evening and as they made their dignified entrance I was struck by what a handsome pair they made. Karen looked confident in a pale green silk coat dress which complemented her golden hair. George handed over his long grey wool overcoat to the uniformed doorman to reveal a smart grey-striped suit, and only his bright eyes and healthily ruddy complexion gave a clue to his open-air life. Still, it was good to hear honest northern accents among the London glitterati.

The Messums, father and son, made a fuss of Karen and by the time she reached me through the dense crowd she had four more red spots, and an art critic in tow. We were chatting away when I caught sight of one of my clients arriving, a sharp-suited young man who works in the City. He had bought a Wallbank painting from Castlegate House the previous year and I'd sent him an invitation for this opening. He made his way towards our little group, I introduced him to Karen and pleasantries were exchanged.

It was going well until…

'How are Elaine and your little boy?' I asked him quietly, when there was a gap in the conversation.

'They're fine,' he replied. 'But she's a bit tired, or she'd be here tonight. We're having another. It's been a long gap, longer than intended. We've been trying for a while. Thought it would never happen so we're really pleased.'

'Oh congratulations,' I said. 'Give her my best wishes…'

At this point George, who had overheard our conversation, broke in.

'We've got a cow like that!'

An awkward silence fell but he carried on regardless. 'Ay, we can't get her into calf. We've been trying for ages but it's no good! And we paid 2000 pund for her. Pedigree breeding cow, you know.'

Karen joined in.

'I think we should tek her back, George. Him that sold her to us must have known.'

'Ay, we've tried everything,' George continued. 'We've put the bull to 'er that many times and we must o' been trying A.I.D - Artificial Insemination you know - as well for a couple of years now.'

'We borrowed Jim Hathaway's bull an all, din't we?' Karen added. 'He's a big 'un but it still did no good.'

'How was the weather up north when you left?' my client quickly asked them, just as I was asking how their train journey had been. Somehow, we successfully managed to change the subject before the various methods were explained in more detail. Was this what might be called conceptual art?

We moved on.

236

I had a lovely sense of contentment that evening. I cast my mind back to my discovery of Karen in 1987, when she was heavily pregnant with her third child. She had given me such poor directions to her isolated, fogbound farmhouse, and was so suspicious of me and reluctant to let me take any of her work, I don't know what had made me persevere. Pure instinct, wilfulness or daftness, I think – and the quality of her paintings, of course. Her natural talent was immediately obvious, even if she was painting on upholsterer's hessian and using skirting board for frames; even if some of her pieces ended up a bit 'mixed media' when they were accidentally dropped, butter-side-down, in the horse hair and cow dung of the yard.

Karen had her first exhibition of paintings a few months after the birth of baby Hannah and wowed the art-loving public from the very start. She was the 'farmer's wife' referred to in the title of my first book, and for the next eleven years we enjoyed a marvellous, intuitive business relationship which was to our mutual advantage. Karen is refreshingly unpretentious, endearingly innocent, and has no delusions of grandeur. She counted on me for advice, encouragement and endorsement and I counted on her for unquestioning loyalty, droll statements and a practical approach to life. We could easily tap into each other's mad sense of humour. We laughed a lot. It was a good partnership.

Karen and George came to all the gallery parties, always joining in, even if they were fancy dress. I particularly remembered George as the Laughing Cavalier and Karen as a Mondrian, wearing a blocked colour dress she'd made herself. They'd been there at the gallery's tenth birthday party but then a year later, Karen disappeared.

Each time I rang, she was either abroad or unobtainable.

'She's globe trottin',' George told me uneasily when I caught him in one day. Their three children must have been grown up by then, I realised, but a vision of Karen on the hippy trail in India wouldn't materialise. A package to Benidorm was more her style than a package to India. I couldn't fathom it.

I sent her invitations to each exhibition and party, but there was no response. Clients were asking after her and I didn't know what to say. We hadn't had a disagreement that I was aware of, but I searched my soul as to whether it was something I'd done or said. I was worried about her, and also annoyed by the thought that she might have been seduced by another gallery. She was mine - I felt possessive and protective. But what could I do? I backed off.

Seven years of silence later, I got a handmade Christmas card: a monoprint of geese combined with collage and glitter. It was a Karen special: there was glue all over the place and it was stuck to the envelope that contained it.

'Happy Christmas. I'm painting again' was all she had written on the card.

This seemed like an invitation to go and see what she was up to - and of course to try to find out what had gone wrong to make her (and me!) lose those seven years.

So, on a cold January day it was with a sense of déjà vu that I tentatively approached the farm. The bumpy track was just the same. So was the farming debris scattered right and left, although a few more wrecks had been added. The parlour was also the same as it ever was – a big, roaring fire, busy William Morris wallpaper of the dark flower variety, and the same sagging sofa with the springs falling out. Karen's husband George - who used to hide from me in the early days, referring to me as 'that posh woman from the gallery' - poked his head round the door and grinned. He told me he was on the way to buy some 'fancy cows'. I'd no idea what made cows fancy, but no matter. Things were relaxed and easy.

'Gosh,' I said, 'Time just goes, doesn't it? The boys must be grown up.'

'Oh aye,' she said. 'Jack and Tom run the farm now.'

'And what's Hannah doing? Has she left school? Is she at work? D'you know I haven't seen her since she was little.'

The last time I had seen Karen's daughter, she was just starting at the village school, and Karen had been pleased because that meant she would have more time for painting. Hannah was a strange, demanding child with bright red hair. She would never talk and pulled funny faces at me a lot - but so do many other children (and adults, come to that).

There was an embarrassed pause.

'She's at my mum's today,' Karen said. She hesitated and blushed. 'She's not right, you know.'

I didn't know.

Shyly, hesitantly, she began to fill me in.

'Well, we got to realise things weren't right when she was little – about four years old - but nobody could tell us how or why. She did all sorts of tests. They couldn't put a name to it. She went to the village school - small classes, mixed ages - and she was fine. They coped with her. They were brilliant. I didn't say owt to you about it. Didn't need to.'

Karen went on to explain how, when Hannah turned eleven, she'd had to move from her small village school into the confusing and frightening world of a large comprehensive a bus ride away. She lasted only a few weeks. It wasn't going to work. She had been protected in her previous school, but the staff at this one found her rude, noisy, and impervious to discipline. She talked all the time and didn't respond to requests and orders. She didn't join in with any projects. She didn't relate to other pupils or to the staff. They put an ASBO on her and sent her home.

Years later, Karen was told that Hannah was probably autistic, possibly with a touch of Asperger's and maybe some Tourette Syndrome thrown in. This accounted for all the behavioural difficulties they had met along the way (and there had been a lot).

Karen had spent seven years caring for her daughter at home with only the help of her mother, who had moved from the city to live a few miles away from the farm, and a home teacher. It was excessively demanding, and put a stop to any creative work. There was no respite – Hannah would wander round the house in the night, chattering away about nothing, waking everybody up – but Karen accepted this with her usual aplomb and crazy variety of dry, northern humour. She also kept it to herself in the typical way of rural, farming folk. They are tight-lipped about personal matters, dealing with anything life throws at them stoically.

In January 2007, coinciding with my visit, Hannah came of age. I'd noticed the cards on the sideboard. Now that she was eighteen, there was respite care and at last Karen could get back into painting. But, like her paints, she had dried up. She had been in the desert for seven years but now the end was in sight. She went straight back to her messy, neglected studio, catching the moments when she could slip in and make a few brushstrokes before some crisis of farm life intervened.

Tentatively, we tiptoed round the subject of another exhibition. Karen was desperate to get back to the gallery world, but we both wondered if she would be able to pull it off again. Would I be able to rekindle an interest in her work and rebuild a client base? Would people remember her? Would she be able to grow and develop her work? As we chattered, increasingly about nothing, my eye strayed again to the canvases ranged round the room. They were leaning inward, facing the wall, just as they had been on my first visit all those years before - an unspoken challenge between us.

At last I could wait no longer. A raise of an eyebrow, a nod of the head got through to her just as it does to a livestock auctioneer.

'Go on,' she said, 'have a look. You can turn 'em round. Tell me what you think – no kidding. Tell me straight. I can tek it.'

One by one, I turned the paintings round. That Karen's reservations were groundless very quickly became blindingly clear. There was a freshness about them, an atmosphere: biting wind, twinkling frost, isolation, loneliness. The sheep were daubs with black heads and improbably thin black stick legs that seemed unable to support the weight of their big, bulky bodies - but they were unmistakably Swaledales, painted by someone who handles them on a daily basis.

Karen has always told me her landscapes aren't real places because she doesn't sit down and sketch what she sees, but I've been out with her on the rough terrain in the lurching Land Rover Defender and splashed through streams and bogs, seen the trees, the shooting box, the marsh grass, the swathes of heather, the profiles of the mountains. They were all there again in these paintings, sometimes in unlikely colours but, by some alchemy, believable. She could still do it. We could do it.

Karen's come-back exhibition took place soon after and was welcomed and applauded. She was back on the road.

When *Hercules and the Farmer's Wife* was launched, my publishers were approached by the *Daily Mail* for serialisation rights. It was a tough decision, but I decided against it because it would put Karen and a few other artists at the mercy of the red tops. They could probe into private lives and thoughts and would probably cleverly edit my words and possibly change the emphasis of stories. But then Karen's chapter was picked up by a glossy magazine who wanted to publish it. I was still doubtful, and once again pointed the pitfalls out to Karen. She had been so protective and private about Hannah's condition and I knew the magazine would want to explore it. It would be the story of a woman succeeding in the face of adversity, with no details spared.

'They'll dig and delve, Karen,' I warned. 'Do you really want to expose yourself and Hannah to the world? What about the community round here? There's sure to be talk and gossip.'

'Hey, let's go for it,' she said. 'Farmers don't read women's magazines.'

So we did - we went for it.

As soon as the story was published in the magazine, Karen realised she'd got it wrong. Too late! Farmers definitely did read women's magazines! And in an isolated rural community, news travels fast. I received this email the day after the issue featuring Karen's story came out.

From: Karen@wallbank.com
To: chris@castlegate.com
Subject: LOL

Dear Chris
The toast of Bentham market – that's me.
Oh yes. We didn't think farmers read the Women's Magazines did we? I would have put money on it! But George has just got back from the Auction and he says the ring hasn't buzzed as much since Harry Price was butted unconscious by a ram lamb! And that was a long time ago.
But no matter – I got some good news about Hannah, I've been fighting for months, for some respite, for me and specially for mum with social services. It's been a long haul since last December. More and more of the same people kept coming to visit, and made reports only to disappear again without trace. Finally they have agreed to a carer to come to the house for 15 hours a week, over 3 afternoons, doing life skills etc. So I've got a little "me" time at last, god I'll be sending paintings up by shipment!
Weather dismal, anyway hope all well your end, and hope to see you shortly.
Love K xx

That January evening, on the way back from Messum's, my grin nearly split my face. My jaws ached. The road to Cork Street had not been easy but she'd got there. Karen had made it!

Crazy Heart

It was a long walk to the caves in Menorca's August heat. My family, who had started out as a cohesive chattering group, had begun to disintegrate into a straggly trail. At the back the grandchildren, typical sulky teenagers, were questioning their very existence and cursing ours, demanding drinks and information like 'Why should we?', 'How much further?' and 'What for?'

Regardless, we pressed on.

The track narrowed and became less distinct. Bushes scratched and bit us as we passed. Insects landed on our moist skin. The last section was a dusty, steep scramble on all fours, but it was worth it: the first cave was large and cool. When our eyes had adjusted to the gloom and our feet had stopped stumbling on the uneven floor, my eldest son Andrew - intrepid explorer, map-reader and team leader - located his torch and shone it round the cavern. Bats got up from their upside-down beds and left, making a big, swooping commotion about their disturbance.

My younger son, Peter, was quite taken with the place and decided he could move in.

'That's the ledge for my bed,' he was saying, 'and here's my cooker. That's a good table over there.' His wife and daughters, scrambling over rocks, were amused by this uncharacteristic display of domesticity.

'This place is so hard to get to - I reckon nobody's been in here for years,' I said, looking round.

I was wrong.

Andrew was still scoping the torch around when I suddenly saw it. My heart gave a lurch of recognition. Among the stalactites and stalagmites I could see the painting that was hanging at home in the English Lake District. Truly, it was there: revealing itself slowly as my eyes grew accustomed to the dimness. Those hazy, undefined rock formations lurking in

243

the shadows were unmistakeably the shape and source of my painting. Or my partner Michael's painting, really. It was he who bought it years ago from his artist friend, Kenneth Draper, long before Michael and I had known of each other's existence. I had first seen it hanging above the fireplace in his house in the Pennines and it had impressed me immediately, not with its size - it wasn't a massive pushy picture - but with its gentle, modest gravitas. It was an abstract piece in subtle shades of blues, lilacs, purples and greys, but I called it the 'King and Queen' because of the regal attitude of the undefined figures that I detected, jagged crown shapes on their heads.

Like a Rothko, the painting demanded time: looking time; time to gradually reveal itself. The best pictures take the longest time. Like a good book, good wine, or a piece of music, the joy is in the savouring and discovery. And it took time for the picture in the cave to slowly emerge from the gloom, but when it did, it was unmistakeable. It was my E. M. Forster moment. I connected.

'The king and queen!' I shouted, and it echoed back to me a thousand times.

Queen, queen, queen.

'Look, there they are!'

They are, they are, they are.

This was to be the first revelation of many.

That evening, I confronted Ken with my discovery when we met at his house in Es Castell for drinks. He was quietly pleased to have been rumbled - and also impressed that somebody could map-read.

'Oh, you got to that cave, did you?' he said. 'I've got so much work from there. It's a great place, isn't it? I never thought you'd get to it – difficult place to find.'

He'd underestimated the Wadsworth clan. If it's there, we'll find it if we want to. We don't give up easily.

Ken Draper and his wife Jean Macalpine know Menorca inside

out. They first came years ago to look after the house of a friend and found themselves drawn back repeatedly until they decided that they had to settle there. At the time they lived on Portland Bill in Dorset, which suited them both. Ken had a plentiful supply of natural stone for his sculpture and Jean, once his student and now a photographer and formidable artist in her own right, also found inspiration, but they felt cut off. They figured out that, door to door, it was easier to get to London from a Mediterranean island than from the tip of Portland Bill. Moreover, a permanent move made sense in terms of Ken's health. He suffers from a chronic and life-threatening heart condition, the Spanish for which translates as 'Crazy Heart'. The milder Menorcan winters would be much kinder to him – not that Ken is a frail man.

From the moment we walked blinking into the sunlight of Mahon Airport's arrivals hall, I was continually being assaulted, enveloped and smothered by his massive bear hugs. It was like being folded into a huge furry blanket, or perhaps a king-size duvet. Ken is a sculptor and sculptors are touchy-feely – they deal in the three-dimensional, they like to get hold of big, chunky material. Well, he got hold of me as though he was seriously assessing my potential: shape, size, mass. Finally, I got out of my twentieth hug to find the way to our hire car, organised by the ever-efficient Jean, and we drove in convoy to our haven of an air conditioned villa, which they had arranged for us.

That evening we stood with them on the balcony in the balmy air, the twinkling lights of Mahon harbour below us, a glass of cold white Rioja in our hands, and watched the teenagers dive cleanly into the pool. Our lovely friends had stocked the fridge, given us a case of wine and a bottle of Menorcan gin, and put their bikes in the garage for our use. But there was more. It was then that Jean presented us with a large-scale map of the island.

'Is it a treasure hunt map?' asked Sylvie, the youngest of

our party, excitedly. Looking at it closely, we saw that some areas had been ringed and scored, 'KEEP AWAY', or 'AVOID' scrawled across them in a thick black felt-tip. Other areas were marked with stars and comments like 'NOT TO BE MISSED' or 'A MUST'. It was intriguing. Ken's five stars had been awarded to quarries, caves, rocky escarpments and a cryptic area marked 'Lunar Landscape'. Hey, we'd come to a Mediterranean island, not the moon! The no-go areas marked were the holiday 'villages' for package tourists. Where were the sandy coves, the beaches, the safe swimming, the harbourside restaurants and tapas bars? Was I on holiday or what?

Er, well actually I wasn't. I had work to do. I had a Kenneth Draper exhibition to arrange. That was what had brought me there – it was my mission. But now a challenge had been thrown down, and it was one the Wadsworths rose to. Each evening, we appointed a Captain who was in charge of getting us all up early the following day before the heat became insufferable and ensuring we ticked off one or more of the places on the map. The Captain could appoint a deputy from the younger members of the family, and the pair would be in charge of the route, catering and transport. When we found time to drag ourselves away from the pool, the wine and the view of the magnificent harbour, we studied the map, and each time we set out exploring, we were surprised.

I began to see Ken's paintings everywhere we went on the island. Suddenly, having been familiar with his work for years, everything joined up and made sense. The shapes and colours of flowers, lichen, rocks, fish, seaweed - anything his eyes fell on - had been used as the basis for his work and was expressed in paint, found objects and textured, malleable materials: glass, metal, plastic or polymer. Meanwhile, the caves and quarries that Ken had highlighted on his map were instantly familiar. We had seen them all before on canvas, on board, in a frame, but hadn't recognised them for what they really were – his ideas, his inspiration.

Jean used the quarries too, but in a different way. These places were vast cathedrals from which the island's golden towns and churches had been built, and inside which the shapes, shadows and colours changed rapidly with the time of day. Such was Jean's devotion to photographing them that she even got into her oven-like car on Midsummer Day to drive to one hidden quarry to record what happened to the light on the one day of the year when the sun was directly overhead.

On this magical island, she was surrounded by picturesque coves and cliffs, cottages and lighthouses, fields and flowers of unbelievable colour, but could often be found taking a close-up shot of a piece of rusting metal plate in a skip. Jean told me that a delicate abstract 'landscape' – suggesting fields of poppies and a watery sun; a few soft, undefined trees in the background - had begun as a photograph of a bit of scrap on a building site. A 'seascape' started as a close-up of a piece of an old gate, and a 'mountain landscape' was another choice piece of rusting metal. Her photographs were serious works of art, digitally manipulated and transformed into an entirely different abstract study.

One day she took her large plate camera – the comical-looking type on a tripod where you have to stand under a 'watch-the–birdie' black cloth to take a photo - to Cuitadella, a town in the west of the island built from golden, burnished stone gleaned from a nearby quarry. She had seen a bit of pitted wall that really beckoned to her. Tourists were walking past with their fancy Nikons, Pentaxes and Canons, happily taking shots of this lovely town and its beautiful cathedral, and were completely nonplussed by seeing her set up her old-fashioned camera in front of an unattractive piece of peeling plaster wall. Surely this strange woman was facing the wrong way, with her back to the view?

An old man – a local - approached and stood watching and waiting. When Jean finally emerged from underneath her black mantilla, she braced herself for the inevitable scornful comments. The man smiled and gestured towards the wall.

'*Tapies,*' he said, nodded, and walked away.

'He got it!' said Jean triumphantly. 'He understood what I was doing.'

The fact that '*tapies*' is Spanish for wall and Tapies is a famous abstract Spanish painter was more food for thought.

Seeing the Drapers on their home ground was exciting, and the atmosphere was intensified by the fact that our visit coincided with the Es Castell Fiesta, which was mainly taking place in the square right outside their front door. Displays of rearing stallions and hazardous fireworks flouted all Health and Safety laws, and Jean cheerfully told me a government official had been killed by a rearing stallion the previous year. The angle of the riders as the horses 'walked' along upright on their back legs looked impossible, defying gravity, and young men showed off by running underneath the animals' raised front legs, daring each other to touch, to push a flank.

A floating platform in the harbour was the launching pad for a spectacular firework display and when an odd rogue firework fell out of the sky into the crowd and set a woman's hair on fire, her husband quickly and calmly doused it out. In Britain they would be taking out a writ – here they continued as though nothing had happened!

We shared tapas and tables with varying groups of locals and artists. Because of his heart condition, Ken had been advised not to travel, but if he couldn't get to see his English friends, they were more than prepared to travel to see him. We met octogenarian Royal Academician Paul Feiler, dapper in his smart suit; Anne Christopher, an Academician and sculptor who is always well represented in the Summer Exhibition; and a lovely bloke also called Ken who did most of the castings for sculptor Elizabeth Frink when she was alive. He tried to coax me to the front end of a rearing stallion to touch its chest – another typically tactile sculptor.

The conversations were riveting to me as a gallery owner, with lots of delicious art world gossip: who's showing with which gallery, who's sold the most, who's died or reached 80, creating a vacancy for a new Academician, and much more discussion about upcoming exhibitions. I was pleased and surprised to find they'd all heard of and respected Castlegate House, and I felt privileged to be part of such distinguished company.

I had first been introduced to Ken and Jean by my partner Michael at the opening of a private show in the East End of London. It was a great evening with a real party spirit but Ken ended up in hospital a few days later, his crazy heart the culprit. He flew over again to his solo show at the Royal Academy and again ended up in St Thomas' hospital. After that, his Spanish doctors had strongly advised him against flying.

A few months after our Menorcan visit, Ken's work arrived at the gallery for his big exhibition. It had travelled over land and sea, via Barcelona, but we weren't expecting him to follow it. So we were astonished when we got an email a few days before the opening saying simply: 'I'm coming! I don't care what the doctors say, I'm coming!'

We insisted he and Jean stay with us, of course, but when Jean asked us where the nearest hospital was, we were alarmed. I hardly dared tell her it was almost 30 miles away. This was nerve-racking. We did not want to be complicit in the death of an Academician, and especially not our lovely friend!

But for Ken the draw of Cumbria was just too strong. The son of a Killamarsh miner, he felt a strong affinity with the north of England. He's a Billy Elliot figure - an artist from a tough family of miners. However, as a teenager, when he bravely announced to his parents that he wanted to go to art college, he received not the opposition and ridicule he anticipated, but the full backing of both his mum and his dad, who were always very proud of him. In 1991 he achieved the height of recognition when he was elected to the Royal Academy.

Ken made the journey to Cumbria for his exhibition opening with no ill effects. He was determined to come. He missed England, he missed friends, and he missed running water. There were no rivers, streams or waterfalls in Menorca, so we seized the opportunity to take him on a Cumbrian waterfall tour. Ignoring possible consequences, we leaped across slippery stepping stones, clambered about on Sour Milk Gill at Buttermere, took the rough path to Dash Falls just up the lane from our house, and watched the power of Aira Force from the bridge that spans it above Ullswater.

Ken also enjoyed his reunion with my partner and his collector Michael, to whom he refers as 'The Man in Black' or 'Designer Man' because of his propensity to dress totally in black. Together, they instantly regressed into naughty boys seeing what they could get away with. Jean and I were forced into strict maternal roles, trying to balance disapproval with a 'just this once then' tolerance. Our men encouraged each other in their bad behaviour, so it was a while after the Drapers' departure before we dared return to certain local pubs and restaurants.

In one restaurant, when asked if everything was all right by a waitress, Ken replied, 'No, the puddings were terrible, Michael and I would like to try a different one now, please.' It was left to Jean to explain to the flummoxed young woman that he was joking.

Ken and Jean's visit coincided with their first wedding anniversary, and lots of friends and clients travelled a long way to the gallery to celebrate with them. Their wedding in Menorca the year before had been a quiet affair – well, relatively so: nothing about Ken is exactly quiet. He had been married twice before and intended to have no guests, no family, no reception, but the news inevitably trickled out and Ken's little granddaughters begged to be bridesmaids. They appeared in their dressing-up box princess costumes and were joined by a young cowboy grandson who had plundered the same box,

250

not wishing to be left out. An Academician - no names! - who had foolishly made a bet that Ken wouldn't ever get married again had to honour his debt and wear a pink tutu. And Jean wore black! Nevertheless, the locals looked on with affection and amusement: Ken was a popular character on the island and of course an artist can get away with anything – even a pink tutu.

After the exhibition at Castlegate House, Ken left England looking happy and well. We were relieved that he had survived a hectic week without any medical help: this was a first for many years. So we were shocked a few months later to hear that he was desperately ill again. At least it was nothing to do with us, I thought - but the prognosis was not good. His crazy heart was going even crazier, working erratically at only twenty per cent its normal rate, and fibrillating almost continuously. The Spanish doctors had done everything they could over the years to keep him alive, including performing several heart and bypass operations, but now they had to advise him that they could do no more. He'd had every treatment and all the surgery available that would ease his situation. All they could do now was administer more and more drugs, which were making him very lethargic. We were devastated.

Fellow Academician John Hoyland, a long-standing artist friend, was one of the many who went over to Menorca to visit him, full of concern. Ken thought he was seeing his old pal and colleague for the last time and John later confessed that he thought that as well. Of course, whatever the circumstances, when two artists get together they always talk about their work, their triumphs and disasters, their sales and prices achieved. John is a very successful artist - Mel Gooding in the *Guardian* described him as the 'greatest abstract painter of all time' - and his works now sell in the London salerooms and galleries for huge sums of money. As the pair chatted, the competitive spirit came out and John mentioned that he had recently sold several paintings to a private client.

'Yes,' said John, 'I sold them to a really nice collector who lives in Cambridge. His house is full of Hoylands! He doesn't buy anything else,' he added with a warning look.

'That's really great. Who is he? He must be rich to be able to afford so much of your work,' Ken teased. 'What does he do for a living? Do you know?'

'He's a doctor - a surgeon actually.'

Jean, who had been sitting with them, looked up from her book.

'What sort of surgeon?' she asked sharply.

'He's a top man – in fact he's a heart surgeon, I think.'

John paused.

'I'll check up on that,' he added, suddenly realising the significance of what he'd said.

It was just a few days later that a leading heart surgeon at Papworth Hospital in Cambridge rang Ken. His condition happened to be the surgeon's speciality. How happily coincidental is that? Things then moved quickly. Ken arranged for his medical notes to be sent over from Spain and within a week he had flown back to England and was under the knife.

We all held our breath, crossed our fingers and toes – and to our delight, the operation was successful. I don't think there are special rates for Royal Academicians, but that skilful surgeon gave Ken back to us to paint and hug another day – and to smoke another fag and eat another cream cake (both of which are strictly forbidden of course).

Two years later, I thought it was time for another exhibition. Jean's work was developing in an interesting direction and I was planning to ask for a Draper/Macalpine joint exhibition. This was also a good excuse to go over to their wonderful island again. Michael and I flew to Menorca in October, when the heat was less punishing, and as we walked through Customs we could see Ken pacing about restlessly in Arrivals. The suffocating hugs, male bonding and badinage began immediately as Jean and I looked on.

After my fifth trial by squeezing, Ken whispered in my ear, 'Loved your book. How do I get in the next one?'

I laughed as I extricated myself. 'You'll have to do something outrageous,' I said. 'Boring doesn't make a very good story.'

I didn't realise my challenge would come back to haunt me. Ken naughtily played the outrageous card as often as he could that week, giving me cheekily defiant looks which said 'Is that outrageous enough for you?' He didn't find it difficult at all.

This was a different Menorca from our sweltering August family visit. It was a cooler, windy place, with some dramatic thunderstorms. We were able to use the whole day this time now that we didn't have to escape from the heat, and consequently we could visit more special places from which these two artists derived so much inspiration. It was an education for us.

Ken and Jean drove us to the place they called 'the red rocks', down lanes so narrow and twisting that I braced myself for a head-on collision at every blind bend. What we saw was remarkable: a ridge of soft red sandstone overlooking the valley that had contorted itself over centuries, with the help of wind and rain, into Francis Bacon-like heads and limbs. There were sunken eyes, gaping mouths, twisted limbs; countless tormented souls overseeing our passage through Hell. I'm sure I saw a Screaming Pope. These were nature's gargoyles stolen from Notre Dame. As an ordinary tourist I would have seen none of these things, even if I'd driven through the place: it's an artist's role to change our perception of things, and with Ken and Jean that happened all the time.

We went to the quarries again and saw different angles, different light and different colours. At La Mola, the massive fort built in Napoleonic times to guard the harbour mouth, yet more of Ken's paintings began to make sense as we saw how shafts of light pierced underground gun emplacements and tiny pinholes of light beckoned down long, dark tunnels.

'I love that fort,' Ken said later. 'It has given me so much work, so many ideas, so much inspiration.'

We once again shared raucous harbourside lunches and uproarious evenings. Ken was a popular figure and vigorously hugged and squeezed everybody he met. He was on a strict low-everything diet, but temptation was all around. There were patisseries and pizzerias *par excellence* within a few steps of their front door and Ken, with his penchant for cream doughnuts, and his sweet-toothed friend Michael were incorrigible. The two of them had a week of escaping from their nurses – Jean and me.

'For a man who sadly declares he is not normally allowed such things,' Michael commented, 'Ken seems to know the cake shop staff very well. He's on Christian name terms with them all. Funny that, isn't it?'

On our final day, Sunday, we went for lunch at a beautiful beach restaurant at Binimel-là, on the northern coast of the island. We settled down at the outdoor tables overlooking the sea and scanned the menus in the October sun. We all agreed we'd have a healthy salad lunch, which would counteract the excesses of the week. Jean's Spanish is better than Ken's, but he insisted on placing the order as 'practice' and this may have explained why five Spanish omelettes, four bowls of chips and two fried eggs mysteriously arrived on our table. Of salad, there was no sign. The drinks were likewise strangely not as 'ordered'.

After lunch, Jean and I foolishly decided to walk off some of the thousands of calories that we had just taken in which were surplus to requirements. We set off over the hill to remote Pregonda, the beach where Mike Oldfield of *Tubular Bells* fame had built an appropriately bell-shaped modern house. This was a big mistake. Once out of sight we think puddings may have been consumed. We couldn't be certain, given that the evidence had probably been eaten, but on our walk back,

Jean's mobile rang. Ken was not feeling good. We ran the last bit, and when we arrived back at the restaurant, he looked awful. He had pains everywhere. He had pains where no pains had ever been before. For a man with a crazy heart this was alarming.

We quickly bundled into the car, Ken groaning beside me in the back, and Jean drove to the main hospital like a getaway driver pursued by the police. At one point the moaning got so bad that I remember shouting 'It's a boy!' in a vain attempt to lighten the desperate atmosphere, but nobody laughed. We were all deeply worried.

At the *Urgencia* (A&E to you and me), Ken was immediately whisked off for tests. Michael and I sat and read ancient back copies of Spanish *Homes and Gardens*, not registering a single word. After a while, Jean appeared, looking worried. She was acting as Ken's interpreter with the medical staff on account of his Spanish only stretching to basic necessities like chips, pizza and cream doughnuts.

'They're doing blood tests now,' she said. 'They've done everything else. We've just to wait for the results.'

Half an hour later she reappeared, looking relieved. 'It's all right,' she said. 'They can't find anything badly wrong. His heart's fine. But we don't know the cause as yet. They are looking further into the symptoms.'

A little while later a rather sheepish Ken appeared. He was wearing a comedy backless floral hospital gown. It was very hard not to laugh.

'So what's wrong?' we asked anxiously. 'Do they think you'll live?'

He hung his head. 'It's constipation. I'm to have an enema.'

We roared with laughter. The nurse came out to see what the disturbance was about, shrugged, and disappeared.

Another half hour and a woebegone Ken appeared again, hobbling.

'They've done it,' he said.

'Great,' we said.

'And it hasn't worked,' he said.

His bottom lip came out. He looked sorry for himself.

'I don't know what they're going to do next,' he said.

At that moment a nurse appeared with an enormous length of red tubing and a bowl. It was all too apparent what they were going to do next.

Ken took one look and he was off at speed in the direction of *les lavabos*.

'Gotta go,' he panted, making off for the toilets at a run. It did the trick: problem solved.

Later that evening, recovering with a glass of wine, I assured Ken that he had secured a place in the next book but I felt it was a rather extreme way to earn it. It has taken him a long time to live it down. We are still working on the 'Carry on up the Urgencia' jokes.

Winter came without any more health emergencies and the Drapers sent some work over for our Christmas show. It came by ferry to Barcelona, north over the Pyrenees through France to Calais, then to London and on to Cumbria, where its arrival coincided with the worst floods ever recorded here. For what seemed like 40 days and 40 nights that November, it had rained. Then on 20th November 2009, the sky fell in. Water was falling vertically out of it with a frightening black intensity. The ground was sodden; like a sponge in the bath it could absorb no more. Overnight, Cockermouth was washed in noxious mud and polluted water and our beautiful Georgian gem town was left in ruins.

We spent the following two days watching live film footage on national television as familiar bridges collapsed, one of them taking a policeman with it to his death. Yellow Chinook helicopters winched frightened people from rooftops and upstairs windows, and rescue workers chugged up and down the streets in lifeboats and amphibious vehicles made unstable by the strength of the current. The water had plunged down from the fells into the rivers and lakes which spilled into even bigger rivers which were swelling all the time. As the River Derwent roared its way into the town it became all-powerful. It had pushed relentlessly through every obstacle in its path and was now joined by its junior accomplice, the River Cocker, fed by the swollen lakes of Buttermere, Crummock Water and Loweswater. They met at Jennings Brewery, situated just down the hill from the gallery, and whenever this extraordinary force found its path blocked or difficult, it rapidly found an easier way out by making roaring tributaries of side streets. Moving and spreading at 40 miles an hour, it quickly destroyed the centre of the town, which was preparing for Christmas. It smashed the shop windows and took possession of the gifts inside, carrying them indiscriminately down towards the sea - a conveyor belt of presents for Poseidon.

The gallery was safe. Mediaeval builders knew a thing or three about site choice and had selected the high ground for the town's castle – and for Castlegate, its dower house, opposite. But there was no satisfaction in being safe and dry: just guilt, despair and a feeling of helplessness when others were suffering so badly (we did what we could by setting up a coffee and soup kitchen for those brave souls who made it to the gallery, and to help those stranded this side of the rivers).

Emergency workers were everywhere, pumping water out of old buildings. The pedestrian bridge was broken, the metal twisted into sculptural shapes supporting masses of debris, and a few cars were haphazardly strewn around the adjoining car park like Dinky toys abandoned by a tired child. A parking ticket machine lay uprooted on the ground with its concrete base still attached, wrenched out by the sheer force of angry water. We were cut off from the centre of town and the simple things in life that we had all always taken for granted suddenly became very difficult.

The Spanish lorry driver bringing Ken and Jean's work was naturally unaware of the problem. As he neared the end of his epic over-land-and-sea journey, he rang for directions to the gallery.

I attempted to explain but didn't know the Spanish for 'very big flood' - coming from such a dry, riverless island, he probably wouldn't have understood anyway. So I gave him directions as best I could and tried to think of a route that didn't require a river crossing. He rang again an hour later, complaining that his satnav still didn't seem to be working: it had guided him to a big river and there was no way across. His satnav was unaware that the bridge had been swept away into the sea. I talked him in via Penrith and the motorway and gave him tea when he arrived: he hadn't had a good day.

As soon as he'd gone, I began to sort through the work. The first piece I unpacked was one of Ken's, called *Embers*. It was a sculptural painting mounted in a box: a deep red, purple, orange and lilac textured abstract piece, pitted and shrivelled in places, with a pendulous blob of red opaque glass suspended through it. It was elemental: red hot and molten. I caught my breath. It took me straight back to Menorca: far away from the depressing, black, watery hell outside the door. It made me smile.

On our way to that last 'fatal' lunch we had passed an area which had recently been swept by fire. It was black and barren. Jean had slowed down. 'Gosh, look at that!' she had marvelled in awe.

We looked. I remembered how I only saw burnt ground - empty - black. Ken stopped the car and got out. He stood looking intently for some time.

'This is wonderful. Just look at it. The colours!' he exclaimed enthusiastically. 'I'll come back with my sketchbook after you've gone next week.'

Meanwhile, Jean had her camera out, taking dozens of shots.

I do wish I could see through an artist's eyes, I thought at the time. All I could see was burnt black stumps. What on earth were they getting so excited about? What was I missing?'

Standing in the kitchen at Castlegate House on a desolate November afternoon, my wish was granted. I held the answer in my hands.

An End and A Beginning

'Hello, Chris. I know it's your day off but...'

It was June Bennett on the phone.

'You know I've always got time for you, June,' I said, smiling, hoping it would disguise my dismay. 'How can I help?'

'Well, we've got a bit of a crisis. I wouldn't have disturbed you today but it's urgent.'

This was the first fine Thursday in weeks. I looked out of the window where my new bike was waiting in the yard. I was looking forward to testing my stamina - and my brakes - over Honister Pass.

'Tell me about it,' I said.

'Well, it's Michael's early works.'

'What about his early works?' I came back sharply. All thought of the struggle from Buttermere up to the slate mine vanished from my consciousness in an instant. This was much more important. Michael Bennett and I had had a dialogue going about his early 1960s works for years. Ever since he had mentioned them briefly years before, I had been curious to know more about them. It had become a perennial joke between Michael Bennett and me. I hadn't ever seen them and he obdurately wouldn't tell me where they were. We engaged in friendly badinage from time to time but it got me nowhere and he had sworn June to secrecy as well. He was guarded and possessive about his current work, and even more so about earlier stuff. He didn't want anyone to see it – he seemed to be embarrassed about it.

'Well,' she went on, 'the council have just dropped a skip in the village and he's going to put his early works on it.'

'What? So where have they been stored all these years?'

'In our garage up in the roof space. He now says they're getting damp and taking up too much room. I can't persuade him not to do it. I think you might be able to do something. Can you come? Now!'

Ah ha! So that was where he kept them. The garage, was it? I didn't know the Bennetts had a garage. They lived in a Georgian terrace. Their car was always parked on the cobbles outside their front door.

I glanced at my watch. It was ten o'clock. It was an hour's drive at least to the Bennetts' house on the marshy flatlands of the Solway estuary, but no matter: I had a mission. I had to go.

'I'll come right now,' I promised. The council were unlikely to collect the skip that day, but if it filled up overnight, it could be gone the next morning. Knowing how slowly and deliberately Michael worked there could be a decade of work there in danger of being thrown away in seconds and lost to landfill for ever.

Goodbye bike ride! Off came the Lycra, back went the bike into the shed. I grabbed the car keys, set the gallery alarms and left at speed, leaving the gate swinging and the garage door open in my haste.

As I drove, I thought excitedly about what I was going to see – the forerunners of Michael's present paintings. These early works would be vital if I, or anyone else, ever mounted a Bennett retrospective - which was a definite possibility. At the moment the Sixties were out of fashion, but that could change at any time. I had the feeling that sometime early in the next millennium they would find their place and be popular again. These things come and go but quality will always have a market at some point. I was prepared to wait. I had the storage space.

June was anxiously looking out for me. 'I'm so glad to see you,' she said, giving me a hug. 'What are we going to do about this?'

'Well, I need to see them first. How big are they?' I could barely contain my excitement. I had no idea what they were like.

'Come and see. They're up here.'

We crept up the garden on meandering pathways, past tiny

lawns, a ceramic horse by Jane Smith, and tumbling groups of sweetpeas. The perfume rising from a group of white lilies was heady. Hidden by trees, and accessed from a narrow back lane, the Bennetts' garage was well camouflaged. No wonder I hadn't known anything about it: I hadn't even known there was a back lane. June pulled open the double wooden doors and beckoned me inside. She looked up. I followed her gaze. There they were. A stack of paintings - about twenty at a glance - were balanced on the cross beams above our heads. At a rough estimate, the maximum dimension looked to be about four feet by five. We then went down the road to the skip. It was half full and already there were two paintings on top.

'See what I mean?'

'Well, we're not leaving those in there, for sure,' I said, nodding at the paintings. 'I can take them all, I think. They'll fit in my estate. But shouldn't we ask Michael?'

'He's upstairs at the back, painting,' June whispered. 'Better not disturb him. Come on, bring your car round: let's get these two before something else gets thrown in.'

'But won't he see they're not there if he looks in tomorrow?' I was still doubtful.

June paused. Then her eyes settled on some old damp sheets of hardboard and a few used rotten canvases against the garage wall.

'Come on: we'll put these butter-side-down at the top of the skip and shove some junk on top. There's quite a lot of stuff in it already. I'm sure more will arrive in the night – it usually does. He'll think his paintings are still underneath.'

It was a clandestine mission. We surreptitiously unloaded the two paintings from the skip into my estate car and then fetched the rest from the garage. They fitted neatly – the larger ones on top at an angle – although when we'd finished, the car was packed to the roof. Mission accomplished, June invited me to stay for lunch. She and I had cooked up a story about my coming for some paintings for an exhibition, which I had – we just didn't specify whose. Michael didn't suspect, although

June may have confessed later; he has since said he knew I'd taken them, though none of us ever referred to his early works again. He didn't know at that time that the exhibition I'd mentioned would be his and many years ahead, in totally different circumstances. I'm glad we can't see into the future.

**

New Year's Day 2012: a new year, a new beginning, and my birthday. And in six months' time, there was going to be another anniversary to look forward to: Castlegate House Gallery would be 25 years old.

I still couldn't believe it. I'd given it five years in 1987. I had never expected it to thrive and survive so long. There would have to be a big, spectacular celebration.

The following day, a surprising email slid silently into my inbox.

'Guess what?' I said to Michael, staring at it, 'The Swallows want to buy the gallery. What a cheek. It's not for sale.'

Christine and Steven Swallow were art collectors who had recently moved north from London where Steven had been a hedge fund manager. They had bought some good paintings from the gallery.

Michael looked up from the paper.

'How old are you?'

'What's that got to do with it?' I bristled.

'Why not think about it? It's worth considering.'

'Hey, the gallery's my life. I love it. I don't want to give it up.'

'Yes, but you know, love, you're well past retirement age...'

'What's that got to do with anything?'

'... and you never get the time to do all the things you want to do – do you? What about the writing? You've had

263

several successful books published and the publishers want more. You've cut back opening hours and put on fewer exhibitions. How much longer can you continue to juggle so many things?'

He paused.

'And you know what? When you feel ready to let go there won't be a hedge fund manager standing in the wings ready to make you an offer. Do you really want to shuffle around the gallery on a zimmer frame?'

***

The sale of Castlegate House was probably the easiest sale of the year. The solicitors handling it were baffled. The Swallows wanted the gallery so badly that there were no petty arguments and power struggles; no quibbling over fixtures and fittings. The only problem was that they wanted it quickly. They just couldn't wait to get in and get on with it. But I insisted that I wanted to hand it over on the seventh of July - the gallery's 25th anniversary.

I wanted to throw a big thank you party and invite all the people who had exhibited, helped and supported Castlegate House over the years.

With the anniversary accelerating towards me like a runaway train, the intervening months were spent frantically clearing out 26 years of reckless, indiscriminate accumulation. Given that we had four floors of Georgian splendour, at least fourteen rooms - I'd never actually counted how many there were: I'd always run out of fingers and given up - a big cellar, outhouses, sheds, and multiples of cupboards, this was a daunting task. You don't ever have to throw anything out if you've got that sort of space - you can put it in a cupboard, close the door and forget it.

I had forgotten a lot of things until I began opening those doors. The time had come to be ruthless.

As the weeks went by and completion day approached, panic set in and I called in the reserves. The Gemjars - my faithful volunteers – had been supporters of the gallery for the last ten years at least and had got me out of many tight corners. Their real names were Gillian and John, but as Gillian's email address began with her initials 'GEM', and John's with 'JAR', when I copied them in side by side they became the Gemjars (which is what posh southerners call those glass things you get marmalade in, and what northerners allegedly drink their tea out of). An SOS email was guaranteed to bring them to the gallery at speed.

While Gill was packing ceramics (her speciality – we don't refer to her as 'Superpot' for nothing), John and I started in the studio on the second floor. I was clearing out old, dried-up art materials and bald paintbrushes in the big room when I heard John's muffled voice.

'Chris, what's this in here?' he called out.

His voice was coming from one of the large walk-in cupboards in the adjoining room. I hadn't looked in there for years.

'Looks like big paintings,' he went on. 'Shall I pull them out?'

I instantly knew what they were. He had found Michael Bennett's early works: the Sixties paintings I had rescued nearly twenty years previously.

Gently, he pulled one out and leaned it against the wall. I hadn't seen it since the day after I had rescued it from the skip. Peter, our gardener, had carried all Michael's paintings up to the studio from my car when he had arrived the morning after the salvage operation, and we had dusted them down, photographed and measured each one, protected them with bubble wrap, then stowed most of them away in the cupboard. I had hung one or two of the smaller ones in the gallery with modest price tags, but only one had sold. They weren't in vogue and the majority were too large to appeal to the domestic market.

But that was then and this was now.

John peeled off the wrapping and stood back. The four-foot-square abstract in ochre and orange, brown and black, reduced me to a reverent silence. 'Red Landscape circa 1964' it said on the back in Michael Bennett's neat, distinctive handwriting. It took my breath away.

We spread the rest out around the studio. They were magnificent: twenty big abstracts on board, very typical of the 1960s.

Art tends to go in waves of popularity, like vintage fashion. Barbara Hulaniki - founder of Biba; Mary Quant; Ozzy Clarke; Celia Birtwell – all were now venerated and enjoying a resurgence. Glossy magazines were full of Sixties furniture and fabrics, and abstraction fitted in with the white minimalist interiors that were now all the rage. Just a few months earlier there had been a successful sale of Sixties paintings at Mitchells, the local auction house in Cockermouth.

The paintings were part of the estate of Derwent Wise, a well-known and well-respected artist who had collected work by his contemporaries, mainly on an exchange basis. Strong abstract works by his friends Kenneth Rowntree, Richard Hamilton and Ian Stephenson RA had been snapped up at very respectable prices. This auction had caused a few ripples on the surface of the market of ubiquitous pale watercolours that normally sell at auctions around here.

'What are you going to do with these?' asked John, bringing me out of my little nostalgic reverie.

'I'm going to do what Michael Bennett does, John – I'm going to sit and look and think and then look again.'

We propped the canvases up around the studio. They looked spectacular alongside pieces of furniture that my husband Michael and I had collected in the Sixties and relegated to the second floor. A round white Arcana tulip table and chairs, a white Arcana coffee table, a Danish studio couch and a Habitat pine table: these too were back in fashion. Much loved, much used, they looked good alongside the paintings. They were talking to each other. Nevertheless, they would also have to go: we already had classic Sixties pieces in the minimalist house where Michael 2 and I now lived. Any more and it wouldn't be minimal any longer. Specialist dealers from London were coming to make an offer for the pieces the following week, and in the meantime I decided I would come up here, sit on the Danish designer teak studio couch and look and think.

The furniture dealers from Hackney were young, trendy and enthusiastic. They cooed over the items and made me a very fair offer for them. As we shook hands on the deal, the focus changed. The young woman noticed the paintings that were stacked against the wall.

'Are those paintings for sale?' she asked, curious. 'Can I have a look?'

I pulled a few out.

'We never buy paintings, do we, Geoff? But those would fit in our flat a treat. I like that one... maybe that one as well. How much are they? Tell me about the artist.'

She couldn't take her eyes off Michael's paintings and was getting very excited at the prospect of owning one – but after I had considered her offer, I turned it down. I'd had a better idea.

The recession had hit Michael's specialist art book/catalogue business hard. He and June were now totally reliant on their paintings for income. He had a studio full of gorgeous canvases which he insisted on referring to as 'work in progress' – he still never considered anything finished – and I had managed to extract a few for my last show ever at the gallery. Titled '25 for 25', it comprised the work of 25 artists who had been important to the gallery's development and success over the 25 years of its existence. The catalogue was an homage to these people and had already gone to print. However, this newly rediscovered treasure trove was too important just to add in at the last moment. It formed a cohesive collection deserving of a proper exhibition with a lavish catalogue, fanfares of trumpets and choirs of angels.

The last time I'd seen June and Michael had been a few weeks prior to my exciting discovery, when they had proudly mentioned that their eldest son, Justin, had an exhibition coming up at the Guggenheim in New York. Justin Bennett is also a talented artist, living and working in Holland. To be offered a show at the prestigious, Frank Lloyd Wright-designed, gallery on Fifth Avenue was career-changing, the tops. Michael and June were planning to go to New York for the summer opening – they were determined to go - but money was, as usual, tight.

All this sitting and thinking had given me an idea. The prospective buyers of the gallery, the Swallows, were keen on Sixties work. They had bought some good pieces at the last auction at Mitchells and would be able to do choirs of angels and fanfares of trumpets big time. However, they were also more than capable of finding their own artists. Understandably, they wanted to put their own stamp on the gallery and I didn't want to push in and insult them.

I rang them nevertheless.

'Would you like to come over for a coffee?' I asked disingenuously. 'I've something interesting to show you.'

I had prepared a speech but knew I had to tread carefully as we looked at the paintings together in silence. The Swallows had bought one of June's works the summer before but they hadn't bought any of Michael's so far – then again, they hadn't seen his Sixties work.

'I reckon Michael Bennett is the most important painter working in Cumbria at the moment,' I told them. 'In the Sixties he exhibited with really important artists - David Hockney, Sheila Fell, Sandra Blow, Lucien Freud, Terry Frost and so on. He had a lot of favourable reviews. But he never pushes himself forward.'

I let them take this in before continuing.

'If I wasn't selling the gallery to you, I'd be planning a Michael Bennett retrospective for next year. It's been on my 'to do' list for ages, but I think the time is finally right. I know you'll want to develop the gallery in your own way and I wouldn't dream of trying to influence you... but these are worth considering.'

'Yes, you're right. These are good,' said Steve after some quiet consideration and a whispered consultation with his wife. 'I really like those three.'

He pointed them out.

'*Falling*,' he said, looking at the title on the back. 'And that one there and those two: how much would he take for those, do you think?'

'Ah. I think they should be bought as a complete body of work. He's not prepared to split them up. That's why I've kept them together all these years.'

(I didn't mention that I'd put them in a cupboard and almost forgotten all about them for two decades!)

'But they are big,' I went on. 'In all honesty, big paintings are harder to place, harder to sell. You really need people with big wall spaces to fill. You've worked in the City for years: I bet you have friends – bankers, City boys - who live in lofts?'

'Have you, Steve?' his wife asked hopefully.

'I can't think of any offhand,' said Steve doubtfully.

'Well, you'd better find some!' said Christine forcefully. I could see she liked the work. She wanted it and she wanted to do the exhibition.

'Michael has a hoard of good recent work in his studio that you can extract from him if you're clever – and you are,' I added. 'You'll just have to go about it gently with him.'

It didn't take them long to decide. The Swallows bought the whole of Michael's early works collection – every single one. Steven made the large cheque out directly to Michael as I requested: I didn't want to make anything out of the deal. All I wanted was to be the messenger, the bringer of good news. It would give me enormous pleasure.

I was nervous when I made the telephone call to the Bennetts because when I actually stopped and thought about it some more, I realised I'd just sold a load of Michael's work that hadn't been mine to sell. Oops! I should have asked his permission first. In mitigation, Michael probably thought they had been lost to landfill. Or, if June had in fact told him what had happened to them, he had evidently completely forgotten about them, just as I had.

I took a deep breath and picked up the phone.

'Are you around later this afternoon?' I asked. 'May I come and see you? I've got a surprise for you - a big surprise.'

I arrived at four o'clock with a bottle of champagne and the large cheque made out directly to Michael in my bag. When I handed it over, Michael's eyes widened. June was on tiptoe, craning her neck trying to see what it was.

'Good God,' she said when she saw the amount, 'where's that come from?'

'Well, Michael - you know your early works...'

'I think they were thrown out years ago,' he said quickly. 'If this is for them, I haven't got them.' His shoulders drooped and he held the cheque back out to me.

I looked at June anxiously. She smiled a secret smile.

'No, I know,' I said. 'June and I rescued them. Trouble was, we'd all forgotten about them. They've been in a cupboard at Castlegate House for years and now the Swallows have just bought them. They want to put on a retrospective when they've taken over the gallery – hope you don't mind. Now, let's open that bottle, shall we? I need a drink.'

I was gabbling now. June and Michael hadn't had a windfall like this for years. They painted because they had to paint, not to make money and certainly not to earn a living: they didn't, they just managed to scrape by. It made them a bit unworldly (and also other-worldly). I loved them – both of them. I would do anything for them.

June brought glasses and there were toasts and tears.

'We can really enjoy New York now without thinking about the cost,' June said with shining eyes.

'This will free me up for a winter of painting without having to worry about money,' added Michael as he looked at the cheque again in disbelief.

Those words are etched in my mind. If only they had come true. I would have liked to make them come true. I would like to give this story a different ending. But it wouldn't be truthful. This is not fiction - it's real life.

Yes, June and Michael did get to New York. They had a wonderful time. They stayed in a nice hotel and saw Justin's name in lights: on posters everywhere and on a big banner outside the Guggenheim. As the artist's parents, they were treated as celebrities. They came back full of it and looking well and happy. It had been a trip to remember.

When they returned home to Cumbria they had so much to look forward to. They came to the gallery's 25th birthday party and the occasion of its handing over to the Swallows: a great day full of memories and laughter.

On reflection, I realised that among all the thousands of artists I'd dealt with, June and Michael were among those few who had been the most loyal to me and to the gallery from the very beginning. They had given me the very best of their work; virtually an exclusive without a written contract. Much of the success of Castlegate House could be attributed to them.

Meanwhile, the Swallows were already planning Michael's retrospective for 2013 and it promised to be a great success. They genuinely loved the work. There would be a beautiful catalogue and masses of visitors were guaranteed. What none of us knew was that June would not be there. An invisible, undetectable cancer had been growing in her mouth and spreading. It was discovered far too late. She died three months before the triumphal opening.

Her funeral was on a glorious day in June – her birthday month. Her wicker coffin was bedecked with wild flowers and there were over 100 friends and family members there. Many people came in her trademark pink lipstick, wearing her silver jewellery. It was a joyful day, a sad day; a desperately unhappy day. Many images of her jewel-like paintings were projected onto a screen at the wake, spanning the whole of her career. It was lovely to hear people recognising pieces they owned. Her work was in my very first exhibition and it was in my very last. We had travelled the past 25 years at the gallery together. June will never be forgotten. She is alive on the walls of galleries and collectors.

Three months later, Michael's retrospective took place. Before she died, June had insisted he go ahead with it. She also insisted he must be at his opening – a big ask, as Michael is very shy and they both knew he would be there without her. It would be the first time he'd been to an opening of his or June's work alone. But he was - he did it.

The Sixties paintings which had lain so long in my dark cupboard had been beautifully cleaned and reframed. Stephen Swallow had managed to get a lot of new works from Michael – some of them simply on loan - that covered his lifetime of painting. They produced a magnificent catalogue which was dedicated to June, who would have loved to have seen it. The joyous spirit of June was palpable at the show.

Afterword

PINK EGG, AUGUST 2015

My journey to work is an enviable commute of about 25 metres across the garden from home to The Pink Egg, the writing room where I work. It was built on the footprint of a leaky old earth-floored garage which was unfit for anything (especially cars). Oh, and by the way, it isn't pink. It is a single-room building of glass and steel and overlooks a stream that skitters past so noisily sometimes it sounds like excited human voices. When the building was finished, Michael - my second Michael - gave me an Arne Jacobsen Egg chair in celebration. He said I could choose any colour I liked as long as it was pink, and after a while we started referring to the whole place as The Pink Egg. Now, it has become a place of the imagination. It is a place to think, a place to observe, a place from which ideas hatch and grow.

There are distractions all around me. The south-facing wall of glass looks straight up the north face of Skiddaw. Red squirrels scamper along the decking and busily bury nuts everywhere in the lawn: they never seem to remember where they've put them so the garden is full of their secret hoards. As darkness falls, Mrs Badger hurries silently past on the track she has paced out at the same time every evening for years. This morning the woodpeckers are knocking hell out of the silver birches. A dipper is nodding its way along the stream, a treecreeper is slowly trawling another mossy birch trunk for his insect breakfast, and Mr Weasel has emerged from his drainpipe and is scouring the bank for baby rabbits. He has rich pickings among the honeycomb of burrows.

Woops, the male buzzard has just swooped low the length of the stream, only lifting his massive wingspan to clear the bridge. The other day I was disturbed by some strange, high-pitched fluted notes from the oak wood to which the buzzards return every year to nest. I hurried out to find the little buzzards were fledging. Both parents were hovering low above them, giving them their first lesson in flying. The little ones were running, hopping, jumping and falling about on the ground until one and then the other took to the air, squealing in delight. It's a wonder I ever get anything written with all this drama outside. It's like an episode of *Countryfile*.

Nothing could be more different from my life at the gallery. Home now is a secret place, a secluded farmhouse which I found a long time before leaving Castlegate House. When Michael 2 and I moved in, it had not been inhabited for many years. It was an escape, a retreat. Invisible from the single-track tarmac road, it is reached by an unmarked gate opening onto a track across a field. That gate is the entrance to heaven. There is no light pollution and the only sounds are animals, birds and the occasional quad bike.

'Do you miss the gallery?' people often ask me when I emerge from writing purdah.

No, I don't. I brought it with me to this lovely place. It is part of me and my life and still all around me here. Across the garden I can see *New Dawn*, arms raised to greet the rising sun. The metal bridge made by super blacksmith Alan Dawson takes me across the stream to Jane Smith's ceramic dragon in three parts. Inside The Egg I have Michael Bennett's dazzling *Bouquet to the Sun* to cheer me on; Charles Oakley's *Vermeer's Floor* box to puzzle me; June Bennett's *Butterfly Garden*, her first painting of the garden at Castlegate; and many of my favourite Percy Kellys. Percy's book press, *Boat and Sun* - a painted floorboard and a papier-mâché plate with a painting of a fully-rigged schooner on top that he had made when he found himself in Norfolk, alone for the first time in his life, sit on top of the chart chest which stores Percy's etchings and sketch books. 'From Roberta To Joan with love, 1983' it says on the underside of the plate.

The larger Kelly paintings of Maryport, Whitehaven and Newlands, together with *Cumberland*, Sheila Fell's largest ever oil painting, hang in the house. Alongside them are Feddens, Scotts, Raes, Peascods, Wallbanks and Nicholsons – all my favourites - as well as all the pots and sculpture we've acquired.

Every one holds a memory. I will never tire of these things but if they were to disappear I could still recreate them in my head in every detail. Maybe I don't need things any more, just living memories. But writing is a lonesome activity and I miss the people who used to come regularly to the gallery and became friends. I miss the artists who always opened my eyes to new wonders and ideas, and I miss all the strange new situations and people that were presented to me on a daily basis. Every one of those 25 years spent running the gallery was a Life Class.

Friends, family and visitors are of course just as welcome here, but this place is so hard to find that I am never overwhelmed or disturbed by them. I have advance warning of anyone who approaches, and Michael is a good gatekeeper if I'm working to a deadline. But life still springs surprises. One sunny Saturday afternoon a few weeks ago, I had a call from Steven Swallow at Castlegate House.

'Hi Chris, I've got some people here at the gallery who'd like to see you.'

'What's their name, Steve?'

'I don't think you know them. They want you to sign their brother's book. You're on his bucket list, apparently.'

'What?!'

My mind raced. How could that be? How could I be on a bucket list? People usually have exotic things like riding an elephant, going to Vladivostok on the Trans-Siberian Railway, or floating over Skiddaw in a hot air balloon as their last wishes.

'This is a first for me, Steve. I've never been on a bucket list before. I'm a bit overcome, to be honest.'

'Thought you might be, so I didn't want to just hand over your details. But they've driven a long way – somewhere near

London - expecting to find you here at the gallery. They didn't know you'd moved on.'

I didn't need to think about it. 'You'd better send them over.'

'I've already told them you're hard to find but they've got satnav and they're absolutely determined.'

'Tell them I'll be in The Pink Egg.'

'Sure.'

'Give them my phone number as well,' I said. 'Tell them not to go into the village on any account – it's the Bermuda Triangle of Cumbria. They can ring me when they're lost.'

They did, and when they finally arrived I willingly signed their brother Bill's well-thumbed *Hercules and the Farmer's Wife*. Bill wasn't strong enough to make the journey himself so his sisters were fulfilling his wishes. They rang him. 'Bet you can't guess where we are, Bill. We're with Chris in a Pink Egg. We've got photos and everything: it's wonderful. There's paintings everywhere.'

His sister passed the mobile to me.

'Hello, Bill. It's good to talk to you. Glad you enjoyed the book.'

'Oh yes, I did. It made me laugh. I'm a Sunday painter,' he went on, 'I sign my paintings "Constable".'

'Oh?' I laughed. 'Why's that?'

'Because I am one – a constable. I'm a policeman with the Met. When will the next book be out, then? I'm waiting for it.'

'Well I'm just writing the last little bit, the Afterword, right now so it will be out very soon. And you know what? You might get a mention in it.'

'Gosh,' he replied, 'that's every reason for me to hang on in there at least until then.'

So come on Bill, wherever you are: I hope you are now reading this book and enjoying it as much as you did the last one. Bless you, your wonderful sisters, and your bucket list.

Acknowledgements

Thank you to Christine and Steve Swallow who took the gallery off my hands, relieving me of the day-to-day running, the dreaded VAT returns and all that entails. I only now realise how much that meant. Thank you to all the artists who had faith in me and allowed me to exhibit their precious work; particularly the late June Bennett, artist and friend, who was in my first show and my last.

Thank you to all the people – friends, family, buyers, browsers - who have given me support, encouragement, praise, laughter (and alcohol) over the last 25 years.

To my steadfast editor Stephanie Cross who has bravely battled not only with me but also with painful RSI throughout the editing of the manuscript. Thank you so much Steph for keeping going and for your infinite patience.

To Prospero Press for having faith in me to write a good book and not let them down.

For Jacquie, Ailsa, Carol and other positive manuscript readers and particularly for my long-suffering partner Michael who does the ironing and other boring domestic jobs when I disappear into the Pink Egg for hours to gaze at a screen – or sometimes at the spectacular view.